Robert J. Rogers is a direct descendant of the second-generation James Rogers who is one of the main figures in RISING ABOVE CIRCUMSTANCES. He was born in Edmonton, Alberta, and from his early life followed an intense interest in the history of his family and in military activities. He volunteered as a leader in the Scouting movement for more than twenty years.

Rogers served 32 years in the Canadian Armed Forces, at first in the militia, then later at sea in the Canadian Navy, travelling in the course of his duties all over the globe. He rose to the position of Operations Officer of a destroyer and Executive Officer of a mine-sweeper. In the latter part of his career he served in Naval Intelligence through the crises of the '80's and '90's.

Rogers retired to Edmonton in 1995, where he has devoted much of his time to historical and genealogical research and to a second career as Administrator of a Minor Hockey Association. He is married and has three children.

Rising Above Circumstances

The Rogers Family in Colonial America

by Robert J. Rogers, U.E.

sketches by Gary Zaboly
cartography by Wendy Johnson
photographs from the collections of
Timothy J. Todish, Horst Dresler
and the Author

Sheltus & Picard

Canadian Cataloguing in Publication Data:

Rogers, Robert J., 1947–
    Rising above circumstances: the Rogers family in colonial America

Includes bibliographical references and index.

ISBN 0-9696296-5-6

First edition

    1. Rogers family. 2. Rogers, James, 1728–1790. 3. Rogers, Robert, 1731–1795. 4. Rogers, James, 1700?–1753. 5. United States–History–French and Indian War, 1755–1763. 6. United States–History–18th Century. 7. Rogers' Rangers. I. Title.

CS71.R73 1998   973.2'6   C98–901293–X

Sketches by Gary Zaboly. Cartography by Wendy Johnson. Photographs by Horst Dresler, Timothy J. Todish and Robert J. Rogers 246 pages. 15.3 cm x 22.9 cm (6″ x 9″).

The photographs on pages iii, 98, 99, 184 and 216 are from the collection of Horst Dresler. Those on pages 8, 9 and 76 were taken by Robert J. Rogers, and the photos on pages 13 and 209 are from the collection of Timothy J. Todish. The photo on page 46 is by K. Gunn from the collection of Robert J. Rogers. Maps, except for the map of the St.-François Expedition, are by Wendy Johnson. The sketches, except for the Rogers coat of arms, are by Gary Zaboly.

Printed in Canada by
**Ginette Nault & Daniel Beaucaire, Imprimeurs
St-Félix-de-Valois, Quebec**

Sheltus & Picard Inc.
PO Box 1321, Bedford, Quebec, Canada J0J 1A0
Tel. 450-248-7319 Fax 450-248-2057
email cp.jas.rm@acbm.qc.ca

Sheltus & Picard is a member of the Small Publishers Group.

Acknowledgements

"No man is an Island": the amateur historian acutely feels the truth of John Donne's observation. We learn and advance our knowledge of the past by climbing on the shoulders of the many writers, scholars and historians who have gone before, gratefully acknowledging their efforts. In this regard it is especially fitting to mention such authors as Francis Parkman, Kenneth Roberts, John R. Cuneo, Burt G. Loescher and Allen W. Eckert. Their books on Rogers' Rangers and other facets of Colonial America have been an inspiration and an indispensable source of data for years.

We must also acknowledge the efforts of family historians. Much of the information on the early history of the Rogers family was compiled by Robert Zacheus Rogers (1842–1911), an avid historian. His papers have been preserved in the Ontario Archives as an invaluable aid for researchers. His nephew, Walter James Rogers (1864–1940), wrote a number of papers on family history based on research he conducted in England, and presented the material to the United Empire Loyalists Association in 1899 and 1921. Another relative, John Arnott Calcutt Rogers (1912–1987), expanded much of the information on the family and was instrumental in promoting history and ensuring that recognition was given to the early pioneers of Ontario. Without the work undertaken by these dedicated amateur historians there would be a void where there is accurate information.

No one individual could undertake a project of such scope and hope to complete it with any accuracy without considerable help, and I have had such superior assistance that I know my words will fail to express my appreciation. It is impossible even to list all who have had a hand in this work. Some provided leads and historical data to fill in gaps in my research just when they were needed. Others gave encouragement and advice at critical stages of the project. A number saw and understood the concept of the project and made generous financial contributions to keep the research going during difficult times. You know who you are and how much your assistance is sincerely appreciated.

While it is not my intention to make a list, a few deserve special mention because of their unique contributions. Gary Zaboly of New York not only provided the excellent sketches seen throughout this work but also shared his immense knowledge of Colonial American history without reservation. Timothy J. Todish of Grand Rapids provided invaluable assistance as much through his friendship and active participation as a member of a recreated unit of Rogers' Rangers as through his detailed knowledge of the period. Horst Dresler and Albert Smith of Saint Jean, Quebec, also shared their friendship and their intimate knowledge of the practical aspects of living in the 18th century as members of a recreated unit of the King's Rangers. The insight of all these individuals made the writing of the book more than an academic exercise, and I hope that the realities of life in the period have been conveyed through the pages of this work. Dr. David Mills, Professor of History at the University of Alberta, conducted a final review of the manuscript and gave me the decisive push to get it published. All of these individuals played a unique role in the creation of this work, and I gratefully acknowledge their contribution.

It would be remiss of me not to thank my wife and immediate family, who put up with years of stress not least from my ill temper when things did not go right. They came amiably on the many field trips that criss-crossed the continent to visit graveyards, historic sites, relatives and at times total strangers, all for a project that started in 1973 as a small weekend undertaking to update the family history but turned into a lifelong obsession. Finally I would like to acknowledge the Lord for granting me the talents I needed to undertake an endeavour of this scope as well as the drive, determination and health to see it through to its conclusion.

The King's Rangers Engaged
Re-enactment of a Revolutionary War battle at St. Jean, Quebec 1992

Preface

This is the true story of a family that lived through the turbulence of Colonial America. It is the story of a family that left their home in Ireland and travelled to North America when the trackless forest of the American wilderness was not far inland from the coastal towns. It tells how they carved a new home out of the deep forests of New Hampshire only to have it destroyed during the Indian raids of King George's War (1739–1748). They survived and rebuilt their home, bearing their children as they struggled to survive in that harsh environment.

The family was caught up in the struggle to free America from the threat of the French and their allied Indians at a time when most settlers were more interested in eking out a subsistence living than in seeing to their own security. Three brothers of the family answered the call to arms to fight in the French and Indian War (1756–1763). One rose to international prominence by creating a unit that fought the enemy on its own terms and whose tactics have been used to the present day. It cost another his life while he and the third fought under their brother's command.

The story continues to the Indian uprising in the Upper Great Lakes and goes on to the Governorship of Michilimackinac, the Gateway to the West. It is also the story of a great vision for the exploration of the continent dashed by the indifference of small-minded men, and by petty ambition and resentment that led to accusations of treason and a court martial.

When it was clear that the French and Indian threat had been eliminated, some influential citizens publicly asked why they should have to participate in the defence of the colonies that was clearly the responsibility of the mother country. Yet when the same citizens were taxed to pay for this defence, they revolted against the country that had defended them. By that time part of the Rogers family had built another home in the wilderness that became Vermont. They were caught up in the American Revolutionary War (1776–1783). The family was torn apart in this conflict; but they again rose above their circumstances and made a fourth new home in the seemingly unending wilderness, this time in what would become Upper Canada. It is also, therefore, the story of the founding of two great nations seen through the eyes of those who lived through those turbulent times.

So much has been written about Robert Rogers and his Rangers that it is time to view his life and accomplishments as the product of his family and as part of their history. His parents and brothers deserve equal attention, to show the accomplishments of the family within their times and culture. Robert undoubtedly made a significant contribution to the history of North America; yet he has become an almost forgotten figure in that history. His older brother James rose to a substantial position and later held major responsibility in the settlement of Upper Canada. He was, however, frequently overshadowed by his flamboyant and at times erratic younger brother.

It is certainly not my intention to replace the excellent works by such authors as Francis Parkman, Kenneth Roberts, John Cuneo or Burt Loescher. It is rather my intention to build upon their work, to round out the story and fill in some gaps: in short, to complete the picture from a new viewpoint, the perspective of the family.

Historians judge from a safe distance of time and tend to interpret events by their own moral and ethical standards. This sometimes results in revisionist history: interpretations of events tainted by personal bias and present-day perceptions for a host of motives, often honest. We cannot change the past, but we can learn from it and, we hope, avoid identified pitfalls while benefiting from perceived successes. One point is that we must not judge a culture of the past by present-day standards. If we can learn from the past and the example of our forebears, we have a chance of not repeating their errors. But we who live at the dawn of the twenty-first century have no right to judge our ancestors by our sensibilities and distinctions. We must view the people of the past in the context of the attitudes and moral standards of the time and place in which they lived.

Although I believe I may justly be proud of my heritage, it is not my intention to establish a bragging bench through this book but to offer an analytical work of use to the researcher and scholar as well as to members of the family. The story flows from the facts, and I have attempted to present the most accurate picture possible. I have not hidden their faults but have tried to present the story of a family that lived in perhaps the most turbulent period in the history of this continent. Their accomplishments are significant to the early history of both Canada and the United States. Their lives, warts and all, teach us something about character and perseverance against overwhelming odds, about rising above circumstances.

This work started out as a small project to update the history of the family for my children, the last such history having been written in 1895. The deeper I got into the research, the more intrigued I became, and a small project turned into more than twenty years of research. The main body of this work is over 800 pages long and details the history of the family to the present day. In 1995 a fellow researcher recommended that the first two chapters be published as a separate document, as it would have appeal beyond the family. The book you hold is the result. The rest will follow in time. I hope all who read this book will enjoy my efforts to bring the past to life.

Robert J. Rogers
11 November 1998

Table of Contents

List of Illustrations

Sketches:

Maps:

Photographs:

RISING ABOVE CIRCUMSTANCES

The Rogers Family Coat of Arms

Motto: *Nos Nostraque Deo*—*We and our God*
Arms: *Argent, a chevron gules between three stags trippant sable*
Crest: *A stag's head couped*

James Rogers (1–1) (1700?–1753)

Family tradition tells that James Rogers was born in the early 1700's of Ulster Scot* lineage, in an area once known as Montelony, believed to be located near the present village of Dungiven. This is a beautiful area nestled in the foothills of the Sperrin Mountains a few miles south-east of Londonderry, Northern Ireland. Tradition also suggests that James was married in Ireland to Mary McFatridge sometime in the early 1720's; for the date and place of the marriage no evidence has been found. In his research, John Cuneo uncovered information intimating that James may have been the youngest son of John Rogers of Gillerthwaite and Ennerdale. This region is located along the Scottish border in the northwestern part of England, near the town of Carlisle. Cuneo also suggests that his wife Mary was the daughter of Robert Macphedran and Mary MacGilderoy of Dumbarton, Scotland. After their marriage in the 1720's, the couple apparently moved to Ireland and settled near Londonderry.

An unpublished family history written in the 1850's advances the theory that the family is of Norman French origin, descended from a Count de Rogier who apparently was an officer in the army of William the Conqueror in 1066. After settling in Britain, the family anglicized the name to Rogers. Descendants subsequently participated in the conquest of Scotland and later Ireland, where they remained until the early 18th century.

These stories and traditions have become part of the oral history of the family. However, extensive research has been unable to prove or disprove any of them, and the origins of the Rogers Clan remain unknown.

However the family came to be established in Ireland, James and Mary, with four very young children (Daniel, Samuel, Martha and James), are known to have immigrated to America sometime during the period 1728 to 1731. Family tradition and documents imply that the four elder children were born in Ireland, James being the youngest in 1728. Records of the birth and baptism in America of the next three children (Robert, Richard and Mary), starting in 1731, support this theory. Birth records for the three youngest children (John, Catherine and Amy) have not been found, but they were undoubtedly born in America. The family thus came to America in the first major Ulster Scot migration (1717–1735), but apparently arrived too late to participate in the initial land distribution. Detailed examination of the records has failed to uncover the name of the

---

* For a definition of the Ulster Scots and the story of their migrations see Appendix I to this section.

vessel in which they arrived, but this is not uncommon with historical evidence of this period.

They apparently had some funds, for they paid for their passage rather than engaging in the common practice of indenture. Indentured servants' records were carefully kept legal documents, because the period of their indenture was rigidly tied to the date of their arrival in America. The arrival of members of the aristocracy and landed gentry, or of prominent and wealthy individuals were also a matter of historical record. We may therefore surmise that the Rogers family fell somewhere between these two extremes: better off than those who had to sell their services for passage but not wealthy or prominent. Tradition holds that they brought with them the family coat of arms engraved on metal plates, an indication they had some status in society. These plates are supposed to be still in the possession of descendants, but their location is unknown to the author and they may long since have been lost.

Before describing how the family became established in America, it is first necessary to summarize the events under which the settlement of New England took place and to show conditions in the colonies when the family arrived. In 1620 King James I (1603–1625) patented the Council for the Planting, Ordering and Governing of New England in America as a means of controlling the foundation of colonies. The first successful attempt at settlement of what is now New England was by the Pilgrims, members of the Puritan sect also known as Separatists. This group had fled from England in 1608 to escape severe religious persecution and had temporarily settled in the Netherlands. After being granted a charter for a new colony, they sailed from England and landed at Plymouth on 20 December 1620, to establish a community where they could practice their religion without harassment. The Massachusetts Bay Colony was afterwards founded in the year 1629 and eventually included not only all of what is today known as Massachusetts, but also parts of the states of New York, Connecticut, Vermont, New Hampshire and Maine. The Council for New England also granted a substantial coastal area between the Kennebec and Merrimack Rivers to Captain John Mason in 1622. This grant was confirmed by the Crown in 1629, although altered to encompass most of the Merrimack River basin and a reduced area of coastline. In 1679 the grant was declared as the "Royal Province of New Hampshire," but was part of the Dominion of New England and governed by the Royal Governor of Massachusetts until 1741. In that year the southern boundary was adjusted to a short distance north of the Merrimack and a royal governor appointed.

The colony of New York was first settled by the Dutch in 1621 as New Netherland but passed to English control in 1664. The area was granted

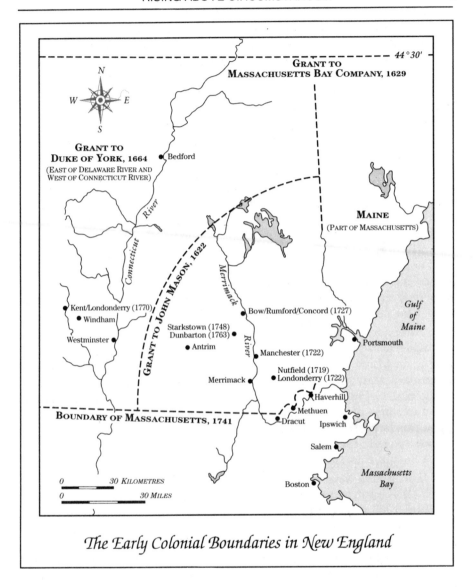

The Early Colonial Boundaries in New England

to the Duke of York and renamed New York. The colony included most of the land east of the Delaware River and west of the Connecticut, a significant area much of which had never been seen or surveyed. The grants and patents of these three colonies did not adequately specify their boundaries and so caused disputes between them until the settlement of 1764. These boundary disputes were of importance to the history of the Rogers family and of the areas in which they settled.

When James and Mary Rogers arrived in the colony some time
around 1729, they initially settled in the town of Methuen, Massachusetts,
where, because they were of the Presbyterian faith, they were probably
given a rather cool reception by the Puritan settlers of the area. Most of the
Ulster Scots had settled farther north and why the Rogers family did not
is uncertain. Possibly they so decided because of the age of the children,
Daniel (2–1) the eldest being only about seven years of age, and James (2–
3) the youngest being an infant. The uncertainty of settling in the
wilderness with such a young family was probably the primary consideration. They remained in Methuen for approximately eight years and it was
here that their next three children were born. The local church registry
records the baptisms of these children by the local minister. This was a
highly unusual occurrence given the faith of the parents, but an indication
of their concern for spiritual matters. Shortly after the birth of their
seventh child in 1736, the family moved onto a small farm on the common
land near the Merrimack River settlement of Dracut. During this period
James and Mary became close friends with Joseph Putney and his family,
who lived on an adjoining farm. The Putney family had come to America
some time before, and Joseph had started as a shopkeeper in Salem.

After a few years James and Joseph felt the urge to move farther into
the wilderness to improve their circumstances, since neither owned the
land upon which they were living. While hunting north of the village of
Merrimack, they stumbled upon a small brook and followed it to its source.
In the midst of high hills and almost unbroken forest, they came upon a
broad expanse of open meadow that had been partly cleared by beaver.
Upon this land stood a luxuriant crop of grass more than waist high. The
two men were so taken by the scene that they resolved to settle in this area,
about 35 miles northwest of Methuen.

The region was known as the "Great Meadows". It was part of
Lovewell's Grant, an area given to the Lovewell family of Massachusetts on
19 June 1735 to recompense the service of Captain John Lovewell of
Dunstable. In the spring of that year, Captain Lovewell had led a party of
armed men in a campaign against the Mohegan Indians who had destroyed
a number of farms in a raid. After some initial success, the mission had
ended in Lovewell's death at Pequawket. The area had been previously
granted to Captain Samuel Gorham of Plymouth, and although he relinquished his claim in favour of the Lovewell family and the Crown in
exchange for another grant in the area which is now the State of Maine, this
area is still referred to as "Gorhamtown" in some sources. There was no
permanent settlement before 1739.

On 12 November 1738, through an agent, James Rogers bought and
received title to an undivided one-sixth interest in the 2190 acres of

Lovewell's Grant. He purchased it for the sum of £11 from Zaccheus Lovewell of Canterbury, England, a brother of Captain John Lovewell. The transfer was subsequently registered in the Massachusetts General Court. Twelve days later Joseph Putney acquired a similar portion, giving each family approximately 356 acres in and around the Great Meadows. In the spring of 1739, the two families loaded all their possessions onto ox-carts and by April had moved onto the land to begin carving homes out of the wilderness. James named his farm Montelony,* after the area in Ireland from which they had come. The village of Bow or Rumford,† some sixteen miles north, was the nearest settlement. After five years of toil the farms prospered, and by 1744 more than 100 acres had been fenced as haymeadow or pasture, with as many more sown to grain. The families had also planted an orchard which by that year was bearing fruit.

The period between the end of Queen Anne's War in 1713 and the commencement of King George's War in 1739 was one of relative peace for the British colonies in America.‡ Even when war erupted, most farmers in the Merrimack River Valley elected to remain on their farms rather than seek shelter and safety in one of the larger settlements. By 1745, however, Indian raids from New France had become so intense that the safety of families outside the towns became a matter of concern. Several homes in the town of Rumford were fortified as places of refuge, and the fields were worked by farmers supported by armed companies, with scouting parties scouring the woods for signs of the enemy.

In April 1746, some thirty-five separate war parties were dispatched by the French from Fort St. Frédéric§ on Lake Champlain to spread fear and destruction to the frontier. The signs of a major war party just north of Rumford in early May caused considerable alarm, and scouts were immediately sent to warn the outlying farms. The Rogers and Putney families were outside the warning circle, and two friends, knowing that James and Joseph would not hear by other means, risked their lives to warn them of a possible raid. They found one family cooking supper and the other churning butter and doing other chores. The meal was left over the fire and the cream in the churn as the families hastened to gather a few belongings. They quickly left for the protection of Rumford under the cover of darkness. The following morning James and his friend Joseph returned to the farms for more of their possessions only to discover the ruins of their log homes still smouldering,

---

* The name is recorded as Mountalona in some sources.

† Bow, also known as Rumford, later grew into Concord, New Hampshire.

‡ For details on these conflicts, see Historical Events, Annex B.

§ Fort St. Frédéric was originally built by the French in 1732 on the projection of land that narrows the southern end of Lake Champlain. It was captured by the British in 1759 and renamed Crown Point.

---

their cattle slaughtered and the orchard of apple trees, some already in fruit, destroyed but for a single tree.*

James and the family were assigned to one of the ten garrison homes in Rumford on 15 May, until the threat of further raids was eliminated. James had five strong sons, two of whom, Samuel (2–2) and Robert (2–4), served in the militia that was formed for the protection of Rumford and the surrounding area. On 26 May 1747 James Rogers signed a petition to the Governor of New Hampshire, Benning Wentworth, "Praying for assistance against the Savages." In April 1748, two years after they had been forced from their farm, the family tried to return; but nature had largely overgrown the land, and the Indian threat made it still far too dangerous to begin again. Disappointed, they returned to Rumford to await the end of hostilities that would permit them to rebuild safely. In October of that year, the Treaty of Aix-la-Chapelle finally brought an end to the war and peace returned to the Merrimack River Valley. It was too late in the season to start rebuilding, however, so the family waited for spring to return to the land.

In October 1748, a group of some 55 settlers, mostly from Londonderry, New Hampshire, petitioned the Masonian proprietors† for a grant of a township five miles square, that would include the entire 2190 acres of Lovewell's Grant. This group included David McGregor, Archibald Stark and another James Rogers.‡ James and Joseph were surprised to discover that their title to the land was void as a result of the resolution of the long-standing boundary dispute between New Hampshire and Massachusetts and a subsequent adjustment of the various grants in 1741. The two men hired an attorney to seek a share with the group of 55 in the new grant and to retain the land and their farms for which they had worked so hard. On the opposite page is part of their petition, taken from the *History of Dunbarton*.

On 17 December 1748, the proprietors granted the township to the original petitioners, and a village was established under the name Starkstown. As a result of their legal action James and Joseph were each awarded a full share equal to that of the other petitioners, and their eldest sons received one share in common. On 2 March 1752, each shareholder finally received approximately 200 acres in the township according to the proprietors' grant.§

---

* The *History of Dunbarton* records that this tree survived and supplied fruit to the community well into the next century.

† The Masonian proprietors controlled the settlement of the lands granted to John Mason in 1622, which were in effect the colony of New Hampshire.

‡ No relation; to distinguish between the two James Rogers families, see Appendix II to this section.

§ The proprietors' grant has been copied as Appendix III to this section.

> *On the twenty-sixth of the same month [October 1748], James Rogers 'now resident of Bow', and Joseph Putney 'now resident of Penacook', by their Attorney requested to the Proprietors 'that whereas the said James Rogers, and six sons: Daniel, Samuel, James, Robert, Richard and John; and the said Joseph, and six sons: John, Joseph, William, Henry, Asa & Obadiah; had purchased a lot of 2190 acres, and had improved it jointly, about eighty acres of meadow and about one hundred acres of up land, and had two dwelling houses and two barns and two orchards, the houses built about nine years past; and that in April last ye Indians burnt and destroyed said houses and barns and cut down ye orchards and killed a heifer and a steer belonging to said James Rogers, ...*
>
> *Wherefore' [referring to the deed from Lovewell] 'they prayed to be included as fourteen persons, among the grantees and the 2190 acres assigned to them as their share.'*

On 10 August 1763, the town was incorporated as Dunbarton after Dumbarton in Scotland, the area from which many of the ancestors of the original settlers had come before their settlement in Ireland and America.* James and his family finally returned to the land in 1749 to rebuild their home.

James had a close friend: Ebenezer Ayer, a resident of Haverhill, Massachusetts, known as a great hunter. For many years Ayer had come to the Dunbarton region in search of game, and he had built a crude, semi-permanent camp there. During the early spring of 1753 when he was about 53 years old, James learned that his friend had arrived and decided to pay him a surprise visit. Ebenezer had been hunting all day when James approached at dusk wearing a bearskin coat. In the failing light Ebenezer saw what he thought was a bear and fired. In the words of a contemporary newspaper:

> Rogers fell mortally wounded and was at once taken by his friend to his cabin . . . . He died shortly before midnight, surrounded by his weeping family and his grief-stricken friend. This was the first death in the township, and the circumstances attending it called together the entire settlement at the funeral,

---

* That area had been initially settled by Alexander II about 1221, who took its name taken from the nearby castle Dumbritton (Fort of the Britons). The town stands at the confluence of the Clyde and Leven Rivers, not far from Glasgow.

James Rogers

which took place a few days afterwards. After a brief service the coffin was brought out and placed neath the trees that all might have an opportunity to view the mortal remains of one whom they all honoured and respected. . . . the coffin was closed. the procession was formed, and the cortege proceeded . . . . to Londonderry, where interment took place.*

A stone marking the grave of James Rogers is located in East Derry, New Hampshire beside a smaller one, possibly that of his youngest son John (2–6), who probably died in childhood. Mary Rogers was appointed administratrix of the estate on 25 June 1753. Her husband left real estate valued at £1500 and personal property of £444, a considerable amount in those days. He appears to have prospered after Starkstown was established. Mary probably remained on the family farm until the time of her death. The date of her death and location of her final resting place are unknown. She was still living in April 1760, we find from a newspaper advertisement for a runaway slave.† A portion of the land surrounding the homestead was sold by James (2–3) in 1772, and it seems likely that Mary died at some earlier time.

The Gravestone
of James Rogers

Located in the
Cemetery
in East Derry
New Hsmpshire

---

* Quoted in *The Snow Flake—The History of Dunbarton,* 1883.
† See newspaper advertisement on Prince, Appendix V to Robert Section 2–4, page 200.

The Dunbarton Historical Society has obtained a 99-year lease on a 25-foot right of way and an acre of land surrounding the site of the second homestead of the Rogers family in the area. A bronze plaque, shown below, marks the location on the farm of Mr. E. N. Noyes in the Great Meadows, near Dunbarton Centre, New Hampshire. Two hundred years later the area is almost overgrown with trees but is an interesting place to visit. The cellar is still clearly discernible.

SITE OF THE SECOND HOME OF
JAMES ROGERS, FATHER OF
MAJOR ROBERT ROGERS
BUILT CIRCA 1749
ORIGINAL ROGERS HOME
IN THE GREAT MEADOWS WAS
BURNED DURING INDIAN RAIDS
OF 1746
DUNBARTON HISTORICAL SOCIETY
1964

James Rogers and his children

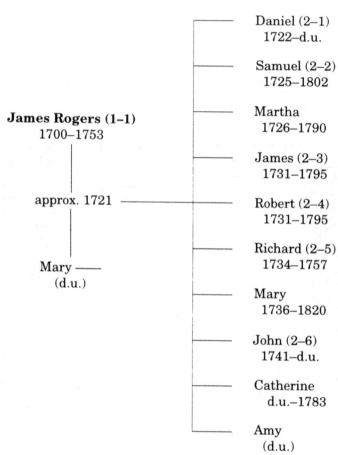

James Rogers (1–1)
1700–1753

approx. 1721 ——————

Mary ——
(d.u.)

Daniel (2–1)
1722–d.u.

Samuel (2–2)
1725–1802

Martha
1726–1790

James (2–3)
1731–1795

Robert (2–4)
1731–1795

Richard (2–5)
1734–1757

Mary
1736–1820

John (2–6)
1741–d.u.

Catherine
d.u.–1783

Amy
(d.u.)

d.u. = date(s) unknown

The parents of James and Mary Rogers have not been entered as research has not determined which of the traditions concerning them are factual.

Sources disagree on the dates of birth of the Rogers children. The dates for Robert, Richard and Mary have been verified from primary sources. The remaining children's birthdates have been deduced from the legal action of 1748, family records and research from historians such as John Cuneo. Where a conflict occurred, dates were taken from primary sources whenever possible.

Children of James Rogers (1–1)

1. Daniel Rogers (2–1) (21 August 1722–?)

Daniel Rogers was born in Londonderry, Ireland, and came with his parents to America around 1729. Several sources state that he was married and had a family at the time of his death. In 1773 Daniel was living in Dunbarton, New Hampshire, and on 29 December, he was appointed chairman of the Committee of Proprietors. Family tradition holds that he went to sea and was drowned off Cuba, leaving a large family at home. Possibly he was involved with his brother James in the privateer scheme and entered on a mercantile seafaring life; however, this is speculation.* Research has failed to uncover any details of his family or descendants.

Children: unknown

2. Samuel Rogers (2–2) (10 May 1725–17 March 1802)

Samuel Rogers was born in Londonderry, Ireland, and came with the family to America around 1729. Some sources indicate that he was the eldest child; however, these do not list the dates of birth of the children. He saw action in the militia in 1745 and was a member of John Goff's scouting company in 1748 during King George's War.† Research has failed to determine if he saw service during the French and Indian War or the American Revolution. His responsibilities for the family may have kept him close to home. He apparently inherited his father's homestead in Dunbarton and lived as a citizen of the United States. His mother lived with his family in the years leading up to her death. According to the "History of Nutfield", Samuel was a resident of Bow in 1758. The town was set apart from Rumford in 1765, and Samuel was appointed moderator and elected selectman in the town, positions he held for many years. The "History of Nutfield" relates that he died on 17 March 1802, at the age of 77 years. He was buried in the East Dunbarton Cemetery, close to the original family homestead. Very little is known about his family other than that he had a daughter, Elizabeth, who died at the age of 83 on 30 May 1839, and was laid to rest near her father. It is thought that there were a number of other children but they are unknown to us.

Children: at least one daughter.

---

* For details on the privateer, see James Rogers, Section 2–3, page 40.
† See Robert Rogers, Section 2–4, page 117 and Historical Events, Annex B.

3. Martha Rogers (1726—07 Sep 1790)

Martha is believed to have been born near Londonderry, Ireland, about 1726, the third child of James and Mary Rogers. She was very young when the family came to America about 1729. Some time around 1750 she married John Miller (03 Aug 1725–23 May 1804), of Londonderry, Ireland. John had also come to America as part of the Ulster Scot migration, but the date of his arrival and the names of his parents are not known. The couple initially lived in Dunbarton, New Hampshire, and later moved to the vicinity of Westminster, Vermont. Both John and Martha died in Westminster, but little else is known about this family.

Children: at least 3 sons and 1 daughter.

4. James Rogers (2–3) (2 Apr 1728–23 Sep 1790)

See Section 2–3 following.

5. Robert Rogers (2–4) (7 Nov 1731–18 May 1795)

See Section 2–4 following.

6. Richard Rogers (2–4) (6 May 1734–22 June 1757)

Richard Rogers was born in Methuen, Massachusetts Bay Colony, about two and a half years after his brother Robert. The register of the First Congregational Church of Methuen records his birth and baptism on 12 May 1734. He was implicated in the counterfeiting scheme with his brother Robert, but escaped punishment when the two of them joined the militia.* On 24 April 1755, he joined the Tenth Company of Blanchard's New Hampshire Regiment as a sergeant, commanded by Captain William Simes. On the regiment's return home from the Lake George area on 4 October, he joined his brother's small unit of volunteer scouts as acting lieutenant. This unit became the eyes of Sir William Johnson's army. When Robert was ordered to raise a company of rangers on 28 November, Richard was appointed first lieutenant. On 24 July 1756 he was promoted to captain and placed in command of his own company of rangers when General Abercromby ordered the corps expanded. Richard played an active role in the winter operations around Lake George in 1756 and assumed command of the existing four companies of rangers during February and March 1757, while Robert was incapacitated with smallpox. During this period he managed much of the recruiting effort, thus effectively contributing to the growth of the corps. On 21 April he received orders to move his company to Fort William Henry, to serve as the scouting arm of General Webb's army, while the remaining companies were sent to New York to embark for the

* For details see Robert Rogers, Section 2–4, page 118.

A company of Rogers' Rangers on a Winter Scout

Members of one of the recreated Companies of Rogers' Rangers during
the winter of 1990. The Ranger in the white coat is Tim Todish,
Adjutant of Jaeger's Battalion. See Appendix II to Section 2–4.

expedition against Louisbourg. He commanded at the Battle of Coutre-
coeur on 6 June. After returning to the fort he came down with smallpox
and died on 22 June 1757.

Shortly thereafter Fort William Henry came under attack by the
Marquis de Montcalm,* who took advantage of the reduced British troop
concentrations in the Lake George area to strike a blow for France. The
siege lasted from 25 July to 19 August. (It is well presented in the strikingly
beautiful 1992 movie *Last of the Mohicans.*) After the surrender of the post,
the French lost control of their Indian allies, who massacred the defenders.
Even the bodies of those who had recently died were dug up and scalped;
Richard's body was one of those so desecrated. In the ensuing weeks a
devastating epidemic of smallpox broke out among the Indians. The braves
carried the plague back to their own territory, and death spread to tribes
as far as the Mississippi. It could be said he had his revenge. Richard was
never married and had no descendants.

---

* See Historical Figures, Annex C.

---

7. Mary Rogers (3 Aug 1736–1820)

Mary Rogers is believed to have been born on the family farm near Dracut, Massachusetts. Although her parents were Presbyterian, she was baptized in the First Congregational Church of Methuen, a Puritan church as were her brothers Robert and Richard. About 1756 she married Hugh Miller (1734–1810), of Dunbarton, New Hampshire. Hugh had served with her brother Robert during the French and Indian War. It is believed that the couple initially settled near Lichfield or Merrimack, New Hampshire, although research has been unable to uncover any details of them in this period. Some time before 1770, the couple moved west among the original settlers of Bradford in the New Hampshire Grants.* There they remained for more than twenty years. Hugh served in the Revolutionary War but made no pension application; consequently few details of his service are available. There can be little doubt that he fought on the side of the United States, and this is likely to have caused friction with Mary's family. In 1795, when Hugh was approximately 60 years of age, he packed up his wife, the youngest children, several of his older children and their spouses, and a few grandchildren, and moved north to become the first settler of the town of Richford. The *Vermont Historical Magazine,* in an article published in 1871, gives the following account:

> They arrived here in March [1795], and the weather was so severe that it was necessary to erect some shelter without delay; they cleared a small patch of ground, left four blue beech staddles standing, for corners, withed on poles, covered with boughs and blankets, and probably carpeted the cold ground with smaller boughs of hemlock. Such was their camp.

The article goes on to describe the hardships of life in those early days in Richford. Mary acted as a doctor and midwife in an area devoid of medical services, and frequently had to travel long distances, often on snowshoes, to help deliver a baby. She made her way through the forest, marking trees that later served as a guide to others. In 1802 Bishop Hedding, a pioneer of Methodism, followed the trail blazed by the early immigrants and preached the first sermon in the town at the Miller home. Hugh died in 1810 of "shock", at the age of 76, twenty days after learning of the death of his son Daniel. He was buried on his farm, and a plaque in the Richford cemetery was later erected by descendants. Mary lived with her son Jacob until her death in 1820 at the age of 84. Her funeral was held in the barn on the family farm, and she was laid to rest beside her husband.

Children: 5 sons, 5 daughters.

---

* The New Hampshire Grants later became the State of Vermont.

8. John Rogers (2–6) (1741–?)

There are several indications of a sixth son born to James and Mary Rogers but there is very little information. The family had five sons when they moved to Dunbarton, New Hampshire, in 1739; but during the legal action of 1748, James indicated that he had six sons, John the youngest. Considering the dates of birth of the other children, this child was probably born around 1741. Extensive research has failed to uncover any information on John. A small grave lies next to that of James Rogers (1–1), however, and as most of the other children are accounted for, this child may have died very young. (The other James Rogers, denoted in Appendix II as James Rogers of Londonderry, also had a son named John, born in 1729. This child eventually became the first settler in Actworth (now Acworth), New Hampshire. He is not the John Rogers of this section as far as we can tell.)

9. Catherine Rogers (?–1783?)

Catherine Rogers was probably born in Dunbarton, New Hampshire. She married Alexander Blair (?–1767), son of Captain James Blair of Londonderry, Ireland. His family probably came to America with the Ulster Scot migration and settled in Londonderry, New Hampshire in 1719. Alexander, like his father, was an officer in the British Army and received a land grant as a reward for service to the Crown. He died by drowning in New Hampshire in 1767. The names of Catherine's and Alexander's children have been taken from the paper "James Rogers of Londonderry and James Rogers of Dunbarton" by Josiah Drummond. This document establishes that they were all of Londonderry and refers to a deed dated 16 April 1787 by which they sold all interest in the estate of their grandfather, James Rogers of Dunbarton. (This deed has been copied on the next page.) By 1792 the boys had disposed of all of their property from both the Rogers and Blair families, and had departed the area. Research has failed to uncover any further details of this family or its descendants.

Children: 4 sons.

10. Amy Rogers (?–?)

Amy Rogers was probably born in the town of Dunbarton. She married Samuel Barnett (?–?), son of John Barnett of Londonderry, New Hampshire. Samuel, with several of his brothers and his sons, served in the Revolutionary War and later became one of the first settlers in the town of Newbury, Vermont. No other information on this family has been uncovered.

Children: at least 2 sons.

Know all men by these presents that we, James Blair, David Blair, Robert Blair and Alexander Blair, all of Londonderry, in the County of Rockingham and the State of New Hampshire, yeoman. For and in consideration of, the sum of twelve pounds lawful money, to us in hand before delivery hereof, well and truly paid by Phineas Bailey of Dunbarton, in the County of Hillsborough, and the State aforesaid, Gentleman. The receipt whereof, we do hereby acknowledge, have given. granted, bargin, sell, aliene, enfiff, convey and confirm unto the said Phineas Baily, his heirs and assigns forever, all rights, title, interest and possessions we have or may forever claim of, in and to all real & state that our honored mother, Catherine Blair, died seized and possessed of, as an heir to the estate of our honored grandfather, James Rogers, late of Dunbarton aforesaid, yeoman, deceased.

In witness whereof we have set our hand and seals this sixteenth day of April A.D., 1787.

Signed, sealed & delivered in presence of us:

Archibald McMurphy   *David Blair*
Moses Rolfe   *Robert Blair*   *Seal*
John Miller   *James Blair*
Oliver Sanders   *Alexander Blair*

Appendix I: The Ulster Scot Migrations

The story of the Protestant Reformation and the religious wars of England, Scotland and Ireland during the 16th and 17th centuries is a significant part of the history of the Rogers clan. They were among the people who emigrated from Scotland to Ireland in the 17th century and thence to America in the early 18th century, becoming known as the Ulster Scots. The chain of events leading to that migration is in part the story of how the Rogers family came to be in North America.

King Henry VIII (1509–1547), vexed at the refusal of Pope Clement VII to annul his eighteen-year marriage to Catherine of Aragon, repudiated the authority of Rome over his kingdom. He induced Parliament to enact a statute that formally separated the English Church from the Roman Catholic Church. The result was the creation of the Church of England and the establishment of the king as its head. This development had the effect of speeding the Protestant Reformation, and religious controversy and strife between Papist and Protestant raged throughout England. The Crown confiscated the lands of the monasteries, and members of the Catholic Church began to suffer severe persecution. During the reign of King Edward VI (1547–1553), influences of religious reform were strongly felt, and the Church of England moved further away in doctrine and sentiment from the Catholic Church, which was increasingly seen as "foreign" and hostile.

Religious reforms were swept away with the accession of Queen Mary I (1553–1558) to the throne. She was a fanatical Catholic who quickly re-established Papal influence and repealed all the anti-Catholic acts except confiscatory decrees. Despite the moderating influence of her husband, King Philip II of Spain, who was also a champion of Catholicism, her actions led to the highly publicized executions of prominent Protestants and her reign was marked by hatred. Philip left her when he realized she would never bear him an heir, and she died a lonely and unhappy woman. She was succeeded by her half-sister, Queen Elizabeth I (1558–1603).

While the day of religious tolerance had not yet dawned, the reign of Elizabeth did bring a measure of stability to the land, at least initially. Later, however, the heavy hand of the re-established Church of England was felt, not only by the Papists but also by Protestants who refused to comply with the prescribed forms of worship. As non-adherents, many Puritans were driven out of England during her reign. In 1588 King Philip II of Spain, in a final effort to carry out a Papal behest to destroy the Church of England, sent a massive naval force, the Armada, against England. It was crippled by a tempest and destroyed by a smaller English fleet.

In 1599, Elizabeth dispatched the Earl of Essex, Robert Devereux, with a large army to Ireland to suppress a rebellion led by Hugh O'Neill, Earl of Tyrone. This army was annihilated, but the rebellion ended in an uneasy truce. O'Neill later violated the truce and subdued the Province of Ulster. Reinforced by Spanish troops, he subsequently threatened the complete subversion of Ireland. An army under the Earl of Mountjoy routed O'Neill's forces at the Battle of Kinsale in 1601 and carried him to London in chains, where he was imprisoned.

O'Neill was pardoned after the accession of King James I (1603–1625), but he immediately returned to Ireland to organize yet another rebellion with assistance from the Earl of Tyrconnell and from Spain. In 1607 the plot was uncovered and both earls fled to Spain: the uprising collapsed. The property of those who took part in the rebellion was seized by the Crown, a total of some two million acres. The land included all the present area of Northern Ireland as well as the counties of Donegal, Cavan and Monaghan in the present Irish Republic, an area collectively known as Ulster.

The Church of Scotland was created in 1590 as a Presbyterian Calvinist church which evolved differently from the Protestant Episcopalianism that was established in England. (The Puritans were a reform group of the Episcopalians who suffered for their principles to keep the faith pure; they later formed their own churches in New England.) With the suppression of the Irish, James thought to populate the new Crown lands with loyal Protestant subjects and looked to his native Scotland. The Scots, not impressed by the idea, consented to go only after receiving a number of inducements. In 1612, a group from Argyleshire, Scotland, crossed the North Channel and settled in the Province of Ulster, in and around the city of Londonderry. Immigration continued for many years and over time led to the severe religious conflict that has plagued Northern Ireland for centuries. It was these Scots and their descendants, as well as others who settled in Ireland over the following hundred years, who became known to history as the "Ulster Scots", and are frequently but incorrectly referred to as "Scotch-Irish".

James was succeeded by his son, King Charles I (1625–1649), whose clashes with Parliament over the question of power ultimately led to the English Civil Wars.* Although he was an ardent Episcopalian, his wife Henrietta Maria was Catholic, and her constant interference in politics did not help his position or endear him to his people. During this war, Irish leaders rose in revolt against the Crown to recover their lands, and in 1641 some 40,000 Protestants were killed. The trial for treason and subsequent

---

* See the English Civil Wars in Historical Events, Annex B.

England, Scotland and Ireland

execution of the King at the hands of Parliament brought an end to the war, and the Commonwealth (1649–1660) was established, governed for the most part by Oliver Cromwell as Lord Protector. Cromwell crushed the rebellion in Ireland, and the Protestants again attained the upper hand. The austerity of the Protectorate and the domination of the army alienated the people, and in 1661 they welcomed back the eldest son of the late king who succeeded to the throne as King Charles II (1649–1685). During his reign Ireland was relatively quiet, and in 1680 the Cargill family* came

---

* In the succeeding generation Captain David Cargill (1661–1734) became a ruling elder in the church and with his son-in-law, the Reverend James McGregor, was instrumental in organising the movement of the Presbyterian church to New England. James McGregor was not only involved with his son, the Reverend David McGregor, in the legal action in re Lovewell's Grant in 1748 but was the grandfather of Margaret, wife of James Rogers (2–3).

from Perthshire, Scotland, to settle at Aghadowey, in the Bann River Valley.

When Charles died with no legitimate heir, he was succeeded by his brother King James II (1685–1688), who had been raised a Catholic. James was uncompromising during his reign, and there was considerable religious persecution, particularly in Scotland and Ireland. The king's first wife was Anne Hyde, by whom he had two daughters who were raised as Protestants. He later married Mary of Modena, who was a Catholic, and the birth of a son James threatened the country with a succession of Catholic kings, the restoration of the Catholic Church and another civil war. Several prominent Englishmen formally invited Prince William of Orange and his wife Mary, the eldest daughter of James, to reign as joint sovereigns. They landed without opposition and James fled to France. They were crowned King William III (1689–1702) and Queen Mary II (1689–1694).

There was then in and around Londonderry a hardy band of Ulster Scots. These people were reverent and of unswerving loyalty, and neither the force of persecution from opposing sects nor the arm of the civil power could deter them from following what they deemed to be true faith and pure worship. In the spring of 1689, James sailed from France and landed in Ireland to gather supporters. He marched north with a combined French and Irish army intending to cross the North Channel to Scotland, where friendly clans awaited his return, then continue south to London to reclaim his throne. Only the town of Londonderry and its population of Ulster Scots opposed his movement. On 17 April the army surrounded the city. The Siege of Londonderry continued for 105 days. The city was eventually relieved by sea, but the original 7000 inhabitants had been reduced to 3000, mainly by starvation and disease. James was forced to withdraw his forces and was finally defeated at the Battle of the Boyne on 1 July 1690. The defenders of Londonderry had thwarted the enemies of the Crown, and King William was not slow to show his appreciation. Thereafter all those who bore arms in defence of that city were exempt from taxation anywhere in the British dominions.

Although the Ulster Scots were gratefully remembered by their sovereign, they were still uncomfortable in Ireland. Protestantism was the rule of the land, but they were surrounded by Irish Catholics who opposed their religion and were hostile to their very existence. Some of the Irish families had been deprived by force of their land upon which the Ulster Scots were settled. In addition, the settlers did not own their farms but held the land on a lease from the Crown; and as Presbyterians they could not in

* After this battle Protestant Ulstermen took the nickname "Orangemen" after their King.

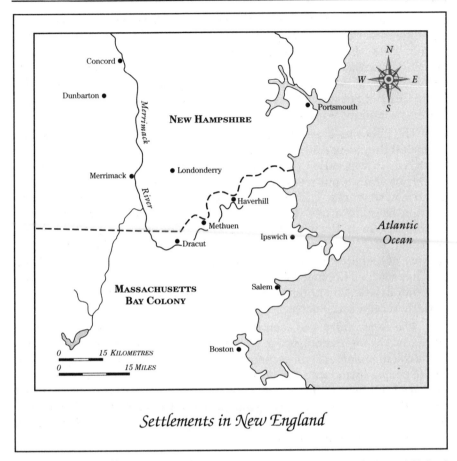

Settlements in New England

conscience conform to the faith and forms of worship of the established Church of England or of the surrounding Catholics. Many of them believed that it was only a matter of time before these difficulties would destroy them. Seeking a home where they might practice their religion without contention and where they could own land, a number agreed to send an agent to America to locate and secure a tract for their occupation.

In 1718 this group signed a memorial to Governor Shute of New England, indicating their desire to immigrate. There were some 320 signatures on the document, representing about 217 families. A portion of the memorial appears on the next page.* William Boyd crossed the Atlantic bearing the memorial and obtained from the Governor of Massachusetts Bay Colony an invitation and a promise of assistance in obtaining the

---

* A copy of the complete memorial may be found in *The History of Londonderry*. See Bibliography.

---

necessary lands upon which to settle. The group converted their assets and sailed for America on the brigantine *Robert*. They arrived at Boston on 4 August 1718 after a six-week voyage. This was the first of five vessels bringing the initial 120 families of Ulster Scots to the New World. On arrival, the immigrants were divided among the existing Puritan towns of the colony until a permanent settlement could be located. Sixteen of these families remained with the Reverend James McGregor at Salem.

The following spring men began to explore west of Casco Bay, and at Haverhill they were told of an area on the Beaver River, about thirty miles north, which was called "Nutfield" because of an abundance of chestnut, butternut and walnut trees. The Reverend James applied for permission to settle in that area, gathered his flock and on 11 April 1719 moved to the location to build a new town in the wilderness, the first Presbyterian community in a Puritan New England. The settlers petitioned the Governor of New Hampshire for incorporation on 21 September but because of disputes involving Indian deeds, a charter was delayed. They then approached Colonel John Wheelwright, who was assumed to have the best Indian title, and purchased the land to obtain clear title. Each settler initially received 120 acres.

The community was soon thriving and prosperous. Their numbers increased through immigration from Ireland and from other communities in the colonies, some of whose members had accompanied them to America. These people introduced the potato into New England, and also began to produce high-quality linen. On 21 June 1722 the town was incorporated under the name Londonderry. From here the Ulster Scots moved farther into the wilderness, founding other towns in New York, New Hampshire, Vermont, Maine and Nova Scotia.

---

*To His Excellency, The Right Honourable Collonel Samuel Suitte,
Governour of New England.*

We whose names are underwritten, Inhabitants of ye North of Ireland, Doe in our own names, and in the names of many others our Neighbours, Gentlemen, Ministers, Farmers and Tradesmen Commissionate and appoint our trusty and well beloved Friend, the Reverend Mr. William Boyd of Macasky, to His Excellency the Right Honourable Collonel Samuel Suitte Governour of New England, and to assure His Excellency of our sincere and hearty Inclination to Transport our selves to that very excellent and renowned Plantation upon our obtaining from his Excellency suitable incouragement. And further to act and Doe in Our names as his Prudence shall direct.

Given under our hands this 26th day of March, Anno. Dom. 1718.

Appendix II: The Two Rogers Families

From various historical records it is apparent that two brothers, James and Hugh Rogers, accompanied David Cargill and James McGregor during the initial Ulster Scot migration to America in 1718. Some historians claim that this family is the one from which the family discussed in this work is descended. While it is remotely possible that there is an earlier connection, so far as research has determined, this Rogers family is not related to the family which is the subject of this book. Details of both families are shown below to illustrate this point. The fact that the two families lived in and around the same area has caused considerable confusion to genealogists for many years. A good reference to detail some of the specific differences is the paper "The Two James Rogers" by Josiah Drummond. This document contains some minor factual errors, but the basic thesis is valid. The evidence clearly shows the two James Rogers families were entirely separate and almost certainly not related.

James Rogers of Londonderry (1686–1755)

James Rogers was born in Ireland in 1686 and came to America with his wife Jean (1694–5 September 1755) in the expedition led by David Cargill in 1718. With his brother Hugh (1683–4 March 1763) and Hugh's wife, also named Jean (1693–28 February 1756), he signed the original memorial to Governor Shute, obtained land in Nutfield and became known as James Rogers of Londonderry or Billerica. James was one of the petitioners for Lovewell's Grant and received a share in the new township. As far as research has determined, however, he never lived in the town of Starkstown, or Dunbarton as the grant later became known, and in 1748 he sold his share to James McGregor, the youngest son of the Reverend James McGregor above. It appears that he lived his whole life in Londonderry and died there on 22 September 1755 at the age of 69 years. A few years later James Rogers (2–3), son of James Rogers of Dunbarton, moved to Londonderry and married Margaret McGregor, daughter of the Reverend David McGregor, thus further confusing genealogical records. James Rogers of Londonderry and his wife Jean had ten children, as shown on the next page.

Name	Date of Birth	Married
a) Margaret Rogers	_____	m. Samuel Thompson
b) Mary Rogers	_____	m. Joseph Scobey
c) Jean Rogers	_____	m. William Morrison
d) Martha Rogers	03 May 1723	m. Robert McClure
e) Thomas Rogers	07 Jul 1724	m. Elizabeth _____
f) William Rogers	15 Sep 1726	m. Jeanet _____
g) John Rogers	25 Jun 1729	m. Jean Ewins
h) James Rogers	22 Feb 1731	unmarried, died young
i) Samuel Rogers	_____ 1739	unmarried, died in 1755
j) Esther Rogers	_____	m. Samuel Houston

James Rogers of Dunbarton (1700–1753)

A full history of James Rogers of Dunbarton, the patriarch of this work, may be found in section 1–1. For the purpose of this appendix it is sufficient to say that James and his wife Mary came to America from Ireland sometime in 1729 or 1730, and that therefore the other family preceded them by at least ten years. They initially settled in Methuen but in 1738 moved into the wilderness and settled on part of Lovewell's grant. They were forced from their land by Indian raids. When they returned in 1748 they became involved in the dispute with the settlers from Londonderry, including the other James Rogers. When the dispute was settled, each received a share in the new township, which caused considerable confusion. As far as records show, this family was known as James Rogers of Dunbarton, Bow or Starkstown. James Rogers of Dunbarton died in the spring of 1753. He and Mary Rogers had the children listed in the main body of this work.

Appendix III: Proprietors' Meeting for the Township of Stark's Town

The first meeting of the proprietors of Stark's Town took place on 2 March 1752 at Portsmouth, New Hampshire. The purpose of the meeting was to take action regarding the settlement and future welfare of the community. The following extract is taken verbatim from the proprietors' records.

Province of New Hampshire

At a meeting of the proprietors of the lands purchased of John Tufton Mason, Esq., at Portsmouth, held on Monday, the second day of March, in the year of our Lord one thousand seven hundred and fifty-two, therefore, voted, That there be and is hereby granted unto Archibald Stark, William Stark, John Stark, Archibald Stark, jr., all of a place called Amoskeag, in the province of New Hampshire; the Rev. David McGregor, Robert McMurphy, William Stinson, John Cochran, James Evans, Hugh Dunshee, John McCurdy, John Carr, John Cochran, Hugh Jameson, David Stinson, Joseph Scoby, Matthew Thorton, Daniel McCurdy, John Carr, John Cochran, Dr. Alexander Todd, William Hogg, James McGregore, David Leslie, George Clark, William Rankin, William Stinson, James Rogers, James Cochran, John McDuffie, James McGregor, Samuel Todd, David Craige, all of Londonderry, in said province; Thomas Mills, Samuel Hogg, Caleb Page, jr., Samuel Richards, Thomas Follansbee, jr., all of Hampstead, in said province; and Jeremiah Page of said place; William Elliott, John Hall, Adam Dickey, all of Derryfield, in said province; Joseph Blanchard, Esq., Joseph Blanchard, jr., both of Dunstable, in said province; Joseph Putney, James Rogers, (their eldest sons for one right), all living on a tract of land hereby granted; William Putney and Obadiah Foster, of the same place, for one hundred acres, and the remaining part of the share or right of Hugh Ramsey of said Londonderry, John Morton of Ports-mouth, in said province, and George Mussey of said Portsmouth, William Stark, (William Stark above named having three rights, being the same man), and Archibald Stark above named, Samuel Emerson, Esq., James Varnum, both of Chester, in said province; John Campbell of Haverhill, William Hyslop of Boston, both in the province of Massachusetts Bay; William Gault of Canterbury, in the province of New Hampshire; Samuel Fulton, late of said Londonderry; equally, as excepting aforesaid, to them and their heirs and assigns, excepting as heretofore excepted, on the terms, conditions and limitations hereinafter expressed, all right, title, estate and property of the said proprietors of in and unto all that tract or parcel of land, about five miles square, more or less, situated in the province of New Hampshire, and bounded as follows: Beginning at the main river on the northerly side of a tract of land lately granted by the said proprietors to Thomas Parker and others, and running westward as far as that tract runs, joining on the same; then running north two degrees west, five miles and one hundred and eight rods; thence north seventy-nine degrees east, till it comes to the Bow line; then southerly by the township of Bow and continuing by that till it comes to the said river; then by that till it comes to the place where it begins;

To have and to hold to them and their assigns as aforesaid in the following terms and conditions, namely: That the division already made and the lots as they have been drawn and numbered shall be and hereby is ratified and confirmed as a full and effectual severance and division of the tract of land, to hold the respective lots to the person or persons to whose name or names the respective numbers of said lots are affixed, and to his and their heirs and assigns, excepting as is hereinafter otherwise mentioned, that the said grantees make a settlement on the said tract of land in the following manner, viz: That thirty families be settled on the said tract of land, each having a house sixteen feet square, or equal thereto, on the same lot belonging to the respective owners of thirty shares among the said grantees, and that each of the said thirty have three acres of land fitted for tillage or mowing on one of the lots belonging to each respective share of the thirty by the last day of May next, and shall clear three acres of land more yearly on one lot of each of the thirty shares aforesaid for a term of two years from the last day of May next; That ten families more shall be settled on the lots belonging to ten other shares of the said grantees, having a house of the dimensions aforesaid and three acres of land cleared on a lot belonging to each of the said shares, by the expiration of three years, to be computed from the last day of May next, which ten families are each to proceed in clearing three acres yearly for two years then next succeeding in manner aforesaid. And that ten families more be settled on the lots belonging to ten other shares of the said grantees each having an house on a lot belonging to the respective shares, of the same dimensions as aforesaid, and three acres of land cleared as aforesaid within five years from May next and to proceed in clearing three acres more yearly the two next succeeding years, as aforesaid;

That David Stinson, David McGregore, James McGregore, David Lesly, Samuel Fulton, Archibald Stark, (Archibald Stark for one more), George Clark, William Rankin and William Stinson make or cause to be made the settlement of the first ten families above mentioned, that Joseph Blanchard, James

Rogers, John Campbell, Samuel Emerson, James Cochran, Matthew Ramsey, James Varnum, John McDuffie, Robert McMurphy and Archibald Stark make or cause to be made the settlement of the second ten families above mentioned, and that William Gault, William Stark, Joseph Blanchard, Esq., William Hyslop, James McGragore, William Stark, Adam Dickey, Samuel Todd, Jeremiah Page and David Craige, in consideration of their having paid a certain sum of money to the settlers to carry on the settlement, be and hereby are exempted from making any settlement on their shares;

That in order to carry on the said settlement to effect, each of the aforesaid grantees pay all such sums of money as shall be voted to be raised by the major part of the said grantees at any regular meeting of them, according to such rules as have been or shall be agreed upon by them for calling the same, to such person or persons and at such times as they shall determine as aforesaid, and in default of such payment, that the part, share and right of the grantee who shall refuse or neglect to pay as aforesaid, in and to said land shall be and hereby is subject to and changed with the payment thereof. And the person or persons appointed to receive such sum or sums of money aforesaid, shall and hereby have full power and authority to sell so much thereof, as near as it can be conveniently done, as will raise money sufficient for such payment with all incidental charges, as occasion shall require from time to time, giving the delinquent person three weeks' notice of such design before the sale is actually made;

That a meeting house of sufficient dimensions be built on the said land within five years from next May, fit for preaching in, and that the grantees maintain the preaching of the gospel there constantly after six years from next May;

That any and every of the said grantees who shall neglect to perform and fulfill every article, matter and thing herein for him to do, shall forfeit his whole right, share and interest in and to the said tract of land to those of the said grantees who shall have done and performed the same for themselves, and they shall have the term of one year after such forfeiture accrues (which shall be reckoned and adjudged to be immediately on the expiration of the time herein allowed for the doing any of the said matters and things) to settle or cause such forfeited right or share to be settled;

That twenty-five of the said rights and shares, be and hereby are issued to the said grantees, their heirs and assigns, and the said share be for the first minister, his heirs or assigns, who shall there continue till he is regularly dismissed or as long as he shall live, that another of the said shares shall be for the use of the ministry forever, and another for the use and maintenance of a school there forever, that these three shares, with twenty-two of those reserved shall be and hereby are exempted and fully exonerated from any and every duty, charge, matter and thing relating to the making of the said settlement, and from all taxes and charges until improved by the owners of each respective right; that all highways that shall be laid out on said land shall be by a committee to be appointed for that purpose by the grantors and grantees, only the person on whose land such way shall run not to be paid for the same;

And if the settlement shall not be made as aforesaid, according to the true intent and meaning thereof, and by the last period of time limited as aforesaid for the doing thereof, the whole grant to be null and void, and the said land to revert, retain or remain the right, estate and property of the grantors, as though the vote had never been passed; reserving also white pine trees standing and growing on said premises, which are hereby granted to His Majesty, his heirs and successors;

That the lots on the aforesaid division, set off and numbered to John Twigg shall be and hereby are appropriated to Archibald Stark, those to John Adams are appropriated to Thomas Mills, John McAllister's to Archibald Stark, William Carr's to John Stark, Archibald Stark's to John Campbell, John Hogg's to William Hogg, Matthew Morton's to John McCurdy, John Starks to William Stinson, Hugh Ramsey's to William Hyslop, Samuel Rankin's to Robert McMurphy, Samuel Stinson's to David Stinson, John Stinson's to William Stark, Alexander Gault's to James Evans, Archibald Cunningham's to James McGregore, John Homer's to William Stark, Thomas Hall's to William Rankin, Samuel Caldwell's to Joseph Blanchard, Esq., John Ramsey's to William Putney, and Obadiah Foster's for one hundred acres and the rest or remaining lots to Hugh Ramsey to hold to them and their respective heirs and assigns;

That four of the said reserved shares being the lots numbered twelve in the first range, two in the second range, twelve in the fourth range, ten on the south side in the seventh range, one and two in the thirteenth range, are hereby granted to the said grantees, their heirs and assigns, upon the conditions aforesaid that the remaining land within the bounds aforesaid which is not comprehended within the said divisions, shall be hereafter divided between the said grantors and grantees in the proportions aforesaid: that is, the grantors having seventeen shares thereof and the grantees being in charge of the division and making the settlement and complying with the terms and conditions herein before limited and expressed, and the lot in said divisions numbered three in the seventh range being one of the said reserved shares be and are hereby granted to Noah Emery of Kittery, gent., his heirs and assigns, exempted and exonerated from duty of settling and paying and charges, tax or expense until improved by him or them; and in the case there shall be an Indian war within any of the times limited for doing the several matters and things aforesaid respectively, the said terms to be allowed for any of the said matters after that impediment shall be resolved;

Lastly, that the grantors do hereby engage and promise to the said grantees to defend them and their heirs and assigns against all and every action and lawsuit that shall be prosecuted, moved and stirred against them and any of them by any person whomsoever claiming the said land or any part thereof by any other title than the title of the said grantors or that from which theirs was derived, with this condition and limitation, that in case the said grantors, their heirs or assigns be ejected and ousted by any such right or title, then they shall recover nothing of and from the said grantors, their heirs, executors or administrators for the land hereby granted, nor for any labor or expense whatsoever which they shall have been or shall be at in consequence of this grant; and the lots in said division called said lot number one be for Matthew Livermore, his heirs and assigns, and that called lot number two be to William Parker, his heirs and assigns.

Attest: Alexander McMurphy
                                   Proprietors' Clerk

James Rogers of the King's Rangers

James Rogers (2–3)
(2 April 1728–23 September 1790)

James Rogers was born in Ireland and immigrated to North America with his parents about 1729 (see Section 1–1). He grew up in Starkstown, New Hampshire; what if any formal education he received is not known. From available evidence and subsequent events it seems certain that he was highly intelligent and that he became literate probably through his own dedicated effort. Very little is known of his early life, and we assume that he remained close to home, no doubt helping the family to defend the homestead. This was in sharp contrast to his brothers Samuel and Robert, who volunteered for military service during King George's War (1744–1748). Throughout his life, James was often eclipsed by his younger and more famous although somewhat erratic brother Robert. It is clear that he was not afflicted with Robert's adventurous spirit as he matured and developed into a stable practical farmer. Unfortunately the circumstances of the times forced him to follow in the footsteps of his brother (whose life is detailed in the following section.) This narrative is intended to isolate the very different experiences of these two men and to accurately describe the life of James, a truly remarkable individual in his own right.

The sketch to the left is an impression of how James would have appeared in 1784, the time of the Loyalist migration to Canada. Still a strong leader in his 50's, James is shown in the uniform of the King's Rangers with his fusil or musket protected in an Indian gun case. In the background, boats being taken up the Saint Lawrence River to what will later become Ontario.

In 1755, at the age of 27 years, James answered the call to arms and volunteered for service in a provincial corps. Hostilities at that time were already under way in what became known in North America as the French and Indian War. A formal state of war between England and France was not declared until 1756 with the outbreak of the Seven Years' War in Europe.* James did not join his brother's ranger corps at its start, and the reasons for this are unknown. When the third company of rangers was formed in the fall of 1756, Lieutenant Humphery Hobbs was promoted captain and appointed to command. James then joined the corps and was appointed as ensign of the company on 17 November. He was with the company during the engagement on 21 January 1757 which became known as the Battle of La Barbue Creek.† During this operation the rangers suffered nearly thirty per cent casualties. On 27 February, Lieutenant

---

* See Historical Events, Annex B.
† For details on this battle see Section 2–4, page 124.

Charles Bulkeley assumed temporary command of the company after the death from smallpox of Captain Hobbs,* and James was promoted second lieutenant. He was promoted first lieutenant and second in command when Bulkeley was made captain and appointed to command the company on 25 April.

With Bulkeley's company, James took part in the abortive attempt to capture the fortress of Louisbourg during the summer of 1757. Robert had been ordered to embark with four companies of rangers from New York for Halifax to join the expedition. By 1 July a British force of about 11,000 men had mustered for the assault. Then patrols around Île Royale† reported the presence of some 22 French warships in the bay. Because of the strengthened garrison, the operation was cancelled and the fleet returned to New York.

James took part in the numerous scouts of the Lake George area during the fall and winter of 1757. The Ranger Corps was expanded in 1758, and James, promoted captain on 14 January, was appointed to command one of four new companies to be raised for a second expedition against Louisbourg later in the year. He was engaged in recruiting for his new command and did not take part in the disastrous Battle on Snowshoes in March.‡

On 2 April 1758, James sailed from Boston with his own company and those of John McCurdy, William Stark and Jonathan Brewer. These units, totalling some 430 officers and men, were the only New England contingent in the expedition; yet they made a significant contribution to the success of the operation. James was senior captain of this detachment of rangers, and by all accounts he was admired and respected by his own troops as well as senior British officers. The rangers, however, were still independent companies at this time, and there was a considerable lack of confidence in "the capabilities of Provincials". It was therefore decided to form a "provisional battalion" commanded by Major George Scott of the 40th Regiment. This unit consisted of the ranger companies, Gorham's Rangers,§ 500 Highlanders and some of the newly created light infantry. This was a temporary arrangement intended for the landing phase of the operation only, as it was appreciated that the rangers would be far more effective functioning independently during subsequent operations.

* The same infection that carried off Richard Rogers (2–5) a short time later.
† Later to become Cape Breton Island, Nova Scotia.
‡ For details on this battle see Section 2–4, page 131.
§ Joseph Gorham was captain of Gorham's Rangers from Nova Scotia. This independent company predated Rogers' Rangers and was not part of the corps. See Historical Items, Annex A.

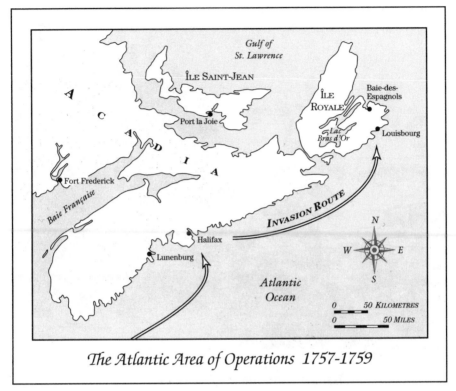

The Atlantic Area of Operations 1757-1759

Major General Jeffrey Amherst,* soon to be Commander-in-Chief in North America, commanded the invasion force of 27,140, made up of 12,370 British regulars, 500 American provincials (rangers), and 270 gunners in the land component, plus an additional 14,000 seamen from the fleet. At Louisbourg, the 7,790 French defenders comprised 2,400 *troupes de terre* (land soldiers or army), 1000 *troupes de la marine* (soldiers of the sea or marines), 400 Canadian militia, 120 gunners and 3,870 seamen from the fleet. They were well entrenched in strongly fortified positions or secure on board the 10 warships that mounted a total of 494 guns anchored in the bay.

The British fleet of 39 warships, mounting 1842 guns, sailed from Halifax on 28 May and sighted Louisbourg on 1 June. The sea was too rough for landing, and Amherst was forced to wait six days before it was calm enough to attempt any landing in small boats. On the evening of 5 June, a small party of rangers made themselves obnoxious to the French when they daringly ventured in a small boat close enough to shore to fire upon the defenders. Only four locations along the shoreline were suitable for

---

* See Historical Figures, Annex C.

Assault Landing at Freshwater Cove

landing, and they were heavily fortified. The battle plan involved a feint against three of these, while Brigadier James Wolfe* directed the real attack at Freshwater Cove.† The Grenadiers were to land first, followed by Scott with the rangers and light infantry, then the remainder of the brigade. The date of 8 June was selected for the assault.

When the first boats approached the beach they were raked by almost continuous fire, and it appeared for a time that the entire assault force would be annihilated. Wolfe passed the order to veer off; but on the right, slightly separated from the rest, the rangers and light infantry were sheltered by a small projecting point and either failed to see or ignored the signal. Ahead lay a rocky shore outside the designated landing area and therefore not initially subjected to the devastating fire from above. Once their intentions were detected, the defenders shifted their fire, but too late.

* See Historical Figures, Annex C.
† Known as La Cormorandière to the French but also as Kennington Cove in some sources.

The landing party forged ahead, boats being crushed on the rocks in a pounding surf, and landed in a storm of grape and musketry. Although some were drowned or sustained injury and many arrived on shore without muskets, they established a beachhead and stormed the enemy positions with bayonets, hatchets and knives, beating back the defenders in hand-to-hand combat. They then covered the landing of the rest of the brigade and turned a potential disaster into victory. According to one newspaper report, the rocks in the landing area "were extremely rough & hard to climb, being almost perpendicular." After the landing, the rangers reverted to their normal scouting duties, acting as skirmishers and protecting the flanks and supply lines of the army.

The sketch opposite depicts the landing with the rangers in the foreground and the light infantry in the middle distance. The sketch also shows the short knife-bayonets, used by the rangers for the first time in this engagement, and a Micmac Indian Chief. The Indians were present in significant numbers. This assault landing was one of the most admirable feats performed by Rogers' Rangers.

Surrounded, under siege with no hope of relief, Louisbourg finally capitulated after sustaining losses of 410 killed and 300–400 wounded. A total of 5,640 French troops were taken prisoner. The surrender took place on 26 July, seven weeks after the assault landing. The British lost 200 killed and 360 wounded in the operation.

While the army consolidated its gains on Île Royale, the rangers engaged in raiding French ports and settlements throughout Acadia and the Gulf of St. Lawrence. From 7–20 August, about 30 men from James' company took part in the capture of Spanish Bay,* while James, with the rest of the company plus another, accompanied Lord Rollo on his 8 August lightning raid on Port la Joie on Île Saint-Jean.† This raid resulted in additional Acadian deportations‡ and the construction of Fort Amherst at this location.

During September, James and his company were engaged in raids of the fishing stations on the Gaspé Peninsula, while the other companies struck along the north shore of Baie Française,§ building Fort Frederick at the future site of Saint John, New Brunswick. The rangers proved valuable

---

* Known as Baie-des-Espagnols to the French; later became Sydney, Nova Scotia.

† Near the present site of Charlottetown, Prince Edward Island.

‡ Rightly or wrongly, the existence of French-speaking Acadians in British territory in time of war was considered a significant security threat, particularly when the numbers included those who refused to sign the oath of allegiance that was required as a condition of their remaining in these territories. The rangers acted as ordered in the light of the military understanding of the time.

§ Later renamed the Bay of Fundy.

---

in gathering intelligence, capturing and interrogating prisoners, seizing vessels and destroying the barns, grain and cattle belonging to the enemy. They proved their abilities through action and became an effective weapon, thus raising in the esteem of senior officers. The King himself learned of their exploits and ordered Wolfe to take no less than 600 on his expedition against Quebec, scheduled for the following spring.

In October, the army went into winter quarters at Louisbourg and Halifax, and some units were deployed to occupy strategic locations in areas of newly acquired territory. Ranger companies were also divided into various areas: Captain McCurdy to Fort Frederick, Captains Brewer and Stark to Halifax, and Captain Gorham to Lunenburg, while James and his company remained at Louisbourg. The rangers were not idle during the winter. James and his company were employed seeking out armed bands of Acadians in the "Lake Labrador region"* according to one source. The rangers were active in at least 24 recorded scouts and actions from the fall of Louisbourg to their departure for Quebec the following June, including a number of skirmishes with the Micmac Indians.

In May 1759, the army was reassembled at Halifax and Louisbourg and departed for Quebec on 5 June, the newly promoted Major General James Wolfe in command. There was also a change in one of the ranger companies. Captain John McCurdy had been killed in an accident in January, and Lieutenant Moses Hazen had been promoted Captain and appointed to command his company.†

On 24 June 1759, Admiral Saunders' fleet of some 200 transports and ships of the line delivered Wolfe's army to Quebec. The British force consisted of some 8,646 troops (6,560 British regulars, 1,190 American provincials, 576 rangers, 330 Royal Artillery and 90 American volunteers) in the land component, and an additional 13,500 sailors and marines in the fleet. The rangers had again been formed into a provisional battalion under the command of Major Scott, made up of the companies shown opposite.

At Quebec, the Marquis de Montcalm‡ was in command of the 14,230 French defenders, including 11,170 Canadian militia, 2,220 *troupes de terre*, 300 Indians, 200 artillery, 200 cavalry and 140 Acadians, with an additional 1,460 naval personnel. Quebec was a formidable obstacle, with very strong fortifications on all sides and a commanding view of the river. The stage was set for what became the most significant battle of the French

* The "Lake Labrador region" cannot be found on contemporary French or English maps, and is perhaps a poor English translation of the French name "Lac Bras d'Or" on Île Royale.

† For a description of the ranger companies see Appendix I to Section 2–4 on page 188.

‡ See Historical Figures, Annex C.

Rogers' Rangers:	
Captain James Rogers' Company	112 officers & men
Captain William Stark's Company	95 officers & men
Captain Moses Hazen's Company	89 officers & men
Captain Jonathan Brewer's Company	85 officers & men
Independent Companies:	
Captain Joseph Gorham's Company	95 officers & men
Captain Benoni Danks' Company	100 officers & men
Total rangers deployed	576 officers & men

and Indian War. The rangers were the initial troops to land on Île d'Orleans and to engage in the first skirmish of the campaign.

From this point, however, the British experienced months of fruitless maneuvering in an attempt to draw the enemy into battle. Wolfe knew that a frontal assault on the fortress would be futile and therefore probed at several points to force a confrontation in the open, where reasonably matched armies would decide the outcome. The rangers participated in all aspects of these operations. Montcalm refused to be drawn, however, knowing both time and position were on his side. By late August, Wolfe was becoming frustrated. He knew that he had to resolve the issue soon or be forced to withdraw before winter trapped the fleet.

Incessant raids waged in the French Canadian "petite guerre"* were having an adverse effect on the troops and disrupting of vital operations. In an attempt to force the French from cover, and to punish the *habitants* for disregarding repeated instructions to remain aloof from the fighting, Wolfe ordered Scott to destroy the villages along the south shore of the river. He was to take the rangers, a detachment from each of the regiments and two men-of-war. With a force of some 1600, Scott departed on his mission on 1 September, landed at Kamouraska and marched the 52 miles back to Quebec, destroying everything in his path. The force returned to Quebec by 19 September. They had missed the battle. On 12 September scouts discovered a lightly defended cove, and by the next morning some 4,500 British troops were deployed on the plateau above the fortress.

---

* The French adapted methods of wilderness warfare from the Indians that they called "la petite guerre". These methods were similar to those employed by the rangers, and were perhaps the beginning of guerrilla warfare. For details on the methods used by the rangers see Appendix II, Section 2–4.

Fearing his supply lines to Montreal were about to be cut, Montcalm ordered his troops to the field, and his defeat at the Battle of the Plains of Abraham sealed the fate of Quebec. Both Wolfe and Montcalm died as a result of the battle, but the British victory forced the garrison to surrender on 18 September 1759.

General James Murray, succeeding Wolfe as the British commander, consolidated the British gains and decided to reduce his forces at Quebec for the winter. Only a single enlarged company of rangers under the command of Captain Hazen would be required, and the remainder would be sent south with the fleet. By the second week of October, a draft of 25 from each of the other companies was added to Hazen's, swelling it to 135 rank and file. James assumed command of the remaining companies and returned to Boston, where they were disbanded on 30 November.

Hazen afterwards played a significant role in the Battle of Sainte-Foy on 28 April 1760. A French force of some 4,200 *troupes de terre,* Canadian militia and Indians, under Brigadier General Levis, attacked from Montreal, and the resulting battle was almost a reverse of the previous year. Although the French in theory won this battle, the British defenders regained the sanctuary of the Quebec fortress after sustaining heavy losses. The ensuing siege was lifted on 16 May when the British fleet appeared in the river and the French were forced to withdraw to Montreal.

On 19 March 1760, James was ordered to raise another company of rangers to join Robert at Crown Point. He rejoined the corps by late May and fought in the Battle of Pointe-au-Fer and other operations along the Richelieu River. By late summer General Amherst had mustered three armies before Montreal, a total of some 17,000 men, and what remained of the armies of France was obliged to capitulate. Governor Vaudreuil surrendered Montreal and all of New France on 8 September, bringing to an end the war in North America.*

On 12 September, Robert was ordered to select two companies of rangers and depart for the upper Great Lakes region to accept the surrender of the French forts and posts of the interior. In the meantime, James assumed command of the remaining companies and was ordered to Crown Point. Here some companies were disbanded on 25 October; the majority were taken to New York, where they were disbanded on 11 November. James was rewarded with a captaincy in the regular army and retired on half pay.

From various land records, it appears that James returned to his

---

* This surrender did not end the war, however, as the hostilities in North America were only part of a much larger conflict, the Seven Years' War, that finally ended with the Treaty of Paris, 10 February 1763.

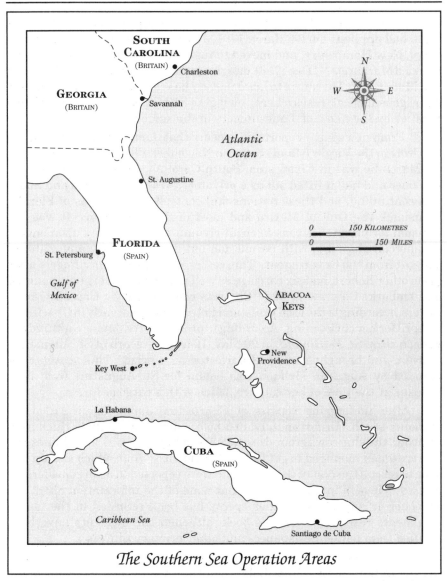

SOUTH
CAROLINA
(BRITAIN)   ● Charleston

GEORGIA
(BRITAIN)   ● Savannah

*Atlantic
Ocean*

● St. Augustine

FLORIDA
St. Petersburg ●   (SPAIN)

*Gulf of
Mexico*

0   150 *KILOMETRES*
0   150 *MILES*

ABACOA
KEYS

Key West ●

●○ New
Providence

La Habana ●

CUBA
(SPAIN)

Caribbean Sea

Santiago de Cuba ●

The Southern Sea Operation Areas

home in Starkstown after the war and engaged in land speculation in this
area as well as maintaining his farm. It is evident that he had a tenant
working the land during his absence, as there was a source of income other
than his military service, and he was certainly becoming prosperous.
During the period 1760–1761, James was a partner with his brother and
Moses Hazen in the firm "Major Rogers & Associates."* This firm was

---

* For details see Section 2–4, page 145.

established to exploit land grants in the Lake George region for which the three had applied. On 24 March 1761, James purchased land in Londonderry, New Hampshire, and moved to that area. During the summer, he married Margaret (?–1 Dec 1793), daughter of the Reverend David McGregor and Mary Boyd. This move to Londonderry has caused vexing problems for later genealogical researchers, owing to the apparent mixing of two families by the name of James Rogers in the same area.*

From newspaper reports, it appears that James spent some time at St. Croix in the Virgin Islands between November 1761 and January 1762. By March he was in Charleston, South Carolina, where he purchased a schooner and had it fitted out as a privateer. War with France and Spain was continuing, and these nations still controlled vast areas of Florida, Louisiana, the Gulf of Mexico and most of the Caribbean. It was not unusual for private citizens to outfit civilian vessels to prey upon enemy commercial shipping, with permission but not necessarily any material support from the Government. This vessel, named the *Major Rogers* after his brother Robert, had six carriage as well as twelve swivel guns mounted and embarked a crew of 50.† She was commanded by Captain James Rogers, according to the local press, and Robert was apparently in Charleston in April for her christening. According to press reports, James captured the French sloop *St. Ferdinand* on 20 May, 10 leagues south of St. Augustine, Florida, and brought her into Charleston as a prize. This vessel, commanded by Augustin Heliqon was bound for St. Augustine from New Orleans at the time of her capture, laden with a cargo of furs.

After undergoing repairs at Charleston, James again sailed his schooner south. Unfortunately, just before dawn on 3 July in thick hazy weather, the ship ran aground on the Abacoa Keys and was lost. James and five crewmen managed to get to New Providence,‡ from which a sloop was sent to rescue the rest of the crew, who were reported to be in considerable distress. (It is of interest to note that none of the information about the schooner or any of these other events has been recorded in the family documents researched for this book, although the incidents have been verified from period newspapers and other primary sources.)

Meanwhile the Ottawa war chief Pontiac§ was organizing and uniting the Indians of the Great Lakes and Ohio Valley against encroaching settlement by the white man. In April 1763 they attacked, and many western posts and small communities fell quickly to the onslaught. By

---

* For details see Appendix II to Section 1–1.

† To provide for manning prizes, privateers' crews were often much larger than normally required.

‡ Now Nassau in the Bahamas.

§ See Historical Figures, Annex C.

The Privateer Schooner MAJOR ROGERS at Charleston

early May an Indian army of some 2,000 braves was laying siege to Fort Detroit. Robert was ordered to raise a company of rangers quickly and proceed with all dispatch to Niagara. There he was to support a relief party of 250 British regulars under the command of Captain James Dalyell, an aide-de-camp to General Amherst. Robert asked James for assistance, and the two soon left Londonderry with forty rangers to met Dalyell's force at Fort Niagara. The expedition arrived at Detroit on 29 July without incident.

Just before dawn on 31 July, the rangers played a conspicuous and heroic role in the skirmish that became known as the "Battle of Bloody Run".* Captain Dalyell had made an ill-conceived attack against overwhelming numbers of the besiegers. His patrol was ambushed and forced to fall back. The rangers covered the retreat, preventing the British from being slaughtered. The siege continued until 31 October, when a truce was signed and the post was relieved. Robert and most of the rangers departed

---

* For details on this battle, see Section 2–4, page 150.

when the garrison was reduced for the winter, but James remained at Detroit during this winter for some reason not known. He returned to New Hampshire the following spring, after conducting business during a brief stay at Niagara.

Little is known of James and his activities during the following two years, but it is assumed that he remained in Londonderry with his family. A son, named David after his maternal grandfather, had been born in 1762 but died of unknown causes in 1766 at the age of four years. In 1763, while he was absent in Detroit, a daughter was born and named Mary after both her grandmothers. A second son was born in 1764 and named James after his father.

On 12 October 1765, James petitioned the New York authorities for a grant of land in the Green Mountains, to the west of the Connecticut River, on behalf of himself and a number of associates. The land was in an area known as the New Hampshire Grants, an area of the wilderness that had been claimed by both New Hampshire and New York for almost 100 years, and parts of which had been granted out by both provinces. This resulted in considerable confusion until an Order in Council, dated 20 July 1764, made the territory part of the Province of New York.* The petition of James to New York, reproduced on the opposite page, was based on a claim that he and others had been granted 26,000 acres on the east side of Lake Champlain, between South Bay and Ticonderoga, by New Hampshire. This land had also been granted to others by New York in 1764, and they had established a legal claim. A grant to James for some 3,000 acres near Ticonderoga, dated 30 May 1764, can be found in the Rogers' Papers,† so there appears to be some truth to his claim. This earlier document is on original parchment, with the seals still attached, but is in very poor condition. The 1765 petition is preserved in the New York Office of the Secretary of State at Albany.

James played an active and prominent role in public affairs. In October 1765, he joined with eleven others in a petition to New York for establishment of a new county between the Connecticut River and the existing boundary of New York, just to the north of the Province of Massachusetts.‡ This was just three days following his petition to form the Township of Kent. On 22 October, James and five others made a further

---

* The area would eventually be admitted to the Union as the State of Vermont in 1791.

† The Rogers' Papers consist of documents of James Rogers and some of his descendants, acquired by the Ontario Archives from Robert Zacheus Rogers (5-3) in 1905 (Finding aid MU 2552/2553).

‡ The area has since been renamed but is believed to encompass the existing counties of Bennington and Windham, Vermont.

---

petition on the same matter, and the County of Cumberland was subsequently created. In the nomination of civil authority for the county dated 11 June 1766, James was named "Ass't Justice in the Commission of the Pleas and Justice of ye Quorum".

To the Honorable Cadwallader Colden, Esq.,
His Majesty's Lieutenant Governor and Commander-in-Chief of the Province of New York and the Territories depending thereon in America.

In Council

    The Petition of James Rogers in behalf of himself and twenty-two other persons Humbly showeth:

    That your petitioner and his associates apprehended they had a good right and title to twenty-six thousand acres of land by a grant from Governor Wentworth, lying on the East side of the water running from South Bay to Ticonderoga. That on the twentieth day of July one thousand seven hundred and sixty-four by the Resolve of his Majesty and his Majesty's Privy Council, the said lands fell within the bounds of this Province and that some time last spring the same lands were granted by your Honor to reduced officers, whereby your petitioner and his associates must inevitably loose their rights unless your Honours will be pleased to make them a grant in some other lands in this Province:

    That there is a certain tract of land lying in this Province bounding on the West side of Tomlinson, beginning at the South Westerly corner of Chester and running West twenty-seven degrees North seven miles and thirty-eight chains; Then South ten degrees West seven miles seventy-six chains; Then East ten degrees South six miles eight chains; Then North twenty degrees East six miles to the place from whence the survey began, containing in the whole twenty-six thousand acres with an allowance of three thousand acres of mountains.

    Your petitioner for himself and associates therefore humbly prays that your Honours will be favorably pleased, by his Majesty's Letter Patent to grant unto them, Under the great seal of this Province, the above bounded and described land and premises to hold to them, their heirs and assigns forever, and that the same be erected into a township by the name of Kent and vested with such powers and privileges as other towns in this Province have and do enjoy.

And your petitioner, as in duty bound will ever pray.

Dated at New York, twelve October,
One thousand seven hundred & sixty-five.

Jas. Rogers.

A List of The Proprietors of The Township of Kent

James Rogers, James MacGregor, Sen., Margaret Rogers, Thomas Creage, James A. Adams, James Miltmer, Jonathan Gillmore, Robert Hunter, William Moore, Garret Schooler, Benjamin Lindner, John McGinnis, James Carroll, David Phillips, Edward Landree, Cornelius Ryan, Andrew Burn, Robert Wallace, Thomas Blaknie, Joseph Cox, John Armstrong, Lewis Hamilton, Patrick Butler.

A draft of the Charter for Kent was created on 29 June 1766 but was never executed. It is currently preserved in a private library in New York. James clearly examined a preliminary draft, for a second petition containing a number of small changes to the eastern boundary was submitted the following day. For some reason the matter rested for about three and a half years.

Finally, on 13 February 1770, a grant was formally made to "Colonel James Rogers and Associates" using the land description in the 1765 petition. (The original charter is in the care of the descendants of the late Ranger Rogers of Denver, Colorado, and has been reproduced as Appendix I to this section.) The grant refers to a third petition to which was attached a list of associates on whose behalf James was acting, and the grant follows this later list of associates. It should be noted that this list differs substantially from that which was appended to the original 1765 petition, and in fact only four petitioners appear on both of the lists. This would suggest both may have been temporary or "straw" lists, and that James had intended from the outset to secure the entire area for himself. This assessment is further supported by the fact that just one week after the grant, all the grantees joined in a deed conveying to him all interest and title to the entire territory covered by the grant.

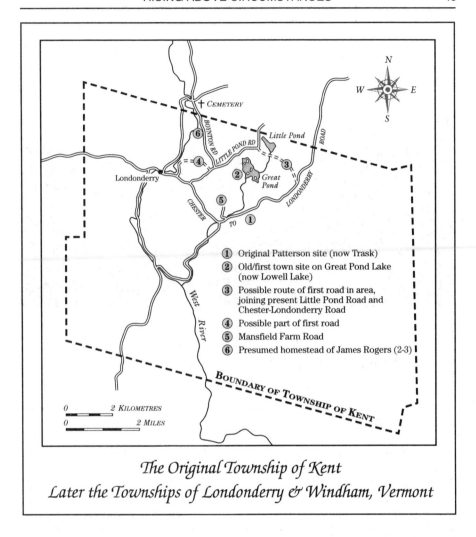

The Original Township of Kent
Later the Townships of Londonderry & Windham, Vermont

This document, dated 20 February 1770, was duly recorded in the Office of the Colonial Secretary in Albany. (The original is located in the Rogers' Papers and has been reproduced as Appendix II to this section.) Through these intricate manoeuvres James became the sole owner of the Township of Kent, some 24,150 acres save for public land of 1,150 acres for a total of 23,000 acres. The plan of the Township makes it clear that most of the public lands were situated so as to fall on the rocky summit or rugged sides of Glebe Mountain in the centre of the township. It is believed that James, using an early survey, set them out in this way so that none of the good land could be used for unproductive purposes.

The West River Valley
A view from the probable site of the Rogers homestead
in Londonderry, Vermont

It is almost certain that James first saw this area on service with the rangers during operations between Lake George and the Connecticut River. It is a mystery that this area alone amid the surrounding territory had not been granted by 1765. James and a party of young men from Londonderry explored and resurveyed the area in 1769, and began to hew out new farms from the forests. This party apparently went home during the winter but returned in the spring of 1770, when the first settlement is said to have been made. James advertised his farm in Londonderry for sale in April 1772 (see opposite), and moved his family to Kent that spring. He also sold lots to others wishing to settle in the area. His son, David McGregor Rogers, was the first child born in the township (23 November 1772). In those early days of the settlement, all that was needed had to be brought in from Number Four (Charleston, New Hampshire) 30 miles to the east. The farm grew, and by the summer of 1776 the family had a substantial home to replace the original log cabin.

To Be Sold The Subscribers Farm, In Londonderry; *

Containing near one Hundred Acres, mostly uncut improvement.
A large Quantity of Stone Wall, Two good Houses and Barns. Two
good Orchards. Is situated on the Border of Chester, and upon the
Main Road: equally handy to Mr. Flag's Meeting House, as to any
in Londonderry. With a Wood-lot of about 150 Acres, and an
exceeding good Brook Meadow. The first about a Mile, and the other
between two and three Miles distance. The whole duely improved,
is well sufficient to support 2 middling Families. Will be sold either
together or apart, as will suit the Purchaser; and upon Lower Terms
than any Farm of the Value in these Parts for a long Time. One Third
of the price paid down, the Purchaser may have Trust for the
remaining two Parts, for a Year, or some longer on reasonable
Terms. — Any Person desiring to know further, concerning the
Premises, may apply to James M'Gregors or James M'Gregors, junr.
both of Londonderry.

N.B. The said Farm, if not sold, will be let a Year, on very
advantageous Terms.

James Rogers

In July 1772, James was appointed Lieutenant Colonel of Militia by
General William Tryon, Governor of New York. In February 1774, he was
elected a member of the "Standing Committee of Correspondence to
correspond with the Committee of Correspondence for the City of New York
and other Committees elsewhere". The First Continental Congress, which
was meeting at Philadelphia that spring, issued a Declaration of Rights as
a strong protest over some of the provisions of the Quebec Act. These
documents served to further inflame tensions between Britain and her
colonies which had been precipitated by taxation issues. On 19 April 1775,
British troops fired upon local militia at Lexington, sparking open rebellion.

On 31 May, the New York Provincial Congress "offered to Colonel
James Rogers a commission of Brigadier General of the Cumberland,
Gloucester and Charlotte Brigade, which he refused due to his political

* The *New Hampshire Gazette,* 10 April 1772.

principles".* It was not that James was unsympathetic to the grievances of the colonies, but he believed that there had to be a way short of civil war to resolve these issues.

In July the Second Continental Congress offered command of all patriot forces to Colonel George Washington.† General Richard Montgomery,‡ commanding an American force, advanced up Lake Champlain on an invasion of Canada, capturing Ticonderoga and other forts on the way. Montreal was forced to capitulate on 13 November, and the governor, Sir Guy Carleton,§ fled to Quebec. The Americans moved toward Quebec; but during the prolonged siege Montgomery was killed, and Benedict Arnold,** his second-in-command, was wounded. In early May the Americans retreated, having failed to secure their objective.

On 4 July 1776, Congress signed the Declaration of Independence, formally separating the colonies from Britain. James Rogers and Edward Aiken were sent as delegates to a General Convention at Dorset (25 July to 25 September), convened to discuss the feasibility of establishing a new province from the area of the New Hampshire Grants. Discussions probably also revolved around the expanding war with Britain and its eventual consequences. While James supported the creation of a new province, he could not accept a challenge to the King's legal authority. He refused to sign the association of the convention,†† or to acknowledge the legitimacy of the various Committees of Safety. In the fall he also refused to sign the "Oath of Allegiance" being administered by the local Committee of Safety.

On 3 January 1777, encouraged by the convention results, the people of the New Hampshire Grants declared their independence from New York and established the province of New Connecticut, which was renamed Vermont in June.

Constantly harassed for his Loyalist stand and principles, James was forced to abandon his family and property in April to seek the relative safety of the British colours. Numerous documents suggest he was the only member of the township to flee; a number joined the American cause. There were no Vermont regiments in the federal army during the Revolution, as Congress and New York refused to recognize the area as an independent province.

---

* Documents of the New York Provincial Congress during the Revolutionary War.
† See Historical Figures, Annex C.
‡ See Historical Figures, Annex C.
§ See Historical Figures, Annex C.
** See Historical Figures, Annex C.
†† A document swearing the delegates to secrecy in the interests of the State.

No evidence of formal confiscation of the Rogers estate in Kent has been found, and it appears that no legal action was in fact taken, although his lands were treated as having passed to the State. His assets were formally seized in New Hampshire and New York, and he was deemed an enemy of these states by acts of the legislatures. (Two documents that describe the action taken by the New Hampshire House of Representatives are recorded in Appendices III and IV to this section.) The lack of any formal or judicial action by Vermont may have been due to its questionable constitutional status.

In October 1777, Captain John Simonds was placed in charge of the estate under the authority of the Committee of Safety; a copy of this order is reproduced on the following page. According to a number of sources, Captain Simonds was a very cruel man who deprived the family of many of the necessities of life, contrary to his written instructions. The Rogers' children, aged fourteen, twelve, eight, five and three years, were all living at home during this period. It must have been very difficult for Margaret, surrounded by those who were once her neighbors and friends but who now treated her family harshly and with contempt. As the conflict continued to escalate, the conditions under which the family was forced to live deteriorated. Like the dependents of many other Tories, they became public charges without any means of support, and local governments were loath to expend any funds for maintenance.

In October 1779, a resolution of the General Assembly of Vermont was passed as follows:

———— for the support of Mrs. Rogers and family, that she is to be put in possession of certain property which is to include the farm upon which she is living, together with farming tools and household utensils.

This resolution was enacted in response to a request based on a report from the "Messrs. McGregors" (believed to be her brothers James and Robert) which detailed the deplorable conditions under which the family was forced to live and the level of their current distress. Further evidence of their suffering is contained in the Memorial of Robert Rogers to General Haldimand, copied as Appendix V to this section. It was about this time that Margaret apparently became disabled, "lost the use of her limbs," although no other information can be found about the incident. It seems she was in good health by 1784 when the family settled in Canada.

Although the State assumed control of the family property, it was not legally confiscated. Consequently, James was unable after the war to secure any reimbursement or compensation from the Crown for the lands seized through the actions of the State of Vermont. On 15 March 1780, the people of the township submitted a petition for the township to be divided along the mountain ridge. The names of the resulting townships were to be Londonderry and Windham. Charters for the new townships were issued 20 April 1780. To the time of his death, however, James always referred to the area as Kent.

State Of Vermont

In Council of Safety
3d Oct. 1777

To Captain John Simonds:

Sir —

You are hereby authorized and empowered to Let or Lease all of the Estate of Colonel James Rogers late of Kent, (now with the King's Troops) both real and personal, and all Real Estate (except so much as humanity requires for the Comfortable Support of the family left Behind) you will Sell at public Venue and Return the Money Raised on such Sail (after the Cost is paid) to the Treasurer of this State. The improved land you will Let or Lease to some proper person or persons as you shall judge will best serve the purpose of supporting the Family & the Benefit of this State, not exceeding the Term of Two Years.

You will return to this Council an account of all the Estate, boath real & personal, that you shall seize. You will Take the Advice of the Committee of the town of Kent with regard to what part will be sufficient to support the family. You are to obey the orders of this Council from time to time, relative to the said Estate and settle your accts. with them or their Successors, or some person or persons appointed for that purpose & you are to do it on oath.

By Order Of The Council

Thomas Chittenden, Prest.

Attest: Joseph Fay, Sec'y.

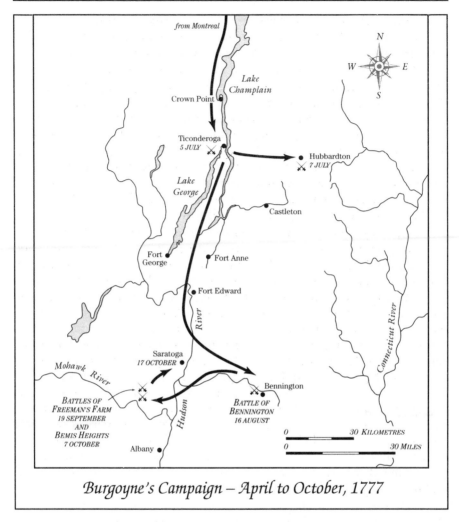

Burgoyne's Campaign – April to October, 1777

In April 1777, James fled to Montreal and was there commissioned captain of an irregular provincial corps made up mainly of fleeing Loyalists. A major military operation was being considered. Senior British officers in England had devised a complicated plan to isolate the New England Colonies "to effectively cut off the hotbed of sedition & revolutionary fervor" and thus quickly bring an end to the rebellion. General Sir John Burgoyne* was ordered to take his army south from Montreal to capture Albany, while General Sir William Howe,† the commander-in-chief of British forces in America, was to march north from New York in support.

---

* See Historical Figures, Annex C.
† See Historical Figures, Annex C.

James Rogers   Section 2–3

It was an excellent plan and might well have worked, but no one thought to inform Howe. Unaware of the northern strategy, he embarked on his own operation to capture the American capital at Philadelphia.

On 17 June, Burgoyne departed Montreal at the head of a 7,500-man army. Lines of supply, the lifeblood of an army, were given little consideration. The British command still believed that the rebellion was led by a small group in New England and that the army would be traversing largely friendly territory. Burgoyne was confident that he could rely on the local inhabitants for supplies of food, information and auxiliary military assistance if required. He was convinced that the area was ripe for recruitment, as the problems concerning boundaries and administration in the area of the New Hampshire Grants were unresolved, and the inaction of Congress on this issue had caused considerable ill will.

By late June the British occupied Crown Point, abandoned by the retreating Americans. On 5 July, they attacked Ticonderoga, and 2,500 American militia were forced to withdraw. About this time, Burgoyne began to realize that much of the country was under the effective control of revolutionary committees, and that supplies were not readily available for purchase by the army's commissaries. Shortages forced the army to forage and take what was required. Leaving the bulk of his army to continue south along Lake George, Burgoyne took 1,900 men and attacked rebel forces at Hubbardton on 7 July, primarily for supplies. Sustaining losses of 40 killed, 50 wounded and 275 taken prisoner, the remaining 650 in the American force retreated to Manchester. British losses in this engagement numbered 35 killed and 150 wounded. By early August, mainly due to the initial success of the army, large numbers of Loyalists began arriving in the British camp, seeking refuge from harassment and an opportunity to contribute directly to the military suppression of rebellion. Some were perhaps seeking vengeance for the treatment they had endured. Many were absorbed into the irregular provincial corps.

On receiving intelligence of a large supply depot near Bennington, Burgoyne dispatched a force of 1,500 men to seize these supplies. By the time they arrived however, the Americans had been reinforced by 3,000 militia under the command of John Stark.* The engagement, which took place on 16 August 1777, became known as the Battle of Bennington. The outcome was an American victory, as the British were repulsed with 780 killed or wounded against only 70 American casualties. Short of supplies but intent on pressing toward his objective, Burgoyne again turned southward along the Hudson River. His advance was checked on 19

---

* Stark was a neighbour and old friend of Robert and James Rogers and had command of a Ranger Company during the French and Indian War. See Section 2–4 and Historical Figures, Annex C.

† Also known as the First Battle of Saratoga.

September by the 7,000-man army of General Horatio Gates at the savage Battle of Freeman's Farm.† Surrounded by ever increasing enemy forces, Burgoyne attempted a breakout on 7 October, but was repulsed with devastating losses at the Battle of Bemis Heights.* This engagement ended in a stalemate, with some 500 British killed or wounded to 350 American casualties. Burgoyne was forced to retreat toward Saratoga, sixty miles from his initial objective. Howe, in the meantime, had success-fully taken Philadelphia and was thwarting all efforts by Washington to dislodge him. He was, however, in no position to come to Burgoyne's relief.

The situation deteriorated rapidly and Loyalist units feared that if captured they would not be treated the same as British or German troops. There is no evidence to suggest atrocities were ever committed against Loyalist forces by regular units of the Continental Army, but rumors persisted. The Americans considered Loyalists not as prisoners of war but as traitors. Fearing that they would be treated harshly by their enemies, Burgoyne released these units, giving them explicit instructions to make their way to the safety of British-controlled territory. James passed through the American lines with some of his men and safely made his way to New York, after a brief stop in Kent to see his family.

By 17 October the American force surrounding Saratoga had swelled to an unprecedented 22,000, and Burgoyne was forced to consider surren-der of his remaining 5,700 troops or face total annihilation. He negotiated the Convention of Saratoga by which his army would lay down its arms but be granted the honours of war. British troops would be safely returned to Britain, Canadians would be permitted to return home, and civilians accompanying the army would be treated as British subjects,: all on the condition that none would bear arms during the current conflict. Once disarmed, however, the troops were imprisoned by the Americans, who were furious that the "traitorous Tories" had been allowed to escape. Congress later refused to honour the terms of the convention.

This surrender was in many ways the decisive turning point in the war. Not only did it lift American morale at a critical time and prove that a major British force could be defeated in open battle, but it persuaded a hesitating France to enter the conflict in support of America. It also resulted in a significant increase in the hardships of Loyalist families left behind in the Colonies, particularly in the area of Burgoyne's operations.

According to an unconfirmed source, James accepted an appointment in the spring of 1778 as major of the Royal American Reformers, a New York provincial corps. On 1 May 1779, Robert received a warrant from General Sir Henry Clinton† to raise a new Loyalist Regiment to be known as the

---

* Also known as the Second Battle of Saratoga.
† See Historical Figures, Annex C.

King's Rangers.* The unit was to consist of two battalions of ten companies (a total of 1,267 officers and men) and be part of the Central Department, under the patronage of Clinton.† James was gazetted Major Commandant of the 2nd battalion of the regiment on 2 June, and he initiated recruiting efforts to assist his brother to raise the corps. It was common practice during this period to permit officers to recruit for their rank and position. Ranks and pay were not confirmed until specific recruiting levels had been achieved. Captains were required to recruit 32 men, lieutenants 16, and ensigns 12, to the established total of 60 men in each company. There were never enough recruits to fill requirements of all officers with warrants, however, particularly at this stage of the war. It was inevitable that the interests of various Provincial Corps should clash and as a result there were many instances of bribery and recruit stealing in all departments.

A return submitted by Robert on 6 July indicated that 130 officers and men had been recruited for the new regiment, all of whom were proceeding to Quebec by various methods. On 8 July, James was sent north on the brigantine *Hawke* with 13 officers and men to receive men coming overland from the south. In a letter dated 17 July, Robert informed General Frederick Haldimand‡ that, for the purpose of carrying out his warrant, he had found it absolutely necessary to send a number of officers to Quebec, "so that they might more easily receive recruits from the Colonies". He asked that these officers be provided with support and permitted to recruit in Canada. When James arrived at Quebec on 22 July and requested assistance from Haldimand, he was told to his surprise that no provision had been made. Nine months before, Robert had been in Quebec in October 1778, seeking permission to raise "a Corps of Royalists upon the Frontiers of this Province" from the Loyalist refugees.§

James was now in a very awkward position. Haldimand had denied Robert's earlier request to recruit in Quebec, seeing no need for yet another unit of questionable military value. Now James was here with a warrant from the Central Department, and Haldimand was plainly displeased. Haldimand suggested that Robert recall his officers, and James was in the middle of the controversy. Eventually James was permitted to receive recruits sent north to the province from the southern colonies, but Haldimand

---

* See Section 2–4, page 181.

† Command of all British Forces in America was vested in the Central Department, with its headquarters at New York. Three subordinate commanders were located in the Northern (Quebec), Southern (Florida) and Eastern (Nova Scotia) Departments.

‡ Governor of the Province of Quebec and Commander in Chief of the Northern Department. See Historical Figures, Annex C.

§ See Section 2–4, page 180.

made it clear that the unit was not to be raised in Quebec. James was also told that there would be no funding to support the unit unless such support came from the Central Department. Not a very good beginning in relations with the senior officer of the area.

By September 1779, the Kings Rangers were stationed at Fort St. Johns on the Richelieu River (now Saint Jean, Quebec). This fort was known as "the Key of Canada", being situated on the primary water passage between Lake Champlain, the Hudson River, Albany and New York to the south, and the St. Lawrence River, Quebec and Montreal to the north. James supported his men from his personal resources until subsistence and pay could be arranged from either the Central or the Northern Department. On 19 September, his officers sent a memorial to the general stating that support was urgently required due to their "absolute distress". The rangers were then given subsistence allowances, but this was to be only a temporary measure; pay was to be arranged and provided by the Central Department. This treatment caused considerable consternation among the rangers. Moreover, their continued presence in Quebec was causing complaints from the other corps.

James became considerably embarrassed by the actions of his brother over the winter. Robert arrived in Montreal claiming to have raised 700 rangers in Nova Scotia, but the number turned out to be very much less. In addition, he was amassing large debts, and his behaviour was placing James in a difficult position with his fellow officers, subordinates and senior military officials in Quebec. There must have been some perhaps heated discussions between the two brothers, as Robert sent a memorial to Haldimand recommending that James be promoted to command another corps under the general's patronage. (This document is attached as Appendix V to this section.) The document also points out the harsh circumstances in which Margaret and the children were living at the time. By spring Robert had left for Halifax, and James continued trying to raise men and seeking authority to send parties to the colonies to recruit and gain intelligence. Permission was granted, but competition with other corps was fierce and some of his recruits were assigned to other units. James wrote Haldimand in April 1780 representing that it was impossible to have men attested in the colonies if they were to be enrolled in other corps after all his effort and expense. To settle these petty recruiting quarrels between regiments, the Governor issued a new set of regulations:

No officer, or other person employed by the various corps at advanced posts, is to enlist a man from the colonies or hold intercourse with him until he has been taken to the Commanding Officer, and declared if already engaged for a particular unit.

If the bickering continued, he warned, all future recruiting disputes would be settled by a board of officers. Later that month, the King's Rangers were temporarily attached to Sir John Johnson's corps, the King's Royal Regiment of New York, and placed on half pay.

On 10 May, James requested permission to resign from the King's Rangers and be allowed to join some other regiment wholly under the command of the general, thereby seeking to distance himself from the actions of his brother Robert. This request was denied because his appointment had been made by Clinton, and Haldimand had no power to grant such a request. In the letter, however, Haldimand extended encouragement to James, mentioned his generally good character, and promised that the "extraordinary behaviour" of his brother would not be held against him. In reply, James wrote: "the Conduct of my Brother of late has almost unmann'd me," and expressed his sincere gratitude to Haldimand.

By September, the Governor had ceased to suggest that the rangers return to the Central Department, and he extended recruiting privileges to include Loyalists in the province who had not joined other corps. He had come to the conclusion that the rangers were there to stay, and if he was going to have them, he would find useful employment for them. Because the corps was very small, he assigned unique tasks for them which included the following:

- scouting and reconnaissance for other units;
- carrying dispatches;
- construction of fortifications and general garrison duties;
- assisting refugees in Quebec and aiding Loyalist families trying to escape;
- responsibility for security of prisoners; and,
- employment in the secret service.

James was instructed to complete two full companies and then a third, all to be employed in Canada. On 8 September 1780, he submitted a muster roll listing 49 officers and men. He also pointed out that some of his men were still using their personal weapons, many of which were no longer dependable, and observed the need for provisions for several women and children who were dependents of his battalion. Shortly thereafter, clothing, arms and provisions were authorized, and James began receiving full pay as a captain. In October, a detachment of rangers accompanied Major Christopher Carleton on his raid of New York outposts along Lake Champlain. Henry Ruiter joined the corps in November and was appointed captain of the third company.

In December 1780, the King's Rangers were mustered and inspected by Major John Nairne, who concluded that James had properly executed all

The Quebec Encampment

This sketch by noted historian and artist Gary Zaboly depicts
the encampment of the King's Rangers at Fort St. John's during an
informal inspection by General Haldimand. The scene is typical of
the period around 1782.

instructions issued to him. Nairne also reported that James "has in his way
much of the air of an old soldier" and seemed to pay great attention to his
men. This was an extremely favourable report for James, considering all
the controversy, but it did not put an end to all his problems and difficulties.
On 16 December the commanders of some of the other Loyalist Regiments
submitted a grievance to the governor complaining about the recruiting
irregularities and insidious methods of the rangers. This document was
typical of the arguments between the various corps. (It has been inserted
as Appendix VI to this section.) A board of officers was subsequently
convened on 4 March to settle the disputes. It dismissed most of the charges
as frivolous and referred the remainder to Haldimand for resolution. In the
end no action was taken against James or his regiment.

On 3 April 1781, James suggested by memorial that the King's Rangers and the Queen's Loyal Rangers, then commanded by Lieutenant Colonel John Peters, might be amalgamated to form a single regiment.* (His memorial has been attached as Appendix VII to this section.) Haldimand could not grant the request, however, as he had not power to combine two corps established under warrants from different departments.

In May, Robert was imprisoned in Halifax for debt and was released only after James gave a bond to cover the amounts. Robert subsequently sailed for New York, but his ship came under attack and captured by Continental forces. He was taken to Philadelphia and imprisoned for the remainder of the war, leaving James in command of the regiment. In late June, James requested authority to seek Clinton's permission to transfer the corps to Quebec under Haldimand's command. While the request was granted, no further action seems to have been taken by either Haldimand or Clinton. James' letters to the Governor during this period are filled with requests for clothing and subsistence for his men and their families.

During the summer of 1781, Ira and Ethan Allen† began to negotiate with the British on the feasibility of making Vermont a Canadian province. Congress had repeatedly refused to admit Vermont as the fourteenth state and was actively considering dividing the territory between the States of New York and New Hampshire. Rather than submit to this injustice, Governor Chittenden directed the Allen brothers to open talks with Haldimand. The talks were known as the Vermont negotiations, and James was involved both by correspondence and in several face-to-face meetings with the Allen brothers and their associates. Chittenden's real objective, however, was probably to force Congress to act. The talks were inconclusive, but Chittenden's move eventually succeeded when Vermont was admitted to the Union in 1791.

On 25 August 1781, the men of the King's Rangers were placed on full pay. In September, with three full companies completed, James was confirmed as major, and the other officers received their official appointments shown on the opposite page.

On 19 October 1781, General Lord Charles Cornwallis surrendered a large British army at Yorktown, Virginia. Although numerous but relatively minor skirmishes occurred during the ensuing months, this event was the most decisive action of the war, as British authorities essentially withdrew their forces into defensive positions. Peace, however, was not to be realized for a further two years.

---

* A short time later the Queen's Loyal Rangers were amalgamated with the King's Loyal Americans to form the Loyal Rangers.

† See Historical Figures, Annex C.

1st Company	Captain/Lieutenant	James Breakenridge
	Lieutenant	Israel Ferguson
	Ensign	William Buell
2nd Company:	Captain	Azariah Pritchard
	Lieutenant	Solomon Jones
	Ensign	Joseph Bettys
3rd Company	Captain	Henry Ruiter
	Lieutenant	William Tyler
	Ensign	David Breakenridge

A small detachment of the rangers saw action in October during an expedition under the command of Brigadier Barry St. Leger. The purpose of the mission was to seize and occupy Crown Point as a show of force probably intended to influence the Vermont situation. Some rangers were detailed for duty at the "Loyal Blockhouse" on North Hero Island in Lake Champlain, where Captain Sherwood had organized and commanded the secret service. In late November all provincial regiments except those designated "Royal" were ordered to wear uniform green coats with dark red facings, to replace the blue coats with white facings that resembled uniforms worn by some regiments of the Continental army.

In April 1782, James requested permission to send someone to the Connecticut River to fetch his eldest son:

He is now in his Seventeenth Year, and I am afraid he will be pressed into the Rebel Service before I can get him from them.......... Mrs Rogers will be sent on here Next Summer, but my oldest Boy will not have the liberty to come with her which makes me wish to have him stolen away before she comes.

Haldimand asked James to postpone the attempt to rescue his son as he had a special assignment for him to perform. He was ordered to go with two highly trusted men to the Loyal Blockhouse, telling no one of his destination. There he would receive sealed orders.

James went as directed and, after reading his orders, discussed this mission with Captain Sherwood and his deputy, Dr. George Smyth. The orders described a complicated plan devised by the resident agent from the Connecticut Valley, Colonel Timothy Bedel, which required a visit by a field officer. Captain Pritchard had been in direct communication with Bedel and was to accompany James on the mission. Sherwood warned that Bedel was one of the most cunning geniuses in America. What was proposed was never revealed, however, as the mission was considered too dangerous, and the Governor cancelled it on 28 April. James was then granted permission to proceed behind enemy lines to gather intelligence and to consider some method to retrieve his son. By 11 June he was back at Fort St. Johns with the young man. The details of this rescue mission are not known, but it could not have been an easy undertaking.

In November 1782, James requested permission to form a fourth company but was refused. He later requested permission to amalgamate his rangers with Major Edward Jessup's corps, the Loyal Rangers and was again refused. Finally, in January 1783, the King's Rangers were officially taken into the Northern Department. The Governor was still very concerned about the possibility of a rebel attack. In May, James petitioned Sir John Johnson requesting that his men be absorbed into the 2nd battalion of his King's Royal Regiment of New York. James was clearly aware that officers of regiments not completed to ten full companies would be denied half pay on reduction and would have no entitlement to other benefits. This policy had obtained at the end of the previous war and had been confirmed by a recent directive from England. James was willing to submerge his command in order to secure the future. His request was denied, but the policy on the entitlement to half pay was later revised, and he became eligible for officer's benefits.

By the spring of 1783, it had become clear that the Loyalists would not be able to return to their homes in the American Republic. On 13 May, James submitted a petition for a grant to consist of uninhabited land between the St. Lawrence River, Richelieu River and the border with New York. The grant was to extend three leagues or about seven miles north of a border that was generally expected would be established at 45 degrees north. (This petition has been copied as Appendix VIII.) James stated in the accompanying letter that the land was for the settlement of his regiment. In June, however, Henry Ruiter made an application for land on the east side of Missisquoi Bay. This must have caused a problem for James, as Ruiter was a member of his command.

The government directed Haldimand to settle the Loyalists in these areas and in others that later became known as the Eastern Townships. The British ministers believed that the Loyalists would institute an effective barrier to encroachments from the south. Haldimand objected, however, for he feared that a Loyalist presence in this area near their old enemies would inflame rather than pacify the border. He argued that the area should be reserved for the natural expansion of the French Canadian population of the St. Lawrence River Valley, and that they would eventually form a far more effective barrier to any incursions from the United States because of their linguistic, religious and cultural differences.

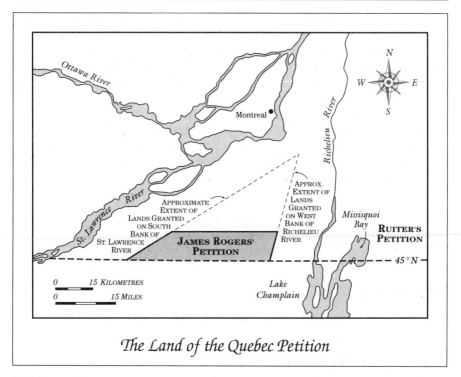

The Land of the Quebec Petition

Haldimand's argument won, and the area of planned Loyalist settlement was shifted west towards the northern shores of the St. Lawrence River and Lake Ontario. About this time, Robert was exchanged and returned to England with the defeated army. There is no record that after James assumed most of Robert's American debts in 1781, the brothers ever again spoke or wrote to one another.

On 3 September 1783, the Treaty of Paris was signed between United States of America and Great Britain. In this document, the Britain recognized the independence of the Thirteen Colonies and made certain territorial concessions. The treaty contained two articles pertaining to the Loyalists. One of these provided that no subsequent seizures of Loyalist property would take place. The other allowed the Loyalists several months in which to collect their debts and straighten out affairs before they would be required to leave the territory of the United States. Congress did not have the power or authority to enforce these treaty provisions, however, lacking a strong central government. As a result, the articles protecting the Loyalists were widely violated, especially in New York and the New England States. During the winter of 1783–84, James made one final journey to his former home in Kent, to settle business affairs and fetch his family. On his return, he informed the Governor of his surprise at the insults and ill treatment he had been forced to endure despite all the assurances previously received from the leaders of the new Republic.

London ordered that Provincial Regiments be reduced by year end, and James was informed that his corps would be disbanded on 24 December. Owing to the very late receipt of the order, however, the Government would continue to provide his men and their families with provisions and lodgings until more seasonable weather arrived. On 22 January 1784, Haldimand ordered all units to submit their completed nominal rolls, so that arrangements might be made to establish a new colony of Loyalists early in the spring. The last return of the King's Rangers was dated 27 January, and detailed three full companies.

The King's Rangers *				
Company	Commander	Officers	Enlisted men	Dependents
Commandant	Major James Rogers	1	—	5
1st Company	Captain James Breakenridge	3	83	81
2nd Company	Captain Azariah Pritchard	3	60	75
3rd Company	Captain Henry Ruiter	3	54	63
Totals:		10	197	224

The return, summarized in the table above, reflected 10 officers, 197 non-commissioned officers and men, with 224 dependants. James indicated in correspondence that he did not know how many of the men in his regiment would settle in the new colony with their families as some were still absent on duty and others might desire to settle elsewhere, particularly in the Missisquoi Bay Settlement then planned by Henry Ruiter. Some men had even expressed a desire to rent the land on which the barracks stood, to lodge their families until they decided where they were to settle finally. This request was denied.

The regiment was disbanded, and the commissioned officers, despite the original policy, retired on half pay. James received £133 per year as a retired major. A captain received £88, a lieutenant £41 and an ensign £32. The payments were to be made for life, and after the death of the officer his widow would receive a smaller pension. In a society where money was scarce these funds were essential. Eventually most of the regiment did

* This table is based on the 27 January 1784 return and other related documents.

settle on the lands allocated, near their old commander. After Britain decided the allocation of land in the new areas of settlement, instructions were sent as follows:

> *To every field officer, 1000 acres;*
> *every subaltern, staff or warrant officer 500 acres;*
> *every non-commissioned officer 200 acres;*
> *every private 100 acres;*
> *and for each member of their families 50 acres.*
>
> *Civilian heads of families are entitled to receive 100 acres,*
> *and 50 acres for each family member,*
> *while every single man is to receive 50 acres.*

During the war, several problems plagued the Loyalist units. Being completely dependent on the British army for all their requirements, they were not able to attain the organizational cohesion nor the independence that might have made them an effective fighting force. The authorities paid scant attention to the military potential of these units, preferring instead to regard them simply as refugees whose material needs were met as well as the current circumstances permitted but whose military plans and ambitions were never taken very seriously.

James organized a band of 120 officers and men from his regiment for settlement on lands to be allocated near Cataraqui. With a group of families comprising altogether 47 women, 118 children under 21 years and 14 servants, the party totalled some 299 persons. The group moved to Montreal to spend the winter in preparation. Sir John Johnson was to be responsible for the entire settlement but was otherwise engaged with the duties for the Indian Affairs Department and delegated the responsibility to Major Edward Jessup, who supervised the movement of more than 3,000 Loyalists to this area. He was assisted by Justus Sherwood, James Grey and James Rogers, the four of them being the only field officers to settle in this part of the colony.

Organizing the resettlement was handled like a military operation. The logistics associated with organizing, moving and administering such a diverse assemblage must have been immense. Every man, woman and child was issued with clothing and blankets. Each group of five people was provided with a tent and a cooking kettle for the journey and the initial settlement. Families were to occupy these tents until cabins could be built, after which they were to be returned to the quartermaster's stores. Each

James Rogers at Pointe des Cascades in 1784

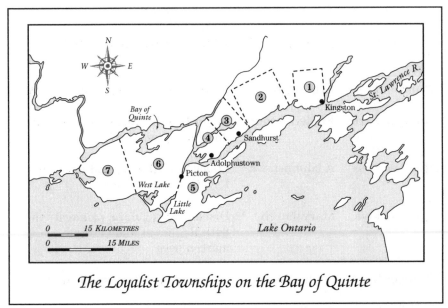

The Loyalist Townships on the Bay of Quinte

family was also issued with provisions for a month with further provisions to be provided when they reached the new townships. Navigation on the St. Lawrence opened on 20 May, and supplies and surveyors were sent forward.

It took ten to twelve days for the journey up the river to Cataraqui by means of small boats built at Lachine known as caudelles or bateaux, later known as Durham boats. Each weighed about two tons and was capable of carrying four to five families. Twelve of these boats made up a brigade under the command of a conductor. Rapids were ascended on foot, with only a few in the boat to pole and the remainder onshore walking or pulling the boat forward by means of ropes. Frequently this required wading in the current upon jagged rocks.

The first Loyalist settlers left Montreal on 2 June, surmounted the rapids and arrived at Cataraqui on 12 June. The last of the settlers had left Montreal by 24 June. When James and his regiment actually moved is not known, but family records indicate that they were at Cataraqui by 17 June. The surveyors laboured frantically to keep ahead of the arriving settlers, but the surveys were not complete. At Cataraqui a town plot, some time later named King's Town, was hastily established to meet the influx of settlers. The Bay of Quinte area was surveyed and divided first into five and later seven numbered townships as shown on the next page.*

---

* Named by Lord Dorchester in honour of the King's children on 24 July 1788.

Number One	Kingston	Captain Grass and Associated Loyalists
Number Two	Ernesttown	Major Jessup's Corps (remainder)
Number Three	Fredericksburg	Major Rogers King's Rangers and 2nd Battalion KRRNY
Number Four	Adolphustown	Major Van Alstyne and Associated Loyalists (remainder)
Number Five	Marysburgh	Disbanded regulars, primarily the 84th Regiment and German mercenaries
Number Six	Sophiasburgh	Reserved for future settlement
Number Seven	Ameliasburgh	Reserved for future settlement

When the Loyalists arrived only the first two of the townships were ready for settlement. By July the third township had been surveyed and was ready, but it was August before the fourth and fifth townships were laid out and surveyed. The waiting and anticipation soon led to rumors of other concerns. Shortly after the groups had left Montreal, an order arrived from England specifying that supplies designated to support the Loyalist families were to be reduced. This caused considerable apprehension among the settlers, which resulted in the memorial copied below. In late July, on his own authority Haldimand restored full rations until further notice. This action helped but did not entirely ease anxiety. There was also a significant issue about the allocation of land, the requirements for which had been considerably underestimated.

To Sir John Johnson, Knight & Baronet, &c., &c., &c.
The Memorial of the Subscribers for themselves and in behalf of the
Loyalists
and others interested therein.

Humbly Sheweth - -

*That your Memorialists being informed that an order is received from
His Excellency General Haldimand directing the Commissary General to
victual them in the following manner, vizt. at two thirds allowance to the
1st of May 1785, and from that Period at one Third Allowance to the 1st
of May 1786, estimating the whole Ration at one Pound of Beef, or twelve
ounces of Pork.*

*That your Memorialists having seriously taken into Consideration the
diminution ordered, beg leave to transmit thro' you to His Excellency
General Haldimand, the following Considerations, so essentially interesting to them, vizt. that thro' unavoidable delays, the Season being already
too far Advanced to permit the least hope of raising anything towards their
Support until next Spring, & even then nothing of consequence - and their
Remote situation, want of Communication with the Inhabited Part of
Canada in the Winter Season, joined to the inability of the greater part to
purchase supplies, even if within reach, justly fill them with the most
gloomy apprehensions, that disorders arising from their wretched situation
and very contracted Allowance of Provisions will fataly frustrate His
Majesty's good intentions towards them, and Ruin a numerous Settlement
in its Infancy.*

*They hope it will not be deemed impertinent here to suggest to His
Excellency a comparison between the situation of the Loyalists settled in
Nova Scotia and those not yet settled at or about Cataraqui, the first settled
early last Summer in a Country, the Coasts of which supply them plentifully
with Fish. They have a communication by Sea to the Plentyfull coasts of
New England &c. whilst the other situation entirely excludes them from
any such advantage, and unless relieved by His Excellency's Humane
Interference (by granting them their usual Ration for as long time after*

taking possession of their Lands Allotted them as were granted to the Loyalists settled at Nova Scotia) have nothing but extreem Misery to expect.

And your Memorialists as in duty bound &c., &c.

Cataraqui, 5th July 1784

       Geo. Singleton, Capt. K.R.R.N.Y.

       Edward Jessup, Major

       Jas Rogers, L.M.K.R.

       Thos. Gumersall, Capt. K.R.Regt.N.York

       G. Baron De Reitzenstein

       H. Spencer, Lt. K.R.R.N.Y.

       T. Thompson, Ens. 2d Batt.K.R.R.N.Y.

       O. Church, Lt. 2d Batt.K.R.R.N.Y.

       Willm. Mckay, Liut.

       William Fraser, Adjt. 2d Batt.K.R.R.N.Y.

To Sir John Johnson, Knight & Baronet, &c., &c., &c.

The Memorial of the Subscribers for themselves & the . oyalists under their respective care. Humbly Sheweth —

That your Memorialists in Conjunction with Major Holland were commissioned by you to superintend the Settlement of the Loyalists of the Late Second Battalion K.R.R.N. York & the King's Rangers upon the Crown Lands allotted to them by His Excellency the Commander in Chief for their Reception. Your Memorialists cannot without the most Poignant concern View the Measures adopted by a Person jointly commissioned with them, which must inevitably (if he is permitted to proceed in the same Track) Occasion the total Ruin of a great Number of Industrious, Loyal, and well disposed People.

Your Memorialists beg your Permission to Point out their Grievances and the causes, also to Represent to you their opinion of the Consequences that will attend a perseverance in the Measures by him adopted Vizt- It was agreed in your presence by Major Holland and your Memorialists that they should have the Third Township and as much of the Fourth as would be sufficient for them, and the Tenor of your instructions to Major Holland & John Collins Esqur. (a Copy of which he Major Holland permitted us to take) Points out the same agreement, but unfortunately for us we soon discovered that Major Holland had directed his Views quite the contrary and proceeded to circumscribe our Boundaries within the limits of a Nine Mile Square Township and to affix Major Van Alstynes People on the Remaining lands without first exploring and ascertaining the Quantity fit for cultivation - After frequent Applications and remonstrances to him of the impropriety of so doing he still persists in his Original plan and now that the Number of Acres are supposed to be known and which he gives in Amounts to 44,054 Acres being all the lands both in the Third and Fourth Townships, which is not sufficient for the late Second Battalion of the Kings Royal Regiment of New York and the Kings Rangers by 10,546 Acres, without including the Familys, and now says that your Memorialists and the People under their care must take it as it is, for he is determined that Major Van Alstynes People shall not be removed or in other words he will not direct them so to do without an express Order from His Excellency the Commander in Chief.

Your Memorialists from your Instructions to Major Holland and John Collins Esqr. (who look up to them for Redress) having neither Tent nor House to Shelter themselves under, added to their scanty allowance of Provisions - Humbly beg your Interference and your Memorialists as in duty bound &c., &c.

Jas. Rogers
Thos. Gumersall
W. R. Crawford

Cataraqui, 7th August 1784

Cataraqui, 8th August 1784

Sir;

We are exceeding sorry to find ourselves under the disagreeable necessity of communicating by way of Memorial, a Number of grievances which the obstinacy of an individual solely occasions. Now that Matters are come to a Crisis after amusing us this upwards of six Weeks & frequently asserting that there was land enough for us & Major Rogers People, he finds himself mistaken and sees the impossibility of making good his assertions, his proposals to us are such that it is impossible for us to contenance such either being considered acessarys.

The Bearer Lieut. McKay whose only Business to Canada is to present to you our Memorial will point out to you his Conduct to us & our People since your Departure.

The Gentlemen with us join in Compliments to you. We are with the greatest respect, Sir, your most obedient Hble Servants.

Jas. Rogers

Thos. Gumersall

W. B. Crawford

Sir John Johnson, Knt & Bart. &c., &c., &c.

In August the King's Rangers and the 2nd Battalion King's Royal Regiment of New York, both incomplete units, were allocated land in the Third Township, plus a strip of twelve lots from the Fourth. The land allocated in each township was drawn by lot to ensure fairness. About 22 August the Rogers family finally reached their land near what is now Sandhurst, Ontario, and set about building yet another new home from the ground up in the virgin wilderness.* Settlers banded together and built shelters for the winter: small houses 15 x 20 feet of rounded logs constructed to a height of seven to eight feet. In many cases these houses served for several years. Each cabin had one door and a window opening covered by blankets until doors could be fashioned and window glass obtained. All supplies and tools were scarce, and the settlers were constantly pleading for further support during the first few years.

---

* One source suggests that Margaret and the children did not join James until 1785, after a basic shelter had been erected. While possible, this is considered unlikely, and it contradicts family documents.

The disputes over land had already been resolved; yet the rebuke shown below was received from the Governor in August. It appears to have had no damaging effect on James and the settlers. On 10 September, John Collins reported to Haldimand that all issues respecting land had been satisfactorily settled among the parties concerned. Frederick Haldimand left Canada on 16 November 1784, never to return. In 1786 Sir Guy Carleton, who was now Lord Dorchester, was appointed Governor-in-Chief of Canada.

Head Quarters Quebec, 23 August, 1784.

Sir,

Major Holland having reported to me the opposition He met with in the Execution of His Duty in laying out the Township No. 4 from Major Rogers, & others Captains of the 2d Battalion of the Royal Yorkers but particularly the extravagant Conduct of Capt. McDonell, so highly disrespectful to the King's Service, and to an officer of Major Holland's Rank and Character, in Consequence whereof and in Consideration of Mr. McDonell being an unfit Person to reside in a New Settlement, you will upon Receipt of this Letter order him away from the Settlement, and at the same time acquaint him that by his Conduct he has forfeited every Pretention to Protection of Government, and that his Name shall be struck out of my Recommendation of the officers for half pay, which you will publish in Orders.*

You will please also to acquaint Major Rogers and Captn. Gumershall and Crawford of my displeasure at a Conduct so opposite to that which they ought to observe in an Infant Settlement, where nothing but the Force of Example can reconcile the numberless Difficulties that must unavoidably occur, circumstanced as they are at present. Nothing but Major Rogers's time of life, and a belief that he and the Parties concerned have been influenced by Capt. McDonell should prevent me from withdrawing from them in like Manner His Majesty's Bounty which Servants are no longer intitled to than while they conduct themselves as dutifull and well-disposed

---

* Captain Allan McDonell's conduct was not specified but was probably that unbecoming an officer. He left as ordered and eventually settled near what would become Hamilton, Ontario.

Subjects. I have directed Mr. De Lancey to repair immediately to Cataraqui in order to settle the Distribution of the Township in question with Mr. Collins agreably to Instructions he will receive from Sir John Johnson. I have referred him to you for your Advice and Assistance, and must desire that you will afford Him all in your Power — the more the Business of the Settlements is transacted under the Sanction of the Civil Power the better it will be relished by these People. I shall send up Commissions of the Peace for Mr. Van Alstine and Capt. Sherwood, which I believe will make a sufficient Number.

Haldimand

Major Ross, Cataraqui

For many years, James supervised the needs of the men of his own regiment as well as those of the 2nd Battalion of the King's Royal Regiment of New York, at the request of Sir John Johnson. Fredericksburg was the most overcrowded of the townships. After settling in the area, James and a brother officer set off to explore the region. Coming to an inlet on the south side of the peninsula, they were so taken by the scenery, land and timber, that they resolved to settle in this portion of the Sixth Township, later known as Sophiasburgh. James moved to the area around 1787 and established a homestead on the shores of an area he called Little Lake, southwest of what is now Picton. Feeling the pressure from Loyalist exiles in Britain, the Government decided to recompense these people for their wartime losses. A Royal Commission was established to examine all the claims for compensation for loss of property and income. Their terms of reference defined a Loyalist as a person who:

- had been born in the Colonies or was living there in 1775 at the outbreak of the revolution;
- had rendered a substantial service to the Royal cause in the war; and,
- had left the Colonies during the war or shortly thereafter.

Though the bulk of the commission's work was done in England, three commissioners traveled to Canada in 1786 and 1787 to hear and settle the claims of the thousands of Loyalists there. The memorial that James submitted is shown on the next page. It is of interest to note that James made no mention of his service during Burgoyne's campaign. His presence with Burgoyne has, however, been confirmed from other sources.

To the Honourable Commissioners appointed by
Act of Parliament for enquiring into the losses
and Services of the American Loyalists.
The Memorial of James Rogers Esqr. late Major Commandant of the King's
Rangers in Canada.
Humbly Sheweth,

That your Memorialist in 1755 Served in His Majesty's Provincial
Troops as Ensign, in 1756 as Lieutenant of a Corps of Rangers and in 1757
was appointed a Captain of an Independent Company of Rangers, Served
on most of the Campaigns during the late French War in North America,
was at the taking of Louisbourg and Quebec.

That your Memorialist in 1763 and 1764 went to the relief of Detroit
and served during the Indian War, after which period Your Memorialist
settled in the Colonies where he purchased and improved Land in the
Provinces of New-Hampshire and New York which he effected with much
expense and labour. His Excellency General Tryon was pleased to appoint
him Lieutenant Colonel of Militia and first Assistant Justice of the Court
of Common Pleas in the County of Cumberland from which he in the Month
of April 1777 made his Escape and at the hazard of his life joined His
Majesty's Troops at New York leaving his Wife and Family to the
resentment of the Enemy, who plundered them of every thing they could
find with their wonted rage and inhumanity a recital of which your
Memorialist avoids as it could not be contained in the compass of a
Memorial. In the Spring 1778 he was appointed a Major to a Provincial
Corps in New York and in the Spring 1779 a Major Commandant of the
Second Battalion of Kings Rangers which appointment he held 'till the
general reduction took place in Canada.

That in consequence of the Loyalty and Services rendered to His
Majesty's Government by your Memorialist he was proscribed his Country
and his property Sold for the good of the State.

Your Memorialist therefore most Humbly prays that his case may be
taken into consideration and such favourable report made thereon as his
Losses and Services may appear to deserve, And as in duty bound shall ever
pray.

Jas. Rogers

Montreal, June 26th 1787

The Commission generally settled claims on a pro-rated basis. Loyalists in Quebec were awarded approximately one-third of all that was claimed. On average, settlements amounted to some £178 sterling, a substantial sum in a pioneer society, particularly when added to the value of the land grants. James received £1048, along with his land grants, in compensation for some 50,427 acres he had forfeited in the United States. The property he owned is listed below but does not include additional land in Londonderry held for him by James McGregor, mentioned in his will.

23,000 acres	in the Township of Kent, Vermont *
12,000 acres	in the Township of Hubbardton, Vermont
8,000 acres	in the Township of Nawarth, New Hampshire
3,500 acres	in the Township of Londonderry, New Hampshire
927 acres	in the Township of Dunbarton, New Hampshire
3,000 acres	in the Township of South Bay, New York

The winter of 1787–1788 was known as the Hungry Year. The rations that had been provided by the Government ceased in June 1786, and the settlers had little to fall back on when their modest crops failed. Remarkable stories are told of how people survived, from soup bones being passed from cabin to cabin, to the faithful cat or dog who daily brought home a rabbit. The settlers took note of the roots eaten by the pigs and thereby avoided those of a poisonous variety. They butchered livestock to survive, and in some cases even the family dog fell victim to help them avoid starvation. By spring, no one had seed or potatoes to plant, for all had been consumed. Lord Dorchester obtained permission from England to acquire relief supplies from the United States. Provisions and seed were rationed to the settlers, averting a major disaster and the collapse of the Colony.

On 9 November 1789, Lord Dorchester informed his Legislative Council that it was his desire and that of the King to put some mark of honour upon the Loyalists of Canada. The result established the tradition of the United Empire Loyalists.

Shortly before his death James was forced by very poor health to return to Fredericksburg, where he died on 23 September 1790, at the age of 62 years. Family documents suggest that he was laid to rest in the "old cemetery", and the records of the Reverend John Langhorn state that he was buried at Fredericksburg on 25 September; but the actual location is unmarked and unknown. His final will, dated 12 August 1790, but not probated until 17 January 1794, has been reproduced as Appendix IX to this section. In spite of the dating of the will within five weeks of his death,

---

* James did not receive compensation for the loss of his estate in Kent due to the legality of the confiscation. His eldest son James later tried to recover some of this property and met with limited success.

The Proclamation of 1789

The Loyalists who had adhered to the Unity of the Empire and joined the Royal Standard before the Treaty of Peace in 1783, and all their children and Descendants by either sex, are to be distinguished by the following capitals affixed to their names:

U.E.,

Alluding to their great principle, The Unity of the Empire.

it appears that it did not fully account for all his property. His heirs later divided the remaining lands by mutual consent on 2 June 1803, and a copy of the legal document is reproduced as Appendix X.

In 1791 the British Government passed the Constitutional Act dividing the Province of Quebec into two new provinces of Upper and Lower Canada. The act also allowed for the creation of colonial government, which balanced the appointed Legislative Councils with an elected assembly. General John Graves Simcoe* was later appointed as the first Lieutenant Governor of Upper Canada.

A short time after James died, the family returned to Little Lake, where they were joined by John Armstrong and his wife, James' daughter Mary. The Armstrong children had been living at Little Lake for some time, taken there by James because of Mary's poor health and John's frequent and prolonged absences. After John died in 1792, it was decided that Mary should move in with her mother and the family. On the evening of 1 December 1793, she became very ill with a fever. At the time her brothers were out hunting, and the closest neighbors, her sister Mary Ann and her husband John Peters, were five miles away. John Peters felt uneasy about them and came early the next day, but Mary had died during the night. Margaret expressed a wish that Mary be laid to rest beside James, but supposed that it was not practicable because there was no road and the ice was not thick enough to support a sleigh. By early evening, she too had died. It is believed that both women were buried on the family farm at Sophiasburgh on 3 December 1793. The Reverend John Langhorn performed the service, according to his records, but they do not identify the location.†

---

* See Historical Figures, Annex C.

† A family tradition suggests Mary and Margaret were buried beside James at Fredericksburg; however, the records of John Langhorn indicate otherwise. Their final resting place is unmarked and unlocated.

Several items of furniture from the Rogers' original homestead have been donated and are currently on display at Barnham House, a Loyalist museum in the town of Grafton, Ontario. In 1963 the plaque shown below was set up at St. Paul's Anglican Church in Sandhurst to commemorate the arrival and settlement of the Rogers family in the area. A second plaque to the settlement of the family in Upper Canada has been erected in the United Empire Loyalists' Church in Adolphustown.

James Rogers was a reluctant soldier in that family and farming were far more important to him than exploration and fighting, so unlike his brother Robert. He nevertheless answered the call to arms at the age of 27 and demonstrated leadership ability fully equal to that of his brother. He was with Amherst at Louisbourg, with Wolfe at Quebec and later with Robert at Detroit during Pontiac's uprising. Although the privateer scheme was a short-lived adventure, it had great potential and could have changed the direction of his life. He built farms from the wilderness at Londonderry, New Hampshire, and at Kent in what is now Vermont. James was recognized as a leader in these communities and was elected a member of the Committee of Correspondence. His decision to remain loyal

Plaque at St. Paul's Anglican Church, Sandhurst

to the Crown was based on principle, and as a result he lost all he had acquired. He firmly believed that there had to be a better way to resolve differences than the spilling of blood, but once he had committed himself to the cause of the Crown, he stayed with his commitment to the end. The Revolution tore the family apart. It appears that only James and Robert chose the King, while their other siblings joined the rebellion. James fought with Burgoyne and again at his brother's side. He was also engaged in operations with the Secret Service. After the war, at the age of 55, he led a part of the United Empire Loyalist migration to Upper Canada and established another new home in untamed country. James had an arduous but fascinating life, and so far as we know he never expressed any regrets during a lifetime of taking responsibility and of service to the community.

Of his children, his daughter Mary was wed to John Armstrong, and their descendants include members of the Larkin, Beatty, Ryerson, Spencer and Baldwin families. Mary Ann married John Peters, and Margaret married Aaron Greeley. James Rogers (3–1) returned to the United States after his father's death in an attempt to recover some of the confiscated family lands and possessions but returned to Canada by 1818. David McGregor Rogers (3–2) saw action during the War of 1812 and was an elected member of the Legislative Assembly of Upper Canada, a position in which he served for more than 25 years. His descendants settled in Grafton and Peterborough and include members of the Caddy, Strickland, Burritt, McNabb, Price and Burnham families.

James Rogers (2–3) and his children

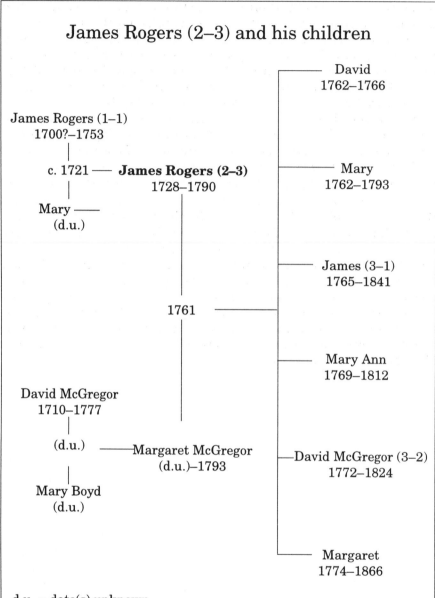

d.u. = date(s) unknown

The first child born to James and Margaret was a son David, born in Londonderry, New Hampshire. He died of unknown causes on 2 November, 1766 when four years old and was buried in Londonderry.

Appendix I   Crown Grant for the Township of Kent

The following Grant for the Township of Kent, signed at New York on 13 February, was recorded in the office of the New York Colonial Secretary on 22 February, and was docketed by the New York Auditor General on 23 February 1770. The original Charter, on parchment with seals still attached, is preserved in the care of descendants of the late Ranger Rogers (7-6) of Denver, Colorado.

CHARTER

GEORGE THE THIRD;

By the Grace of God, of Great Britain, France and Ireland; KING, Defender of the Faith, and so forth.

To All To Whom These Presents shall come, Greeting;

WHEREAS our Province of New York in America hath, ever since the Grant thereof to James, Duke of York, been abutted and bounded to the East in part by the West Bank or side of Connecticut River; AND WHEREAS of late years, a great part of our said Province lying to the Westward of the same River, hath nevertheless been pretended to be granted by divers instruments under the Great Seal of the Province of New Hampshire, as tho' the same Lands had then belonged to, and were within the Bounds and Limits of the said Province of New Hampshire, and within the powers and jurisdiction of the Government thereof;

AND WHEREAS our loving Subject James Rogers, by his humble petition in behalf of himself and twenty two other persons presented unto our late, trusty and well beloved Sir Henry Moore, Baronet, then our Captain General and Governor-in-Chief in and over our Province of New York, and the Territories depending thereon in America, and read in our Council for our said Province of New York on the second day of June which was in the Year of our Lord one thousand seven hundred and sixty six, did set forth: THAT the petitioner and his associates apprehended they had a good Right and Title to twenty six thousand acres of land lying on the East side of the Water running from South Bay to Ticonderoga, under one of the pretended Grants above mentioned; THAT the said Lands had since our Royal Order in our Privy Council of the twentieth day of July, in the Year of our Lord one thousand seven hundred and sixty four, been granted to reduced Officers, whereby the petitioner and his associates must inevitably lose their Rights, unless a Grant should be made to them of other lands in our said

Province of New York; THAT there is a certain Tract of Land lying in our said Province of New York, bounded on the West side of a certain Tract of Land commonly called & known by the name of Tomlinson, beginning at the Southwesterly corner of Chester, and running West twenty seven degrees North seven miles and thirty eight chains; then South ten degrees West seven miles and seventy six chains; then East ten degrees South six miles and eight chains then North twenty degrees East six miles to the place of beginning containing twenty six thousand Acres;

AND THEREFORE the petitioner did humbly pray our Letters Patent under the Great Seal of our Province of New York, granting unto him and his associates their heirs and assigns, the Tract of Land bounded and described as aforesaid, and that the same might be erected into a Township by the name of Kent, and vested with such powers and privileges as other towns in our said Province of New York have and do enjoy.

WHICH PETITION, having been then and there read and referred to Committee of our Council for our said Province of New York, our same Council did afterwards, on the same day, in pursuance of the report of the said Committee, humbly advise our said late Captain General and Governor-in-Chief of our said Province of New York to grant the Prayer thereof under quit Rent Provisoes, Limitations and Restrictions prescribed by our Royal Instructions; the quantity of three hundred and fifty Acres of the said Tract of Land to be granted to the use of the Incorporated Society for the Propagation of the Gospel in Foreign Parts; like quantity thereof to be granted as a Glebe for the use of the Minister of the Gospel in Communion of the Church of England, as by Law established, for the time being residing on the said Tract; and like quantity thereof to be granted for the Minister of the Gospel who shall first settle on the said Tract; and the quantity of one hundred acres thereof for the use of a Schoolmaster residing on the said Tract.

AND WHEREAS the said James Rogers by his humble petition in behalf of himself and his associates presented on the sixteenth day of January now past unto our trusty and well beloved Cadwallader Colden, Esquire, our Lieutenant Governor and Commander-in-Chief of our said Province of New York, and the Territories depending thereon in America, Hath set forth, among other things; THAT having procured an actual Survey of the said Tract of Land at considerable expence, the same was found to contain twenty four thousand one hundred and fifty Acres; THAT the said Tract of Land tho' within the Lands formerly claimed

---

by the Government of New Hampshire had not been granted by that Government and remains still vacant and vested in Us;

AND THEREFORE the petitioner, in behalf of himself and associates, did humbly Pray that the Letters Patent ordered on the said first recited Petition might issue for the Lands so surveyed as aforesaid, in the name of the petitioner, and in the names of his associates mentioned in the Schedule or List at the foot of the said last recited Petition.

IN PURSUANCE WHEREOF and in Obedience to our said Royal Instruction, our Commissioners appointed for the setting out of all Lands to be granted within our said Province of New York, have set out for the said James Rogers, and his associates named in the Schedule aforesaid, to wit: Daniel Goldsmith, Daniel Goldsmith, junior, Henry Shute, Garret Vandenbergh, Joseph Cox, David Philips, Cornelius Ryan, Cornelius Van den Bergh, Andries Riglear, Adam Vandenbergh, Caleb Hyatt, George Hopson, William Shooler, Benjamin Betts, James Smith, John Woods, Edward Laight, Thomas Ivers, Adolph De Grove, Joshua T. De St. Croix, Alexander Wilson, and James McCartney; ALL that certain Tract or parcel of Land situate and being in the County of Cumberland within our Province of New York, BEGINNING at the Northwest corner of a Tract of Land lately granted to John Hall late Lieutenant in our eightieth Regiment of Foot and runs thence South eighty degrees East five hundred and seventy two Chains; then North seven degrees East three hundred and sixty Chains; then North sixty three degrees West five hundred and seventy nine Chains; then South, ten degrees West five hundred and twenty nine Chains to the Place where this tract first began, containing twenty four thousand one hundred and fifty Acres of Land and the usual allowance for Highways;

AND ALSO our said Commissioners have set out the several Lots herein- after described parts & parcels of the larger tract, for the several and respective uses and purposes herein before mentioned, that is to say: FOR the use of the Incorporated Society for Propagation of the Gospel in Foreign Parts, ALL that certain Lot or parcel of Land, part of the larger Tract herein before described, BEGINNING at the distance of two hundred and seventy five Chains, measured on a course North seventy degrees East from the said Northwest Corner of the said Tract lately granted to John Hall, and this lot runs from the said place of beginning South eighty degrees East sixty Chains and three Rods, then North ten degrees East sixty Chains and three Rods then North ten degrees West sixty Chains and three Rods, then South ten degrees West sixty Chains and three Rods, to the place where this Lot first began, containing three hundred and fifty Acres of Land and the usual allowance for Highways;

FOR a Glebe for the use of the Minister of the Gospel in Communion of the Church of England, as by Law established, for the time being residing on the said larger Tract, ALL that certain Lot or parcel of Land part of the said larger Tract herein before described, BEGINNING at the North East Corner of the Lot set out for and granted to the Society for Propagating the Gospel in Foreign Parts, and runs from said place of beginning North eighty degrees West sixty Chains and three Rods, then North ten degrees East sixty Chains and three Rods, then South eighty degrees East sixty Chains and three Rods, then South ten degrees West sixty Chains and three Rods to the place where this Tract or Lot first began containing three hundred and fifty Acres of Land and the usual allowance for Highways;

FOR the first settled Minister on the larger Tract aforesaid, ALL that certain Lot or parcel of Land, part of the larger Tract described as aforesaid, BEGINNING at the North East Corner of the lot set out for the said Society and runs thence South ten degrees West sixty Chains and three Rods, then South eighty degrees East sixty Chains and three Rods, then North ten degrees East sixty Chains and three Rods, and then North eighty degrees West sixty Chains and three Rods to the Place where the Tract or Lot first began, containing three hundred and fifty Acres of Land and the usual allowance for Highways;

AND FOR the use of a Schoolmaster residing on said larger Tract, ALL that certain Lot or parcel of Land, part of the aforesaid larger Tract, BEGINNING at the Southeast Corner of the Lot set out for the Glebe and runs thence North ten degrees East sixty Chains and three Rods, then South eighty degrees East seventeen Chains and one Rod, then South ten degrees West sixty Chains and three Rods, and then North eighty degrees West seventeen Chains and one Rod, to the place where this Lot first began, containing one hundred Acres of Land and the usual allowance for Highways;

AND in setting out the said larger Tract of Land, and the several Lots and parcels of Land last described, our said Commissioners have had regard to the profitable and unprofitable acres, and have taken care that the length of any of them doth not extend along the Banks of any River, otherwise than is conformable to our said Royal Instructions, as by a Certificate thereof under their hands bearing date the seventh day of this instant Month of February, and entered on Record in our Secretary's Office for our said Province of New York may more fully appear.

    WHICH said Tract of twenty four thousand one hundred and fifty Acres

---

of Land and usual allowance for Highways so set out aforesaid according to our said Royal Instructions, WE, being willing to grant to the said petitioner and his associates above named, their heirs and assigns for ever, with several powers and privileges and to and upon the several and respective use and uses, Trusts, Intents, and Purposes, Limitations and Appointments, and under the several Reservations, Exceptions, Provisoes, and Conditions, hereinafter expressed, limited, declared, and appointed of and concerning the same and of and concerning every part and parcel thereof; KNOW YE that of our especial Grace, certain knowledge and meer motion, WE have given, granted, ratified, and confirmed, and do by these Presents for Us, our Heirs and Successors, give, grant, ratify and confirm unto them the said James Rogers, Daniel Goldsmith, Daniel Goldsmith junior, Henry Shute, Garret Vandenbergh, Joseph Cox, David Phillips, Cornelius Ryan, Cornelius Van den Bergh, Andries Riglear, Adam Van den Bergh, Caleb Hyatt, George Hopson, William Shooler, Benjamin Betts, James Smith, John Woods, Edward Laight, Thomas Ivers, Adolph De Grove, Joshua T. De St. Croix, Alexander Wilson and James McCartney, their heirs and assigns, ALL that the aforesaid large Tract or parcel of Land set out, abutted and bounded, and described by our said Commissioners, in manner and form as above mentioned, including all the aforementioned several smaller Tracts or Lots of Land set out and described by our said Commissioners, as parts and parcels thereof, Containing in the whole twenty four thousand one hundred and fifty Acres of Land besides the usual allowance for Highways; TOGETHER with all and singular the Tenements Hereditaments, Emoluments, and Appurtenances to the same and every part and parcel thereof belonging or appertaining. AND also all our Estate, Right, Title, Interest, Possession, Claim, and Demand whatsoever of in and to the same Lands and Premises, and every part and parcel thereof. AND the Reversion & Reversions, Remainder and Remainders, Rents, Issues and Profits thereof and of every part and parcel thereof; EXCEPT and always reserved out of this present Grant unto Us, our Heirs and Successors for ever, ALL Mines of Gold and Silver, and also all White or other sort of Pine Trees fit for Masts of the Growth of twenty four Inches Diameter and upwards at twelve Inches from the Earth, for Masts for the Royal Navy of Us, our Heirs and Successors.

TO HAVE AND TO HOLD the said Tract of twenty four thousand one hundred and fifty Acres of Land, Tenements, Hereditaments, and Premises by these Presents granted, ratified, and confirmed, and every part and parcel thereof; with their and every of their Appurtenances (Except as is herein before excepted), unto them our Grantees above mentioned, their heirs & assigns for ever, to, for and

James Rogers   Appendix I to Section 2–3 upon several and respective use and uses, Trusts, Intents and Purposes hereinafter expressed limited declared and appointed of and concerning the same and of and concerning the said respective Lots herein mentioned and expressed to be set out by our said Commissioners as parts and parcels thereof and to and for no other use or uses, Intent or Purpose whatsoever, that is to say:

AS FOR and concerning ALL that the before mentioned small Tract, Lot or parcel of Land, so set out for the Incorporated Society for the Propagation of the Gospel in Foreign Parts as aforesaid being part and parcel of the said large Tract of twenty four thousand one hundred and fifty Acres of Land and Premises, hereby granted ratified and confirmed and every part and parcel of the same Lot of Land with the Appurtenances to the same belonging (Except as is hereinbefore excepted), To and for the only proper and separate use and Behoof of the Society for Propagation of the Gospel in Foreign Parts above mentioned, and their Successors for ever, and to and for no other use or uses, intent or purpose whatsoever.

AND AS FOR and concerning ALL the beforementioned small Tract, Lot or parcel of Land so set out as and for a Glebe, for the use of a Minister of the Gospel in Communion of the Church of England as by Law established, being part and parcel of the said large Tract of twenty four thousand one hundred and fifty Acres of Land and Premises hereby granted ratified and confirmed, and every part and parcel of the same Lot of Land with Appurtenances to the same belonging (Except as is hereinbefore excepted), IN TRUST as and for a Glebe for ever to and for the only proper and separate use, Benefit and Behoof of the first Minister of the Gospel in Communion of the Church of England as by Law established, having the Cure of Souls and residing in the said large Tract of Land hereby granted, and Successors for ever, for the time being residing as aforesaid and to and for no other use or uses, Intent or Purpose whatsoever.

AND AS FOR and concerning ALL that the before mentioned small Tract, Lot or parcel of Land, so set out for the first settled Minister in the said large Tract of Land hereby granted, the same being part and parcel of the said large Tract of twenty four thousand one hundred and fifty Acres of Land and Premises hereby granted, ratified and confirmed, and every part and parcel of the same Lot of Land, with the Appurtenances to the same belonging (Except as herein before excepted), IN TRUST to and for the sole proper and separate use, Benefit and Behoof of the first Minister of the Gospel that shall settle and officiating on the said large Tract of Land hereby granted, his heirs & assigns for ever. AND IN TRUST also that our said Grantees their heirs or assigns, shall and do well and truly by good and *sufficient assurances in Law, convey the same last mentioned small Tract or Lot of Land with the Appurtenances to such Minister of the Gospel as shall be first settled and officiating as aforesaid, his heirs and assigns for ever, in fee simple as soon as may be after such Minister shall be settled and officiating as aforesaid and to and for no other use or uses, Intent or Purpose whatsoever.*

AND AS FOR and concerning ALL that other small Tract, Lot or parcel of Land, so set out for the use of a Schoolmaster, being also part and parcel of the said large Tract of twenty four thousand one hundred and fifty Acres of Land and Premises hereby granted, ratified, and confirmed, and every part and parcel of the same Lot of Land with the Appurtenances to the same belonging (Except as is herein before excepted), IN TRUST for ever to and for the sole and separate use, Benefit & Behoof of the first publick Schoolmaster of the Township, by these Presents constituted and erected, officiating and resident in the same Township and Successors Schoolmasters as aforesaid for ever, and for no other use or uses Intent or Purpose whatsoever.

AND AS FOR and concerning ALL the rest, residue and remainder of the said Tract of twenty four thousand one hundred and fifty Acres of Land, Tenements, Hereditaments, and Premises by these Presents granted, ratified and confirmed, TO HAVE AND TO HOLD one full and equal twenty third part (the whole into twenty three equal parts to be divided) of the said rest, residue and remainder, and every part and parcel thereof, with all and every Appurtenances to the same belonging or in any wise appertaining, (Except as is herein before excepted) unto each of them, the said James Rogers, Daniel Goldsmith, Daniel Goldsmith junior, Henry Shute, Garret Van den Bergh, Joseph Cox, David Phillips, Cornelius Ryan, Cornelius Van den Bergh, Andries Riglear, Adam Van den Bergh, Caleb Hyatt, George Hopson, William Shooler, Benjamin Betts, James Smith, John Woods, Edward Laight, Thomas Ivers, Adolph De Grove, Joshua T. De St. Croix, Alexander Wilson and James McCartney, their heirs and assigns respectively; TO their only proper and separate use and Behoof respectively for ever as Tenants in Common and not as Joint Tenants, and to and for no other use or uses Intent or Purpose whatsoever, ALL and singular the said Tract of twenty four thousand one hundred and fifty Acres of Land and Premises hereby granted and every part and parcel thereof, TO BE HOLDEN of Us, our Heirs and Successors in free and common Socage, as of our Manor of East Greenwich in our County of Kent, within our Kingdom of Great Britain. YIELDING, rendering and paying therefore yearly and every year for ever unto Us, our Heirs and successors, at our Custom House in our City of New York, unto our Collector or Receiver General, there for the time being, on the Feast of the Annunciation of the blessed Virgin Mary, Commonly called Lady Day, the yearly rent of two shillings six pence Sterling, for each and every hundred Acres of the above granted Lands, and so in proportion for any lesser quantity thereof, saving and except for such part of the said Lands allowed for Highways as above mentioned, in lieu and stead of all other Rents, Services, Duties & Demands whatever for the hereby granted Lands and Premises or any part thereof. AND WE DO of our especial Grace, certain knowledge and meer motion, create erect and constitute the said large Tract of Land containing twenty four thousand one hundred and fifty Acres as aforesaid, hereby granted and every part and parcel thereof, a Township for ever hereafter to be, continue and remain, and BY THE NAME OF KENT for ever hereafter to be called and known.

AND for better and more easily carrying on and managing the Publick Affairs and Business of the said Township, Our Royal Will and Pleasure is, And we do hereby for Us, our Heirs & Successors, give and grant to the Inhabitants of the said Township, All the Powers, Authorities, Privileges, and Advantages heretofore given and granted to or legally enjoyed by all, any or either our other Townships within our said Province of New York; AND we also ordain and establish that there shall be for ever hereafter in the said Township Two Assessors, One Treasurer, Two Overseers of the Highways, Two Overseers of the Poor, One Collector and Four Constables, elected and chosen out of the Inhabitants of the said Township yearly, and every year on the first Tuesday in March, at the most publick place in the said Township by the majority of the Freeholders thereof then and there met and assembled for that Purpose; Hereby declaring that wheresoever the first Election in the said Township shall be held, the future elections shall, FOR EVER thereafter, be held in the same place as near as may be, and giving and granting to the said Officers so chosen, Power and Authority to Exercise their said several and respective Offices during the whole Year from such Election, and until others are legally chosen and elected in their room and stead as fully and amply as any the like Officers have or legally may use or exercise their Offices in our said Province of New York; AND in case any or either of the said Officers of the Township should die, or remove from the said Township, before the time of their annual Service shall be expired, or refuse to act in the Offices for which they shall be respectively chosen, Then Our Royal Will and Pleasure further is AND we do hereby direct, ordain and require the Freeholders of the said Township to meet at the place where the annual election shall be held for the said Township, and chuse other or others of the said Inhabitants of the said Township, in the place and stead *of him or them so dying, removing or refusing to act, within forty days next after such contingency; AND to prevent any undue election in this case, We do hereby ordain and require that upon every vacancy in the Office of Assessors, the Treasurer and either of the other Offices, the Assessors of the said Township, shall within ten days next after any such vacancy first happens, appoint the Day for such Election, and give publick notice thereon in writing under his or their hands by affixing such notice on the Church Door or other most publick place in the said Township at least ten days before the Day appointed for such Election; AND in Default thereof, We do hereby require the Officer or Officers of the said Township or the survivor of them, who in the order they are herebefore mentioned, shall succeed him or them so making Default, within ten Days next after such Default to appoint the Day for such Election, and give notice thereof as aforesaid, hereby giving and granting that such person or persons as shall be chosen by the majority of such of the Freeholders of the said Township as shall meet in manner hereby directed, shall have hold exercise and enjoy the Office or Offices to which he or they shall be elected and chosen, from the time of such Election until the first Tuesday in March then next following and until other or others be legally chosen in his or their place or stead, as fully as the person or persons in whose place he or they shall be chosen might or could have done, by virtue of these Presents. AND WE do hereby Will and direct that this method shall, for ever hereafter, be used for the filling up all vacancies that shall happen in any of the Offices between annual elections above directed.*

PROVIDED ALWAYS, and upon condition nevertheless, that if our Grantees, their heirs or assigns, or some or one of them shall not, within three years next after the date of this our Present Grant, settle on the said Tract of Land hereby granted so many families as shall amount to one family for every thousand Acres of the same Tract; OR if they, our said Grantees, or one of them, or one of their heirs or assigns, shall not, within Three Years to be computed as aforesaid, plant and effectually cultivate at least three Acres for every fifty Acres of such of the hereby granted Lands as are capable of cultivation; OR if they, our said Grantees, or any of them, their or any of their heirs or assigns, or any other person or persons by their or any of their Privity, Consent or Procurement, shall fell, cut down, or otherwise destroy any of the Pine Trees by these Presents reserved to Us, our Heirs and Successors, or hereby intended so to be, without the Royal Licence of Us, our Heirs or Successors, for so doing first had and obtained, that then and in any of these cases; THIS, our Present Grant, and every thing therein contained, shall cease and be absolutely void, and the Lands and Premises hereby granted shall revert to and vest in Us, our Heirs and Successors, as if this, Our present Grant, had not been made, anything hereinbefore contained to the contrary in any wise notwithstanding.

PROVIDED FURTHER, and upon condition also nevertheless, and We do hereby for Us, our Heirs and Successors direct and appoint that this our present Grant shall be registered and entered on Record within six months form the date thereof, in our Secretary's Office in our City of New York in our said Province of New York, in one of the Books of Patents there remaining; AND THAT a Docquet thereof shall be also entered in our Auditor's Office there for our said Province of New York; AND THAT in default thereof, THIS, Our present Grant, shall be void and of none effect, any thing before in these Presents contained to the contrary thereof in any wise notwithstanding.

AND WE DO moreover, of Our especial Grace, certain knowledge and meer motion, consent and agree, that this our present Grant being registered and recorded and Docquet thereof made as before directed and appointed shall be good and effectual in the Law to all Intents, Constructions, and Purposes whatsoever against Us, our Heirs and Successors, notwithstanding Misreciting, Misbounding, Misnaming, or other Imperfection or Omission of, in or in any wise concerning the above Granted or hereby mentioned or intended to be Granted Lands, Tenements, Hereditaments, and Premises or any part thereof.

IN TESTIMONY WHEREOF, WE have caused these, our Letters to be Patent and the Great Seal of our said Province of New York to be hereunto affixed. IN WITNESS, our said trusty and well beloved CADWALLADER COLDEN, Esquire, our Lieutenant Governor and Commander-in-Chief of our said Province of New York, and the Territories depending thereon in America, at our Fort in our City of New York, the thirteenth day of February, in the Year of our Lord, one thousand seven hundred and seventy, and of our Reign the Tenth.

Appendix II: Quit-Claim Deed for the Township of Kent

The following quit-claim deed is deposited in the Rogers' Papers* at the Ontario Archives. By the document the entire 24,150 acres of land, granted as the Township of Kent in Cumberland County, Province of New York, was conveyed to James Rogers by all the other grantees, on 20 February 1770.

---

* The Rogers' Papers consist of documents of James Rogers and some of his descendants, acquired by the Ontario Archives from Robert Zacheus Rogers (5–3) in 1905 (Finding aid MU 2552/2553).

THIS INDENTURE, made the twentieth day of February, in the Year of our Lord, one thousand seven hundred & seventy, in the tenth year of the reign of our Sovereign Lord, George the Third, by the Grace of God, of Great Britain, France and Ireland, KING, Defender of the Faith, and so forth;

BETWEEN Daniel Goldsmith, innholder; Daniel Goldsmith junior, painter; Henry Shute, wheelwright; Garret Van Den Bergh, innholder; Joseph Cox, an upholsterer; David Philips, innholder; Cornelius Ryan, breeches maker; Cornelius Vandenbergh, innholder; Andreas Riglar, butcher; Adam Vandenbergh, yeoman; Caleb Hyatt, yeoman; George Hopson, butcher; William Shooler, surgeon; Joshua T. D. St Croix, mariner; Benjamin Betts, weaver; Alexander Wilson, merchant; James Smith, carpenter; Adolph De Grove, hatter; Thomas Ivers, ropemaker; John Woods, weaver; Edward Laight, merchant; and James McCartney, Tavernkeeper; ALL of the City of New York, of the first part; AND James Rogers, formerly of Londonderry in the Province of New Hampshire but now of the Province of New York, Esquire, of the second part.

WHEREAS our said Sovereign Lord the King by Letters Patent under the Great Seal of the Province of New York, bearing the date the thirteenth day of February instant, did give, grant, ratify, and confirm unto all the said parties to these Presents, both of the first and second part, ALL that certain tract or parcel of Land situate, lying, and being in, the County of Cumberland and within the Province of New York, BEGINNING at the North West Corner of a Tract of Land, lately granted to John Hall, late Lieutenant in his Majesty's Eightieth Regiment of Foot, and runs thence South eighty degrees East five hundred and seventy two chains, then North seven degrees East three hundred and sixty chains, then North sixty three degrees West five hundred and seventy nine chains, then South ten degrees West five hundred and twenty nine chains to the place where this Tract first began, containing twenty four thousand one hundred and fifty Acres of Land and the usual allowance for Highways.

TO HOLD the said Tract of twenty four thousand one hundred and fifty Acres of Land with all the Tenements, Hereditaments and Premises thereunto belonging and appertaining, unto them, the said Grantees, their heirs and assigns, for ever, to, for and upon the several and respective use, uses Trusts; Intents and purposes therein expressed, limited, declared and appointed, that is to say: THREE hundred and fifty Acres of Land part and parcel of the said larger Tract of Land to and for the only proper and separate use and Behoof of the Society for Propagation of the Gospel in Foreign Parts, and their successors for ever; ONE other three hundred and fifty Acres of Land part and parcel of the said larger Tract of Land, for a Glebe for ever to, and for the only proper and separate use Benefit & Behoof of the first Minister of the Gospel in Communion of the Church of England as by Law established, residing in the said larger Tract of Land thereby granted, and his successors for ever, for the time being residing as aforesaid; ONE other three hundred fifty Acres of Land, part and parcel of the said larger Tract of Land, to and for the sole, proper, and separate use, Benefit and Behoof of the first Minister of the Gospel that shall be settled and officiating on said larger Tract of Land thereby granted, his heirs and assigns for ever, to be conveyed by the said Grantees, their heirs or assigns to such Minister of the Gospel as shall be first settled and officiating as aforesaid, his heirs and assigns for ever, in fee simple; AND ONE hundred and fifty Acres of Land, part and parcel of the aforesaid larger Tract of Land to and for the sole and separate use, Benefit & Behoof of the first publick Schoolmaster of the Township thereby constituted and erected, officiating and resident in the same Township and his successors Schoolmasters as aforesaid for ever.

AND as for and concerning all the rest, residue & remainder of the said Tract of twenty four thousand one hundred and fifty Acres of Land, Tenements, Hereditaments and Premises, by the said Letters Patent granted ratified and confirmed, TO HAVE AND TO HOLD one full and equal twenty third part (the whole into twenty three equal parts divided), of the said rest, residue and remainder of the said Tract of Land and Premises unto each of them, the said Grantees their heirs & assigns respectively, to their only proper and separate use and Behoof, respectively, for ever, as Tenants in Common and not as Joint Tenants.

WHICH said Tract of twenty four thousand one hundred and fifty Acres of Land was also, in and by Letters Patent aforesaid, erected into a Township by the name of KENT with usual privileges as by the said Letters Patent or the Record thereof in the Secretary's Office of the Province of New York, reference being there unto had, may more fully and at large appear.

NOW THIS INDENTURE WITNESSETH that they, the said Daniel Goldsmith, Daniel Goldsmith junior, Henry Shute, Garret Vandenbergh, Joseph Cox, David Philips, Cornelius Ryan, Cornelius Vandenbergh, Andreas Riglear, Adam Vandenbergh, Caleb Hyatt, George Hopson, William Shooter, Benjamin Betts, James Smith, John Woods, Edward Laight, Thomas Ivers, Adolph De Grove, Joshua T. D. St Croix, James McCartney and Alexander Wilson, the Parties to these Presents of the first Part, and each of them severally and respectively for, and in consideration of, the sum of fifty Pounds current money of the Province of New York to each of them severally and respectively in hand paid by the said James Rogers at, or before, the ensealing and delivery of these Presents, the Receipt whereof they DO, and each of them DOTH, hereby severally and respectively acknowledge and thereof, and of, and from every part and parcel thereof, DO and each of them DOTH hereby severally acquit, release and discharge him, the said James Rogers, his heirs, executors, and assigns, for ever by these Presents HAVE, and each of them severally and respectively HATH granted, bargained, sold, alieved, released and confirmed, AND by these Presents DO and each of them severally and respectively DOTH clearly and absolutely grant, bargain, sell, alien, release, and confirm unto him, the said James Rogers, ((in his actual possession now being, by virtue of the Letters Patent aforesaid, and also of a Bargain and Sale to him thereof, made for one whole year by Indenture bearing date the day next before the day of the Date of these Presents and by force of the statute made for transferring Uses into Possession)) and to his heirs and assigns for ever: ALL their and each of their said several and respective part of the Tract of Land aforesaid, so respectively granted to them, the said parties to these Presents of the first part, and the said James Rogers, as abovementioned; AND all other their several and respective share, shares, and proportions thereof; AND all their several and respective Estate, Right, Title, Interest, Use, Trust, Property, Possession, Claim, and Demand, whatsoever, both in Law and equity to the same respectively, and every part and parcel thereof; AND the Reversion and Reversions, Remainder and Remainders, Rents, Issues and Profits, of them respectively, and of every part and parcel thereof;

TO HAVE AND TO HOLD the said several and respective, share, shares, and proportions of each and every of them, the said parties to these Presents of the first part, of in and to the said Tract of Land, Tenements Hereditaments and Premises, and every part and parcel thereof, with their and every of their Appurtenances unto the said James Rogers his heirs and assigns, TO the only proper use and Behoof of him, the said James Rogers, his heirs and assigns, for ever, SUBJECT to the Quit Rents due, or to become due, to his Majesty, his Heirs and Successors, for the same, and to the Conditions, Provisoes, Limitations, and Restrictions in the said Letters Patent expressed and contained. AND the said parties to these Presents of the first part, severally for themselves, their heirs, Executors, and Administrators respectively, DO hereby covenant and grant to and with the said James Rogers, his heirs and assigns; THAT they are respectively Owners of the Premises, hereby by them respectively granted, and have power to grant the same in manner aforesaid; AND

THAT the said Premises are free from all Incumbrances, by them respectively made and shall, and may be for ever hereafter, peaceably enjoyed by the said James Rogers, his heirs and assigns, without any disturbance from any person claiming, or to claim the same by, from or under them, the said parties to the Presents of the first part, or any of them respectively.

IN WITNESS whereof, the parties to these Presents have hereunto interchangeably set their hands and seals the day and year first above written.

<< signed by all 22 parties of the first part >>

Sealed & Delivered in the Presence of us:

<< signed Alexander Whyte & Obadiah Wells >>

Received on the day and date of the within Deed, from the within names James Rogers, the sum of Fifty Pounds each, being full for the consideration money within mentioned.

<< signed as follows >>

Witness:	Alexander Whyte	Daniel Goldsmith	Henry Shute
	Obadiah Wells	Benjamin Betts	John Woods
		Adolph De Grove	Andreas Rigler
		Edward Laight	Cornelius Ryan
		James McCartney	Joseph Cox
		David Philips	Garret V. D. Bergh
		Daniel Goldsmith Junior	James Smith
		William Shooler	Thos Ivers
		A. B. Van Den Bergh	Cornelius V. D. Bergh
		Caleb Hyatt	Alexander Wilson

City of New York:

Be it Remembered that in the Day & year first within written, personally came and appeared before me, Daniel Horsmanden, Esquire, The Chief Justice of the Province of New York, Alexander Whyte of the said City, Gentleman, and being duely sworn on the Holy Evangelist of Almighty God, Deposeth and saith that he did see the several persons named in the within Deed, as parties thereto of the first part, sign, seal and deliver the same as their Voluntary Act and Deed, for the uses and purposes therein mentioned, and that this Deponent, together with Obadiah Wells, subscribed their names as witnesses thereto in the presence of each other. I having perused the same and finding no Razures or Interliveations therein, Do allow the same to be Recorded.

<< signed Daniel Horsmanden >>

New York Secretary's Office, 20th February, 1770
The within Deed and Indorsments are Recorded in the Office, in Lib Deeds commencing 16th May 1768 page 288.

<< signed W Banyar, D Secry >>

Appendix III: Expulsions from the State of New Hampshire

The following Act of the New Hampshire House of Representatives was similar to actions of other states designed to seize and incarcerate those deemed to be a threat to the state. Although James Rogers was not specifically mentioned, his name appears with many others in documents naming those who were deemed to be enemies of the United States. The reason for the omission of his name in this case may be that he had long since left the Dunbarton area. The consequences of returning, however, would have been the same. In many states, the first return usually resulted in expulsion as indicated below, but a second return generally meant death.

State Of New Hampshire

In the year of our Lord one thousand seven hundred and seventy-eight

SEAL   *AN ACT to prevent the return of certain persons therein named and of others who have left or shall leave this state or either of the United States of America and have joined or shall join the enemies thereof.*

Dunbarton — William Stark, Esq.; John Stark, yeoman, son of the said William; John Stinson, yeoman; John Stinson, jr., yeoman; Samuel Stinson, yeoman; and Jeremiah Bower, yeoman.

*BE IT THEREFORE ENACTED by the Council and House of Representatives in General Court assembled and by authority of the same, THAT if the said ****

William Stark, John Stark, John Stinson, John Stinson jr., Samuel Stinson or Jeremiah Bower **** or any or either of them and all other persons, though not specially named in this Act, who have left or shall leave this State, or either of the United States, and joined or shall join the enemies thereof as aforesaid, shall, after passing this Act, voluntarily return to this State with out leave first had and obtained therefore from the General Assembly of this State by special Act for that purpose, IT SHALL BE THE DUTY of the Sheriff, his under sheriff and Deputies of the County, and of the Selectmen, Overseers of the Poor, Committees of Safety, Grand Jurors, Constables and Tythingmen, and of all others, Inhabitants of the Town, Parish or District wherein such person or persons presume to come, and they are hereby respectfully impowered and directed forthwith to apprehend and carry such person or persons before some Justice of the Peace within the same county, who is hereby required to commit him or them to the Common Gao l within the same county there in close custody to remain until he or they shall be sent out of the State as hereafter directed.

State Of New Hampshire

In the House of Representatives, Nov. 11 1778, this bill having been read a third time, voted that it pass to be enacted.

Sent up for concurrence;

John Langdon, Speaker.

In Council, November 19, 1778.

This bill read a third time and voted that the same be enacted.

M. Weare, President.

Appendix IV: Confiscation of Estates in New Hampshire

By 1778, revolutionary authorities in the various states, short of cash, began to turn to the property owned by the Royalists as a source of revenue. Some states, including New Hampshire, passed acts in the state legislature to confiscate these properties. These acts later helped some Loyalists obtain at least partial compensation from the Crown for their losses because they had been documented and had been under the force of law. By this document, James lost all the lands he owned in New Hampshire in his own name, but he did have some protected in the care of relatives under their names and thus did not lose all he possessed in the state.

State Of New Hampshire

In the year of our Lord one thousand seven hundred and seventy-eight

SEAL   AN ACT to confiscate the estate of sundry persons named therein.

WHEREAS William Stark, Esq., John Stinson and James Rogers have, since the hostilities between Great Britain and the Untied States of America, left this and the other United States and gone over to and joined the enemys thereof, whereby they have justly forfeited all right to protection from either of said States and also their right to any farther enjoyment of their interest and property being within this State.

BE IT THEREFORE ENACTED by the Council and House of Representatives, and it is hereby enacted, that the whole estate, both real and personal, of the said William Stark, John Stinson & James Rogers, and each and every one of them, lying and being within this State, be and hereby is declared forfeited to this State, and that the same be for the use thereof.

State Of New Hampshire

In the House of Representatives, November 27th, 1778. The foregoing bill having been read a third time, voted it pass to be enacted.

Sent up for concurrence;

John Langdon, Speaker pro tem.

In Council, November 25th, 1778.

This bill was read a third time and voted that the same be enacted.

M. Weare, Prest.

Some states including New York, appointed special commissioners to control and administer properties formerly owned by Loyalists and to lease or rent the farms to people "of proper revolutionary sympathies," intending perhaps to derive some continuous economic benefit for the State. The Crown did not consider these actions legal, as there was no formal legislative act. In these cases, compensation was generally disallowed later, as it was still possible to recover property through the courts. Though apparently less harsh than outright confiscation, this policy had the same practical effect, pauperizing the families that remained behind. In this way James lost the income and control of his property in the States of New York and Vermont.

Appendix V: Memorial of Robert Rogers on the King's Rangers

The following memorial to General Haldimand, was written by Robert Rogers in 1780 during the period when he was at Quebec. In the document he recommends James for command of another regiment and highlights the difficulties experienced by the family. Robert was given a very cool reception in Quebec and subsequently ordered to leave and rejoin his regiment. James, however, was permitted to remain and continue the efforts to raise the King's Rangers.*

To his Excellency Frederick Haldimand Esqr., Captain General & Governor in Chief of the Province of Quebec & its dependencies, Vice Admiral of the same &ca. &ca. &ca., General & Commander in Chief of His Majestyis forces in said Province & the frontiers thereof &ca. &ca. &ca.

The Memorial of Lieut. Colonel Rogers

Your Memorialist being confident that your Excellency is not unacquainted that he has spent many Years in His Majesty's Service, in this Country, in which he has been exposed to the greatest fatigues and a Continual Series of Dangers, Received Several Wounds, has Strength of Constitution and willingness to execute any orders ever received from his Superiours, in all which he distinguished himself through a Career of many Years Service, with the Approbation of the several Officers (who he served under) that had the Honor to Command His Majesty's Troops in these parts. - and has the fullest Testimonies of his Character and Capacity of Executing whatever he had the Honor to undertake to The advantage of His Majesty's Service in America.

The Meml. thinks it his duty to Represent to your Excellency that since he received the orders of the first of May last from His Excellency General Clinton to raise two Battalions of Rangers for His Majesty's Service, that he has been very attentive to, and prosecuted them with the utmost assiduity, made every enquiry in his power in respect to the Situation, temper and Intentions of the Inhabitants in the Colonies in New England now in Rebellion, and ventures to Affirm that there is a Certainty that a Battalion can be drawn from thence to serve His Majesty. The Inhabitants Settled near Lake Champlain, Connecticut River and that of Hudsons &ca. - which may seem the more probable for his Success on the Eastern Frontiers of New England at Penobscot.

* British Library Additional Manuscripts No. 21874, Folios 146–147.

That his Brother, Major James Rogers, was a Captain of a Company of Rangers during the whole Course of the Last War served part of that time under the Memorialist's Command on the Northern frontiers of New York, After at the Siege of Louisbourg, and was with his Company at the Reduction of this important place. - and has been totally ruined Since the Commencement of this present Rebellion in America, plundered of his Estate, Driven from a Wife & Six helpless young children, who are now in the greatest distress & want, not being more than forty eight Miles Eastwardly of Ticonderoga and Confined to a Hutt or rather a sml Hovel (by the Rebels) with only the Milk of one Cow for their sustenance with the addition perhaps of a few Ears of Indian Corn, the produce of Lands which my brother once Could Justly Call his own Consisting of more than Twenty Thousand Acres - And that his Wife & Children are Obliged to gather this Corn, thrash it themselves and carry it on their backs to a Rebel Mill, the Miller who extracts an Extraordinary tole; and many more families of Loyalists are in the same or worse Situation in the four Colonies of New England watched by the Committees and Rebel Guards (which together (with their present poverty) Cannot get to the King's Army.

The Memorialist begs leave to acquaint your Excellency that from his own Knowledge of his brother, is fully convinced he is a man of honour, and a brave soldier, and the Meml. prays that your Excellency will be pleased to appoint him (the said Major Rogers) a Lieutenant Colonel Commandant of a Battalion to be raised under your Excellency's Command, and that he may have the liberty solely to recommend the Officers to your Excellency with full authority to send them out to the frontiers of the Colonies & take Rebels that Oppress the Loyalists and Exchange either on the Spott, or here as your Excellency may think most Convenient.

The Meml. further begs leave to Set forth the Lieutenants Insley & Waller, with Ensigns Anderson and Insley of the Rangers left New York with orders to Carry such Loyalists as were desirous & willing to fight for the Honor of the Crown and Recover His Majesty's Just rights in America - to Carry their Recruits to Niagara or the most Convenient Post on Lake Champlain or elsewhere on the Southern frontiers of Canada - The Memorialist had previous to that time obtained a Letter from Lord Rawdon to your Excellency requesting that they might have provisions &ca. It is Impossible for any Loyalist- to get to New York, the Jerseys being guarded either by the Committees or Rebel Soldiers, the Coast to Eastward and quite through Connecticut and all round Rhode Island in the same Situation.

Camp and Battle Scenes: a Recreated Unit of the King's Rangers

Robert Rogers

Several Loyalist Regiments including the King's Rangers have been recreated by amateur historians. These units conduct re-enactments in period dress and provide an excellent vehicle to teach about our heritage. Families are often involved, living in a camp setting of the 18th century. These photographs were taken between 1993 and 1997.

Robert Rogers

Section 2–4

- *Capt. Stevens with two Volunteers was directed to Come up Country and down Lake Champlain with their Recruits. Those partys Could in a Dark Night by passing to the Jerseys up the Sound land on the Main and pass the Rebel Guards, but to the memorialists knowledge no large party could come to the British Army, many being Kill'd in attempting it.*

The Memorialist therefore most respectfully asserts to your Excellency, that such men as have, or may Come through the Country, never have, neither will they sett out, with an Intention to Join either Sir Johns or Major Butlers Corps for this plain Reason, it is the Relations & acquaintances of those Officers now gone through the Country to bring Recruits to Canada, Those men depending Intirely on Different families that have not much Acquaintance with Sir John or Major Butler, - and the Meml. begs leave to Assert to your Excellency that if any one or number of such Recruits that comes with an Intention to Join any other Corps, or has the least inclination so to do, the Meml. will with your Excellency's Consent discharge them & Enter them in the Corps he or they Chuses to enter into in His Majesty's Service.

Therefore the Memorialist with Great respect most humbly begs that the Recruits for his Corps may be order'd to be given him, if any such are detained by the Officers either at Niagara, or out posts, that they may attend the Memorialist on his return to Penobscot, and prays Arms may be delivered to them &ca. And further most humbly Intreats your Excellency to order a party of your Indians to Join him, as he is fully assured that the Machias may be easily destroyed with his Recruits party on his return if Assisted by Indians. The Preservation of the Kings Masts haul'd this Winter to the banks of the River St. Johns will depend as the Meml. Verily believes on the destruction of Machias and the few Rebels that are there; And at the same time a blow given to Machias may prevent an intended attack by the Rebels on the Kings Garrison at Penobscot.

The Memorialist begs further to mention his Wish to go to St. Johns to Visit his Brother, which Gentleman if not promoted by your Excellency, it is the prayer of the Meml. that he may have leave to remain in this Province, to receive the Recruits Coming in 'till the Ensuing Campaign is over, then that he may either pass through the Country to Join the Meml. or other Persn as directed. - The Meml. has received from your Excellency's Secretary by the hands of Captain Babington an account of money advanced some of the Officers of the Rangers here, and they been sent through the Country. As it must be deducted from our pay, hopes it may be done at Halifax where Mr Thomson the Paymaster for Provincials resides.

The Memorialist most Humbly prays that your Excellency will be pleased to take this his Humble Memorial into Consideratyion and do as you think meet in Respect to him & his brother, whose sole ambition is for the Good of His Majesty's Interest & Government. And your Memorialist will as in Duty bound ever Pray

Robert Rogers

1st Feby 1780

Appendix VI: Petition on Recruiting Disputes with the King's Rangers

There were never enough recruits to fill all the requirements of Loyalist Regiments during the course of the Revolution, and this led to disputes between the various corps. The following document, dated 16 December 1780, is typical of those in the Northern Department. A Board of Officers was convened on 4 March 1781 which dismissed most of the charges as frivolous. Others were submitted to the Governor for resolution but no further action was taken.

To Frederick Haldimand Esquire, Captain General & Governor in Chief of the Province of Quebec, General and Commander in Chief of His Majesty's Forces in the said Province & the Frontiers thereof &c. &c.

The Memorial of Messrs. John Peters, Edward Jessup & William Fraser Humbly Sheweth

That your Memorialist having lately seen some of your Excellency's Instructions to Major Rogers & having the happiness to find that your Excellency considers Sir John Johnson's Regiment & the different Corps of Royalists to be under your Excellency's immediate patronage in preference to Major Rogers or any other Corps of Royalists not belonging to this Province beg leave to point out the following facts & submit them to your Excellency whether such proceedings are agreable to the Letter & Spirit of your Excellency's Instructions to Major Rogers, & whether they have not already and will not in Future much retard your Excellency's intention of giving Sir John & the Royalists the first chance of recruiting from the Northern Frontiers.

James Rogers   Appendix V to Section 2–3

Witnesses
Refer'd to Major
Rogers's Returns
Capt. Sherwood
Calib Clauson
Saml. Sherwood
_____ *Griffis*
Thos. Sherwood
Messrs.
John Jones
John Morehouse
Anthony Phillips
Lemuel Brooks
Levi Warner
Barhibas Huff
Abraham Hiet
Gideon Adams
Martin Kelly, Serjt.
James O'Neal

Facts as follows

1st — Major Rogers did in 1779 give a Warrant to Israel Ferguson of Sir John's Regiment, by which he was to be a Lieut. on condition of enlisting a certain number of men; & encouraged a Calib Clauson, Soldier in Jessup's Corps, that he should be an Ensign with him on the same Conditions: That Mr. Ferguson & Clauson went to Kinsbury near Fort Edward where they well knew there was a number of Loyalists who intended to come in and Join the Loyalists; & Ferguson & Clauson informed them that Major Rogers was Raising a Regiment of Rangers at 2/6 pr. day to do no other duty, & never to leave the Province during the War; That the Royalists were a Rediculous Sett, would never be formed nor in any Credit; That Sir John's Regt. would be established and the Men held for Life; That if they Joined the Loyalists, their Officers would sell them to Genl. McLean or Sir John for one Guinea Pr. Man. Mr. Tayler belonging to Kingsbury was promised a Lieutenancy, three Sergeants and upwards of twenty men joined Major Rogers, who, most of all of them had previously promised to join the Royalists. On some of them hearing that the Regiment was to go to Halifax, Major Rogers told one of the Officers of the Loyalists that "whoever would presume to Mention such a thing for the future he would call him to a severe Account, for it was false, as his Regiment would never be moved from Canada."

2ndly. — Mr. Tyler had leave from Major Carleton to go to Massisco Bay, at a time when the Commander in Chief was pleased to prohibit any recruiting parties being sent out, but in place of going to the Bay, he went directly to Kingsbury and persuaded away a Number of Men for Major Rogers; Major Carleton having reason to suspect Mr. Tyler was gone into the Country sent to know whether Major Rogers had reason to think he intended to go into the Country? - was Answered in the Negative. When Mr. Tyler came in, he was examined whether he had been into the Country or not: said

"Upon" Honor he had not. was then asked - Where he found the Men who came in with him? he reply'd "they met him on the Lake." It since appears by the Inhabitants who have came in, that Mr. Tyler had been in the Country.

That it is the constant practice of the Recruiters under Major Rogers, to tell the people who come in, that if they engage with the Loyalists, they will be obliged to go into the works like Slaves and be removed into the back Settlements with the Canadians. That Major Rogers Regiment is to Continue at St. Johns during the War for the sole purpose of Ranging at half a dollar Pr. day; That they will have three Guineas Bounty; That the Royalists will have none; That the Families belonging to Major Rogers get full Rations of provision; That any who enlist with Genl. McLean or Sir John Johnson will be held in the Service during Life &c. &c. &c.

On those promises a Number of Loyalists who have been long in the Province before Major Rogers came to it, have enlisted with him, especially those at St. Johns many of whom would not have engaged but for the above promises; nor even those would have induced them had they the least Idea that they must be ordered out of this Province, and now would be very unhappy had they the least suspicion it would be the Case, as their Families & Connections are on the Frontiers of the Province of New York.

3rdly. — As none of Major Rogers Men have yet been employ'd in the Works, nor put on any kind of Garrison duty, & as his Women & Children have drawn full Rations - while others had the usual allowence: this so far corroborates with their general Declaration that it has a great tendency to induce Strangers and ignorant Soldiers to believe the whole is true.

The following Men have all received Warrants or promises for Warrants with Major Rogers:

Lieut.	Israel Ferguson	Soldier Ks. Rl. Yorkers
Do	Azariah Prichard	Pensioner
Do	Wiliam Buel	C. Peters Corps
Captain	Henry Ruiter	Leakes Corps
Lieut.	Conrad Pest	Do. Do.
Lieut.	Haramanus Pest	Do. Do.
Do	John Platt	Royalist
Ensign	Roger Stephens	Pensioner
Lieut.	_____ Tyler	Royalist
Do	Solomon Jons	Pensioner
Captn.	Jos. Bettys	Soldier McAlpines
Ensign	George Camel	Do. Do.
Do.	Calib Clauson	Do. Jessups
Do.	Calib Green	Pensioner
Serjt.	Peter Tayler	((Blank))

Your Memorialists are convinced by unhappy experience that the above Facts have much Retarded the Recruiting Plan in general; but the principle weight of the hindrance proceeding from the above stated facts falls on the different Corps, to which your Memorialists are at present attach'd, as they not being fully acquainted with your Excellency's Intentions on this Subject have consequently the less power to evade or oppose them; Your Memorialists conceive they have reason to view the above Facts in many Respects contrary to your Excellency's Instructions to Major Rogers, and the favorable intentions your Excellency has been pleased to exhibit to the Royalists Recruiting in this Province; Your Memorialists therefore, in the most humble manner, request your Excellency will please to signify your pleasure, how, or in what manner those unhappy disputes between the different Corps recruiting in the Province may in future be avoided, which your Memorialists will always invariably observe.

Appendix VII: Request to Amalgamate the Rangers with another Corps

James Rogers requested that his regiment be amalgamated with another corps on several occasions during the period when the King's Rangers were in Quebec; one such request is the petition printed next. The reasons for this action probably centred around the difficulties with his brother's reputation, recruiting disputes with the other corps and concern over the fate of incomplete units at the end of hostilities. All his requests were denied, and the Rangers were eventually reduced at the end of the war as an incomplete unit. In one sense, General Haldimand could not grant these requests, as the King's Rangers were formed under a warrant issued by the Central Department, beyond his control and authority. It is likely, however, that he chose to ignore the issue, having a poor opinion of the capabilities of Loyalist forces in general and a desire to be rid of these King's Rangers in particular. Other corps were amalgamated in the Department, and the same could have been done in this case with a small amount of effort and coordination with the Central Department. The original petition is located in the British Library, Additional Manuscripts, No. 21874, Folio 205.

To Frederick Haldimand Esqr. Captain General and Governor in chief of the Province of Quebec General and Commander in Chief of his Majesty Forces in Said Province and frontiers thereof

&c: &c: &c: ———

The Memorial of James Rogers Humbly Sheweth;

That your Memorialist during the short time he had to recrute last fall has Compleated three Companys of good men fit for the Ranging Service and hopes by next fall to Compleat one Battallion, if his Excellency is pleased to give him full Liberty to send to the Colonies for Recrutes and at such times as may be thought Necessary, and likewise to Recrute here, such as will not ingage in any Other Corps. Since your Memorialist has been at St. Johns, he has taken due care to make every inquiry in his Power in Refferance to the temper and intention of the Northern Collonies in New England now in Rebbelion, and ventures to assert that there is almost a Certainty that he can soon Compleat a Battallion from the Collonies, with the help of his friends there. Your Memorialist humbly begs your Excellency will take him under your Excellency's immediate Patronage, and allow him and the officers with him to be commissioned here under your Excellency's Command. Your Memorialist further begs leave to Inform your Excellency that for a more speedy Execution of His Majesty Service it is agreed between your memorialist and John Peters, Esqr., who now commands a Corps of Loyallists, to unite our two Corps into one; first to Compleat one Battallion and afterwards a Second; Your memorialist further begs leave to Inform your Excellency that Colonel Rogers has no objection to my being Commissioned here as I have it from under his own hand Dated first of August last, and his Letter is now in my Possession ready to Produce. Your Memorialist can Certainly be of more use in this Quarter as his Conections lieys on the Frontiers of New England. Your Memorialist Humbly begs your Excellency will take the above Primisses into your wise Consideration, and give orders as in your Wisdom shall think meet,

And your memorialist, in Duty bound Shall Ever Pray ————

Quebec 3d April 1781

Jas. Rogers

Appendix VIII: Petition for Land in Quebec

Realizing that the Loyalists would be unable to return to their lands, James drafted the following petition in an initial attempt to settle all the men of his Regiment at one location. The request was denied, as the lands in question were reserved for the natural expansion of the French Canadian population along the St. Lawrence River Valley. The Loyalist Regiments were later settled along the north shore of Lake Ontario.

To his Excellency Frederick Haldimand Esqr., Governor and Commander in Chief in and over the Province of Quebec &c: &c: &c : —

The memorial of Major James Rogers, Commanding the Corps of Kings Rangers and his asociates Humbly Sheweth —

That Whereas your Excellency's Petitioners, having been Driven from our Estates and Respective Places of abode for our Loyalty to his Majesties Government by this unnatural War and have in the Event Lost our Earthly all; Therefore Doth most Humbly Pray that your Excellency Will Graciously be Pleased to take our case into your Wise Consideration and Grant unto us that Tract of uninhabited Lands Which is Situate Between the Waters of Lake Champlain and the River St. Lawrence, to be bounded on the South by that Line that Divides this Province of Quebec from that Province or State of New York, and is Commonly Called the Line in the :45: Degree of North Latitude, to Extend North from the Said Line of :45: Degrees North Latitude Three Leagues, and to Extend from the West Line of those Lands Which have been Granted on the West Banks of Lake Champlain to those

---

that are *Granted on the Waters of the Grand River of St. Lawrence, or So much of the Same as your Excellency Shall in your Great Benevolence Shall think Just. As in Duty bound Shall Ever Pray* —

St. Johns, 13 Mar 1783

Jas Rogers

St. Johns, 13 Mar 1783
May it Please your Excellency,

By the Enclosed Petition you Will understand my Wishes. Should it be agreeable to your Excellency, it is my Design to have those Lands, When obtained Distributed between and among my officers and Soldiers, agreeable to your Excellency Directions. Perhaps it may be thought That our tract is too Extensive but as those Lands are Considerablely Incumbered with Cedar Swamps & Morass Ground &c; &c; &c: Should our Petition meet your Excellencys favourable Reception I shall think it best to Make a farther Search and Report to you a more accurate Description of the afforesaid Lands. It is our Intentions to begin Settlement as Soon as may be Consistant With his majesties Service and your Excellency's Permission. A few Lines to Signify to me your Disposition on the Subject Will be most Thankfully Recved by your Excellency's most obedient and Most humble Servant.

Jas Rogers

His Excellency Genrl Haldimand

Appendix IX: Last Will & Testament of James Rogers

The following is a copy of the Last Will and Testament of James Rogers written 12 August 1790. James died 23 September 1790, but this will does not appear to have been settled until January 1794. The original will is located in the Rogers' Papers, deposited in the Ontario Archives.

IN THE NAME OF GOD, AMEN. I James Rogers, Lieut Colonel of the Fredericksburg Militia, being weak in body but of sound memry (blessed be God) do this twilfth day of August in the year of our Lord, one thousand seven hundred and ninety, at Fredericksburg, Make and publish this my last Will and Testament in manner following:

First I give and bequeath unto my well beloved Wife Margaret Rogers the sum of two hundred pounds Sterling, at present in the hands of Robert Ellice and Co, which said two hundred pounds Sterling is to be deposited in the hands of Executors and by them to be put at Interest and to be paid by them to her as her necessitys may require. Also all my household furniture Together with a Mare, a Milch-cow, and a Hefor, to her the said Margaret Rogers, her sole use, benefit and Behoof. I also give and bequeath unto my dear beloved Wife Margaret Rogers the Easternmost half of Lot. No7 in the first concession of Fredericksberg containing one hundred acres of Land together with the Appurtenances thereto belonging, to be disposed of by her as she, the said Margaret Rogers, may think proper.

I also give and bequeath unto my Oldest Son, James Rogers Junior, four hundred acres of Land whereon he now lives, situated on half of Lott No18, the whole of Lott No19, and the half of Lott No20 on the Northeast end of the Little Lake, together with all my right and title to two hundred acres of Land as Lord Dorchesters bounty to him, the said James Rogers Junior, his heirs or assigns, forever.

Also I give and bequeath unto my son David Macgregore Rogers four hundred acres of Land whereon he now lives, situated in Lott No1 and Lott No2 in the first concession and on the East side of the abovesaid Little Lake and imeadiately opposite to the four hundred acres of Land above Bequeathed to my son James Rogers Junr, to him, the said David Macgregore Rogers, his heirs and assigns, forever.

I also give and bequeath unto my daughter Margaret Rogers, two hundred acres of Land situated in Lott No6 and Lott No17 in the third Concession of Fredericksburg containing four hundred acres of Land which said 400 acres, to her, the said Margaret Rogers, her heirs and assigns, forever.

I also give and bequeath unto my Grandson James Rogers Armstrong, Lott No12 on the West side of West Lake containing two hundred acres of Land, to him, the said James Rogers Armstrong, his heirs and assigns, forever.

Also I give and bequeath unto my Grandson Edmund Westhrope Armstrong, Lott No3 on the East side of the Little Lake adjoining Lott No2 and butting on Lott No1 bequeathed to my son David Macgregore Rogers containing two hundred acres of Land, to him, the said Edmund Westhrope Armstrong, his heirs and assigns, forever.

Also I give and bequeath unto my son in Law John Peters, Lott No1 and Lott No2 containing four hundred acres of Land on the East side of the Little

Lake, Lott No one butting on Lott No twenty bequeathed to my son James Rogers Junr and Lott No two butting on the water of the Little Lake and adjoining Lott No three bequeath to Edmund Westhrope Armstrong, to him, the said John Peters, his heirs and assigns forever.

Also I give and bequeath unto my Well Beloved Wife Margaret Rogers, my Oldest son James Rogers, my son David Macgregore Rogers, my daughter Mary Armstrong, my daughter Margaret Rogers, and my daughter Mary Ann Peters, all the profits of monies arising from the sale of my Lands lying (formerly in Kent) now Londonderry in the State of Vermont. Also all the profits and monies arising from the sale of my Lands in Hubarton in the said State of Vermont now at present under the care of Mr. James Macgregore of Londonderry in the State of New Hampshire. Also all the monies for my compensation of loses (Except two hundred pounds Sterling already bequeathed to my Well beloved Wife Margaret Rogers) remaining in the hands of Messrs Robert Ellice and Company, which said profits of monies arising from the sale of my Lands in Londonderry and Hubarton together with the remainder of the monies for my compensation of losses remaining in the hands of Messrs. Robert Ellice & Compy to be equally divided between my well beloved Wife Margaret Rogers, my Oldest son James Rogers, my son David Macgregore Rogers, my daughter Mary Armstrong, my daughter Margaret Rogers, and my daughter Mary Ann Peters, to their sole use, Benefit and behoof.

It is also my desire that the dividend of my daughter Mary Armstrong in the profits of monies arising from the sale of my Lands at Londonderry and Hubarton together with the remainder of the money for my compensation of losses remaining in the hands of Messrs Robert Ellice and Compy be deposited in the hands of my Executors and the profits arising from her dividend to be appropriated to the maintenance of the children of the said Mary Armstrong and the overplus, if any, to be by the Executors, equally divided between the children of the said Mary Armstrong.

I also give and bequeath unto my Well beloved Wife Margaret Rogers, my oldest son James Rogers, my son David Macgregore Rogers, my daughter Mary Armstrong, my daughter Margaret Rogers, and my daughter Mary Ann Peters, all my right and title to the Lands yet undrawn as a field Officer, Agreeable to Lord Dorchestors Instructions.

It is also my Will and desire that if my servantman, John Miller, shall and will remain with my Well beloved Wife Margaret Rogers and deport himself as becometh, that then at the expiration of his Servitude he shall receive one hundred dollars from my Executors who are hereby required to pay him.

I also give and bequeath to my son in Law John Armstrong, the sum of five pounds Sterling, which said sum of five pounds Sterling is to be paid to him by my Executors.

I do hereby constitute and appoint James Rogers Junior and Captain Oliver my sole Executors to see my will full filled.

In Witness whereof, I, the said James Rogers, Lieut Colonel of the Militia of Fredricksburg, have to this my Last Will and Testament set my hand & seal the day and year first above written.

Jas Rogers (LC)

Signed, Sealed & delivered by the said Lieut Colonel) *Archd Macdononlle*
James Rogers as and for his last Will and Testament in) *Timothy Thompson*
the presence of us who were present at the Signing and) *John Hourtes*
Sealing thereof   *)* *Mattw Dies*

Be it remembered that, on Wednesday, the seventeenth day of November in the year of our Lord one thousand seven hundred and ninety, personally came and appeared before us, Richard Cartwright Junior and Neil McLean, Esqrs., Judges of the Common Pleas for the District of Mecklenburg, Archibald McDonile of Marysburg, Esqr., and Matthew Dies of Fredricksburg, two of the subscribing Witnesses to the Original Writing of which the above is a literal and exact Copy, compared by us with the Original, and declared upon Oath that they, the said Archibald McDonile, Esqr. and Matthew Dies, did see Colonel James Rogers Sign and Seal the Original aforesaid writing and that he was, to the best of their Judgement, at the time of sound mind.

Archd McDononlle   *Richard Cartwright Junr. J. C. P.*
Mattw Dies   *Niel McLean J.C.P.*

Be it remembered that on Saturday, the twelfth day of February in the year of our Lord one thousand seven hundred and ninety one, personally came and appeared before me, Richard Cartwright, Esquire, one of the Judges of the Court of Common Pleas for the District of Mecklenburg, Timothy Thompson of Fredricksburg, one of the subscribing Witnesses to the Original writing of which the foregoing is a true copy, compared by me with the Original, and declared upon Oath that he, the said Timothy Thompson, did see Colonel James Rogers Sign and Seal the aforesaid Original writing and that he was, to the best of his Judgement, at the time of sound mind.

Timothy Thompson   *Richard Cartwright, Junr. J. C. P.*

DISTRICT OF   )   I do hereby Certify that the foregoing is a true and
MECKLENBURG)   Extract from the Registrar of His Majestyis Court of
Common Pleas for the said District.

In Testimony whereof, I have put my hand and the Seal of the said Court at Kingston this fourteenth day of February in the year of our Lord one thousand seven hundred and ninety one.

Peter Clark, Clk

PROVINCE OF QUEBEC   IN THE COMMON PLEAS
DISTRICT OF   *Be it remembered that on Saturday the third*
MECKLENBURG   *day of March in the Year of our Lord one thousand seven hundred and ninety two, Personally appeared before us, Richard Cartwright Junr and Niel McLean, Esquires, Judges of the said Court, James Rogers Junr and made Oath that he would well and truly discharge the Office of Executor to the last Will and Testament of the Late Colonel James Rogers, to the best of his skill and ability for the benefit of all concerned.*

Peter Clark, Clk.   *Richard Cartwright Junr. J. C. P.*
Neil McLean J. C. P.

These are to Certify that James Rogers Junior of Sophiasburg, is the only Person that hath been Qualified to act as Executor to the last Will and Testament of his father, the Late Colonel James Rogers

Peter Clark, Clk.   *Richard Cartwright Junr. J. C. P.*
Neil McLean J. C. P.

The foregoing is a true Copy of the last will and Testament of My late father and a true Copy of the Probate thereof made from the Originals.

Montreal, 22nd October 1793   James Rogers,

Sole Executor of the last will and Testament of my father the late Col. James Rogers

---

I, John Reid, Clerk of the Court of Common Pleas for the District of Montreal in the Province of Lower Canada, do hereby certify that the within is a true copy of the original will of the late James Rogers; and that the Probate of the same and certificate of Administration are true copies of copies certified by Peter Clark, Esquire, Clerk of the Court of Common Pleas for the District of Mecklenburg, filed in the said Court of Common Pleas for the District of Montreal, in a cause wherein James Rogers as Executor of the said last will is Plaintiff, and Thomas Forsyth and John Richardson, Defendants. In Testimony whereof I have hereinto set my hand at Montreal, this twenty second day of October, one thousand seven hundred and ninety three.

John Reid

Entered in the Office for Auditing the publick Accounts - 14th January 1794
Entered in the Paymaster General's Office on account of Half Pay
17th January 1794

Appendix X: Supplement to the Will of James Rogers

For some reason, the will of James Rogers in the preceding Appendix did not account for all the land he owned at the time of his death. As a result, his heirs divided the remaining land between them by mutual consent. The following is a copy of that document, the original of which is located in the National Archives.

We do hereby Certify that the lands of the late Major James Rogers have by mutual consent been divided as follows:

To James Rogers, Lot number fifteen second concession, Lot number one and eleven in the third concession and the north east quarter of eight hundred acres in the first concession Military Tract, Township of Hallowell, also the northernmost three fourths of Lot number four at the east end of the east Lake, Township of Hallowell.

Mary Ann Peters, the east part of Lot number one and the south west quarter of eight hundred acres in the first concession and Lot number eleven in the second concession of the Military Tract, Hallowell, and the northernmost three fourths of Lot number six at the east end of the east Lake in the Township of Hallowell.

David M. Rogers, the northwest quarter of eight hundred and eighty acres of land in the first concession, Lot number nine in the second concession, and Lot number nine in the third concession of the Military Tract, Township of Hallowell, and Lot number seven second concession of the Broken Front, Township of Haldimand in the District of Newcastle.

Margaret Rogers, Lot number fourteen second concession, Lot number seven and twenty two in the third concession Military Tract, Hallowell, and the northernmost quarter of Lot number six and the southernmost half of Lot number five at the east end of the east Lake in the Township of Hallowell.

Margaret McGregore Armstrong
James Rogers Armstrong   Children of the late Mary Armstrong deceased
Edmund Westroop Armstrong

Lot, number sixteen second concession, number twenty third concession, and the southeast quarter of eight hundred and eighty acres in the first concession of the Military Tract, Hallowell, also the southern most quarter of Lot number four and the northern most half of Lot number five at the east end of the East Lake, Township of Hallowell.

All the said Land being located in the name of Major James Rogers and are divided by us agreeable to the Will accompanying this Certificate.

DMG Rogers   for James Rogers and
the heirs of Mary Armstrong

Mary Ann Peters
DMG Rogers
Margaret Rogers

I do certify that James Rogers personally appeared before me and acknowledged that he had appointed his Brother, David McG. Rogers his agent for the purposes contained in the above Instrument of writing.

2d June 1803   G. J. Thompson J. C. P.

Robert Rogers of the Rangers

Robert Rogers   Section 2–4

Robert Rogers (2–4)
(7 November 1731–18 May 1795)

Robert Rogers was one of the most remarkable men to emerge from the American Colonial period. He possessed vision and energy far exceeding the majority of his contemporaries, and probably benefited his country more substantially than others of greater fame. A backwoodsman of modest origins, he overcame the constraints of low birth and lack of formal education that destroyed the hopes of many men and rose to international prominence through exceptional ability, perception and charismatic personality. He studied the cunning ways of the Indians, modifying, adapting and perfecting their expert tactics for his own survival. He persuaded senior British officers to allow him to employ his methods first in his own company and later at regimental level. In short, he proposed to use the enemy's tactics to defeat him and secure a British victory in the untamed forests of America.

European military tactics at the time were completely inflexible and would remain so for decades to come. Opposing armies formed up in rigid lines to shoot at each other with inaccurate weapons at short range, or fearlessly march toward each other with fixed bayonets. Rogers' proposals were certainly unconventional for his day. They were, however, perfectly suited to the wilderness type of war unique to North America. He did not create the notion of companies operating with great mobility, widely separated from supporting units and bases, but he perfected the concept and techniques of the hit-and-run tactics that would be employed by commando and guerrilla units for more than two centuries. For his time he was a military genius; a man destined to do well in periods of conflict but to suffer from inactivity and other aspects of peace. He inspired intense loyalty; yet he is perhaps the least known of North America's military heroes. Robert, for all his ability as a military commander, was prone to human frailties and flaws. He was a dreamer, a man of vision who tended to ignore some of the mundane aspects of life such as record-keeping. He had a fiery temper and at times acted on impulse without fully considering the consequences, particularly in his youth.

Much has already been published on Robert Rogers' life and exploits, and while it would be pointless to detail this information yet again, some errors in earlier documents can be corrected. This narrative will provide a brief but historically accurate account of his life and accomplishments, warts and all. The bibliography at the end of this work contains more extensive references which can be consulted for additional information.

Robert was born to James and Mary Rogers in Methuen, a small frontier town in the eastern part of the Massachusetts Bay Colony. The foundation of the house where he was born has been preserved as a historic site with an appropriate marker (although it has not been well maintained and is in need of considerable repair). His parents, although Presbyterian, took him to the local Puritan minister for baptism seven days after his birth, an event recorded in the town records and those of the First Congregational Church of Methuen on 14 November 1731. In 1739, at the age of eight, his family moved to a new homestead about sixteen miles southwest of Rumford, New Hampshire.* As this new home was on the very edge of the frontier, it is likely that Robert received little if any formal education. What he learned was probably taught by his parents, local Indians and frontiersmen, as well as what he managed to teach himself about survival in the dark endless forests of America. He learned these lessons well. He studied and became literate, certainly to a higher standard than was common for his class, and is said to have had an excellent working knowledge of French and several Indian languages. Later in life during a visit to London, he stated that in his youth he gathered shoots of alder and yellow birch which he bound into Indian brooms and subsequently "carried them over ice and snow" to sell in Rumford.

From numerous original and highly descriptive sources, it appears that Robert was endowed with a hardy physique and tremendous energy packed into a six-foot frame. He was self-reliant, alert, fearless and intelligent; he was endowed with a natural ability to lead and an aggressive desire for action. No authentic likeness of Robert is known to exist, although many that claim to be such have been published over the last 200 years and have confused descendants, researchers and historians alike. The sketch at the start of this section by noted historian and author Gary Zaboly is an artistic impresson of Robert's probable appearance at the height of his career, the end of the French and Indian War.

The rivalry between the French and English in North America began when both arrived on the continent and essentially ended with the conquest of Canada, although the cultural struggle can be seen even to the present day. The virtually continuous colonial warfare from 1689 was also a reflection of the long bitter struggle between the mother countries for imperial and commercial supremacy in Europe and the world. Few areas in America were exempt from the effects of European politics. From the beginning the French enjoyed a distinctive advantage not recognised or clearly understood by the British: the techniques of fighting in a rough forested country. The British could think only of highly disciplined armies

---

* Also known as Bow, this town grew into the city of Concord, New Hampshire. The area around the homestead eventually became Dunbarton, New Hampshire. For details on this period in the family history see James Rogers, section 1-1.

---

fighting shoulder to shoulder supported by cavalry and artillery, forces wholly unsuited to frontier America. The French quickly learned Indian techniques, refining a style of action they called *"la petite guerre,"* the beginning of guerrilla warfare. They used their native allies to great advantage, permitting sudden devastating hit-and-run attacks on English frontier settlements.

In 1745, after one of these frequent raids on the Merrimack River settlements, Robert volunteered to help seek out and destroy the marauders. He thus began, at the age of fourteen, what was to become a highly distinguished military career. He continued to serve in the militia for the duration of King George's War (1739-1748).* He joined Captain Ladd's scouting company and served from 16 July until 2 October 1746. The following year he served as part of Captain Eastman's scouting company from 1 August until 12 September. Both of these units were formed of local men having little or no military training but an excellent knowledge of the frontier. The results of this conflict were inconclusive, but local tension dissipated with the signing of the Treaty of Aix-la-Chapelle in 1748. The war had been a political and commercial disaster for both France and England, and nothing had been resolved.

The Rogers family had been driven from their homestead by the threat of Indian raids. They returned to their land in April 1748. It is likely that Robert was with them and helped to rebuild the farm that had been destroyed during the war.† Not much is definitely known of Robert's activities from 1748 to 1753. There can be little doubt, however, that he spent a great deal of his time engaged in occupations that increased his knowledge of the wilderness; perhaps some trapping, or trading between English and French settlements, possibly a little smuggling. He probably also learned much from the trappers and traders who frequented the northern areas of the colonies. It is likely that he developed his ideas on frontier fighting during this period.

In the spring of 1753, shortly after his father's death, Robert bought a tract in Dunbarton for £50 and began clearing the land. By early summer he had erected a cabin and started planting. It soon became evident that farming was not to be his chosen profession. By autumn he had a tenant on the land and was off again exploring the wilderness. He also served for a period in Captain John Goff's Company of militia, employed to survey a road through the northern and western parts of the Colony. Governor Wentworth authorized this survey in December 1752 to open the Cohase Meadows to settlement, 100 miles up the Connecticut River.

---

* In Europe the conflict was known as the War of the Austrian Succession. See Historical Events, Annex B.

† See James Rogers, section 1-1.

The expanding settlements caused apprehension amongst the Indians allied to the French, and the threat of raids on the frontier began again. Emotions were strained and tensions ran high for a number of reasons; only a spark was needed to inflame the frontier. The incident came on 28 May 1754 when Provincial troops from Virginia, under the command of Lieutenant Colonel George Washington,* attacked what the French claimed was a courier party, led by Ensign Coulon de Jumonville, in the Monongahela River Valley. These were the first shots fired in the French and Indian War. War was not officially declared between the two mother countries until the outbreak of the Seven Years' War in Europe in 1756, but by that time hostilities were well advanced in America.† Robert initially served in the New Hampshire Regiment from 23 August until 21 September 1754. During this period the regiment was posted near the Connecticut River.

In January 1755, Robert recruited twenty-four men into the Massachusetts Regiment for service in Nova Scotia. On 7 February, however, he and his brother Richard, along with fifteen others, were taken into custody on suspicion of distributing counterfeit tender, apparently with some justification. This was a very serious crime, punishable by death, and even those who escaped the maximum penalty were branded (both ears cropped), the customary lighter sentence of the day. Robert was given a preliminary trial before the Inferior Court at Rumford, which heard sufficient evidence to bind him over for trial before the Superior Court at Portsmouth. Records of this first trial, including the evidence presented, have been preserved in Concord and amplification can be found in the book *The History of Rogers Rangers* by Burt Loescher.‡ Mysteriously, all charges were dropped on 12 February. Shortly thereafter Robert broke his contract with Massachusetts and took his men into the service of New Hampshire at the request of Governor Wentworth. Although fresh evidence of the offences later came to light which would seem to confirm his guilt, he was not further harassed, probably because he was then under the protection of the Governor.

On 24 April, he was commissioned captain of the first company in the New Hampshire Regiment to be designated a ranger company. His brother Richard was appointed his first lieutenant. During June 1755, Robert and his men were employed in the construction of Fort Wentworth at the fork of the Connecticut and Upper Ammonoosuc Rivers, according to some sources. A stone monument marking the site near Groveton records the event, but there is considerable controversy over this claim. Modern historians contend that the fort was not built until some time around 1780 and that the rangers played no role in its construction.

---

* See Historical Figures, Annex C.
† See Historical Events, Annex C.
‡ See Bibliography.

In his journals,* Robert simply states that he made several patrols along the northern and western frontiers of the province under special orders of the Governor, but does not mention building a fort. If modern historians are correct, this fort could not have been used as a rendezvous during his return from the Saint-François expedition in 1759, as suggested in many sources. The position is simply identified as a point some sixty miles from Number Four in his records of the expedition, but he does not refer to a fort there. This controversy demonstrates the difficulty of separating fact from fiction in the life of a folk hero.

On 20 August the New Hampshire Regiment, including Robert and his company of rangers, now numbering 50 men, was despatched to Lake George to join the forces under the command of Major General William Johnson.† The company was shortly detached to serve as the scouting arm of the army in the expedition against Fort Saint-Frédéric.‡ Robert and his rangers quickly proved their worth, completing several successful patrols and obtaining vital intelligence concerning details of the French fortifications and troop concentrations. Just before the planned assault, however, the French army, under Baron de Dieskau,§ surprised the British at the foot of Lake George. The engagement later became known as the Battle of Lake George (8 September 1755). Robert was leading a scout at the time and so missed the engagement. The action was inconclusive, but the French withdrew after their commander was taken prisoner. This incident was just two months after the disastrous British defeat at the Battle of Monongahela (9 July 1755) and the unfortunate death of General Braddock.** The British then decided against any further movement during the year and built Fort William Henry at the southern end of Lake George.

In early October, at the end of their enlistment, the regiment returned home. Robert and twenty-eight of his men remained as volunteers to continue scouting for the army during the fall and winter. Johnson was so impressed that he wrote to Sir Charles Hardy, Royal Governor of New York:

---

* In 1765 Robert published the journals of his experiences during the war in America. These have been used as a primary source for this work. For titles see the bibliography.

† Later Sir William Johnson, See Historical Figures, Annex A.

‡ Fort St.-Frédéric was originally built by the French on the projection of land which narrows the southern end of Lake Champlain in 1732. After seizing the position in 1759, the British built there a large stone fort later named Crown Point.

§ See Historical Figures, Annex C.

** See Historical Figures, Annex C.

Captain Rogers' bravery and veracity stand clear in my opinion, and that of all who know him. Though his Regiment is gone he remains here as a volunteer, and is the most active man in our army. I believe him to be as brave and as honest a man as any I have equal knowledge of, and both myself and the army are convinced he has distinguished himself since he has been among us, superior to most, inferior to none of his rank.

13 October 1755

On 25 November, Robert was ordered to raise a new company of rangers for winter scouting operations, and by 14 December he had recruited some forty-three men to serve under his command. On 14 January 1756 he led a patrol of seventeen men down Lake George, far behind enemy lines, and captured a sleigh and two prisoners. In early February he led another patrol to ascertain troop strengths and the nature of operations at Fort Saint-Frédéric. On this excursion he climbed a tree and made a complete sketch of the French fortifications. His men also set fire to several houses and barns in a village near the fort, destroying a large quantity of grain and more than fifty head of cattle.

The British were notably lacking in victories during the early part of the war, mainly becaise of incompetent leadership, and Robert's activities captured the attention of senior officers on both sides of the conflict. Time and time again he led his men into the very heart of enemy territory, in freezing weather and under severe combat conditions, always returning with his unit intact and the mission accomplished. At times his men were battered, exhausted and starving, but they did return with their lives and their scalps. The press in New England turned Robert into a popular hero as news of his exploits grew with each report. In February 1756, the New York Assembly showed their appreciation by voting him 125 Spanish milled pieces-of-eight as "a gratuity for his extraordinary courage, conduct, and diligence against the French and their Indians."

In March 1756, Robert was summoned to Boston by Major General William Shirley,* the Governor of Massachusetts Bay and Commander-in-Chief of all British forces in America. Here he received a commission as captain of His Majesty's Independent Company of American Rangers. The commission, dated 23 March, reads in part as follows:

. . . . From time to time, to use your best endeavours to distress the French and Allies by sacking, burning and destroying their houses, barns, barracks,

---

*   See Historical Figures, Annex C.

---

canoes and battoes, etc., and by killing their cattle of every kind; and at all times to endeavour to way-lay, attack and destroy their convoys of provisions by land and water, in any part of the country wheresoever they could be found.

Independent establishment meant that the unit was no longer a rag-tag band of provincial volunteers, performing special duties under local commanders. They were instead part of the regular establishment, assured of steady pay for officers and men. This independence gave Robert greater command and control in operations and training.* One company quickly grew into two, then two into three, and thus was born one of the world's most effective fighting forces: a model for commando units to the present day.

The corps was officially named "The Independent Companies of American Rangers," but became popularly known as "Rogers' Rangers" as the war progressed and stories of their exploits were told and retold, perhaps with some embellishment. All men were hand-picked; each was required to excel in backwoods skills and have the ability to endure long difficult marches on short rations. Even with these attributes, few were chosen, and these had to undergo intense training to learn the art of wilderness warfare over all types of terrain and in harsh conditions. Companies originally consisted of a captain, a lieutenant, three sergeants and sixty privates. The following year the complement of each company was increased to a captain, two lieutenants, an ensign, four sergeants and one hundred privates.†

Robert quickly recruited his initial company and by early May had rejoined the army at Fort William Henry by way of a patrol toward Fort Saint-Frédéric. General Shirley, concerned about a build-up of troops at Fort Carillon,‡ sent Robert to disrupt French lines of communication to the Saint Lawrence. Shirley had ordered six lightweight whaleboats brought in from the coast for the rangers, and this was an opportunity to prove their worth. Robert took fifty men part of the way up Lake George and then

---

* For a definition of Independent Companies and how Rogers' Rangers differed, see Historical Items, Annex A.

† Appendix I of this section holds a list of all ranger companies established during the war, with their commanders. This list also shows those officers who rose to senior rank and later fought on opposing sides during the American Revolution.

‡ Fort Carillon was built by the French in 1755 on the strategic point that controlled the only convenient portage between Lake George and Lake Champlain. After its capture the British renamed it Ticonderoga, and its guns played a significant role in the American Revolution.

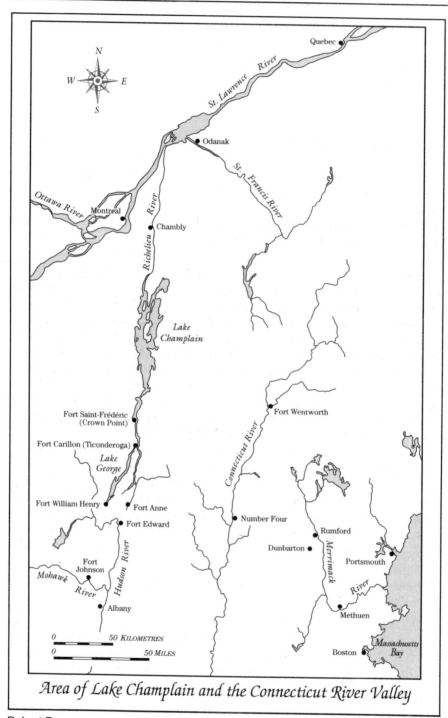

Area of Lake Champlain and the Connecticut River Valley

Robert Rogers

carried five of the boats six miles over the mountain to South Bay.* This was a considerable feat, taking more than three days in enemy territory during the heat of summer. From South Bay they had a clear water route up Lake Champlain. Hiding by day and travelling at night, the rangers continued their mission. On 7 July they attacked a convoy of battoes§ just north of Fort Saint-Frédéric, capturing the crews and destroying a large quantity of cargo. They carefully concealed their boats and returned to Fort William Henry by land with eight prisoners and valuable intelligence. News of the successful mission spread quickly and gave a much needed boost to morale. It proved that British forces could strike deep into enemy territory seemingly at will, and disrupt vital supply lines. Several weeks later the rangers returned to their boats and made another patrol even farther north before hiding them again and returning on foot. Eventually the boats were discovered, and the French were propably mystified as to how the boats came to be on Lake Champlain. During the remainder of the summer and early fall, the rangers went on more than twelve patrols.

In July 1756, Lord John Campbell, Earl of Loudoun,† arrived in America and assumed command of all British forces on the continent. Major General James Abercromby was appointed second in command.‡ By November the ranger corps had been increased to four companies. Two, commanded by Robert's brother Richard Rogers and Captain Thomas Speakman, were posted to Fort William Henry. The remaining two, commanded by Robert and by Captain Humphery Hobbs, were stationed at Fort Edward on the Hudson, fifteen miles to the southeast. The headquarters of the rangers was established on an island in the Hudson River opposite Fort Edward, which was known as Rogers' Island.§ Initially Robert commanded only his own company, while the others were independent. By the end of 1756, however, all companies were unofficially under his command as senior captain and known collectively as Rogers' Rangers. As the effectiveness of the rangers grew the French-allied Indians coined a name for Robert: *"Wobi-Madaondo"* (The White Devil).

On 15 January 1757 Robert left Fort Edward with 52 rangers to reconnoitre the French forts, which were rumoured to have been reinforced. Two weeks' rations and sixty rounds of powder and ball had been issued to each man. The patrol remained a few days near Fort William

---

* Although exact dimensions are unknown, these boats were probably about 1.7m (5 ft) wide and 9m (27 ft) in length with long pointed stem and stern. Each weighed approximately 2000 lbs and when used by the rangers carried ten men with all their supplies.

† See Historical Figures, Annex C.

‡ See Historical Figures, Annex C.

§ This island has been designated a historical and archaeological site, and a monument to Robert and his rangers was erected in 1964.

Henry making snowshoes, and 33 men from other companies joined their ranks. Shortly, however, eleven men were forced to return, lame due to the bitter cold, leaving Robert with 74 effectives. On 21 January, at a point about halfway between Fort Carillon and Fort Saint-Frédéric, the rangers attacked a provisions train of ten horse-drawn sleds. Three sleds and seven men were captured, but the remainder escaped to warn the garrison at Carillon. That afternoon the patrol was ambushed by a force of some 250 French regulars, Indians and coureurs-de-bois.* Robert was grazed along the forehead and left momentarily stunned, but he continued in command against odds of more than three to one. In his report of the battle dated 25 January he recorded:

> . . . . *the french often calling to us and disiring us to accept Quarters, promising that we should be used with humanity & treated kindly, as at the same Time called me by Name, and threatened us that if we did not embrace their Offers, as soon as the Party joined them from the Fort which they expected every Moment they would Cut us to Pieces; but we absolutely refused to recive their proffered Mercy and I told them that we had men sufficient to repel any force that could come against us and that we should have it in our Power to Cut them to Pieces & Scalp them.*

This action, which became known as the Battle of La Barbue Creek, lasted more than three hours. Near sundown Robert was wounded a second time when a French ball slammed into his wrist, passed through and carved a deep furrow in his palm. He could no longer load his musket, and as dusk was approaching, he ordered his men to disperse. Under cover of darkness they made their way to a prearranged rendezvous and then by forced march to Fort William Henry. The patrol had been reduced to 48 effectives and six wounded. Fourteen had been killed and six more were missing or captured, but the rangers had acquitted themselves well. Robert reported that fifty of the enemy had been destroyed; other reports suggest that as many as 116 had been killed. This was the first large-scale skirmish of the rangers and the first in which they suffered casualties.

Robert's wounds became infected, and he was sent to Albany for better medical treatment. While there, he attempted to recover some of the expenses and pay for those who had served with him during the fall and

---

* Canadian partisans, the coureurs-de-bois were the unlicensed fur traders of New France. The term is often translated as bush-lopers or runners of the woods. They are also at times mistakenly referred to as voyageurs (the licensed professional fur traders of the colony).

Lying in Ambush

This sketch by Gary Zaboly, based on historical evidence, depicts Robert and a ranger patrol lying in ambush near Fort Carillon during the summer of 1756. The rangers were not yet in their famous green uniforms, and Carillon was still a wooden structure.

winter of 1755-56 before the establishment of the Independent Company. It was an accepted practice in the colonial period for commanders of provincial regiments and smaller units to outfit and pay their men from personal funds, and later to seek compensation from colonial governments. The New England Committee of War, established to oversee financial aspects of the war, refused to hear Robert's claim. He wrote to Sir William Johnson and Lord Loudoun for assistance in supporting his position, but this necessitated long delays. He received no satisfaction for the claims and was becoming frustrated. During this time he also came down with smallpox, probably contracted at Fort William Henry where the deadly disease had become epidemic. This illness kept him bedridden from 5 March to 15 April. In the following months the disease would claim a large number of fighting men on both sides of the conflict, particularly the Indians, who had no natural defences against this white man's plague.

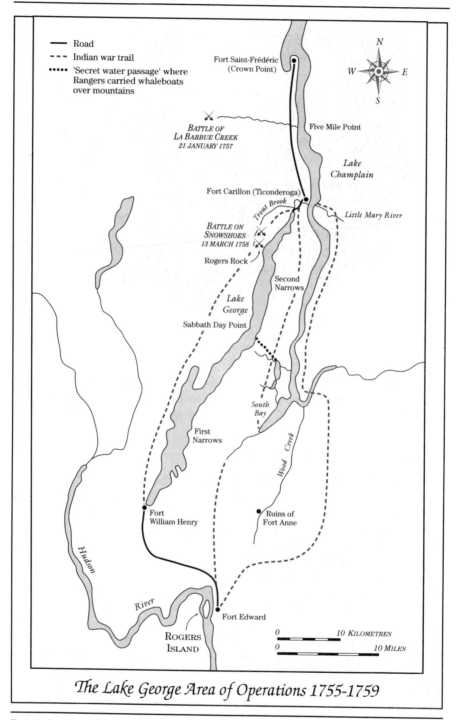

Road

Indian war trail

'Secret water passage' where
Rangers carried whaleboats
over mountains

N
W   E
S

Fort Saint-Frédéric
(Crown Point)

Five Mile Point

BATTLE OF
LA BARBUE CREEK
21 JANUARY 1757

Lake
Champlain

Fort Carillon (Ticonderoga)

Trout Brook

Little Mary River

BATTLE ON
SNOWSHOES
13 MARCH 1758

Rogers Rock

Second
Narrows

Lake
George

Sabbath Day Point

South
Bay

First
Narrows

Wood Creek

Fort
William Henry

Ruins of
Fort Anne

Hudson

River

Fort Edward

ROGERS
ISLAND

0   10 KILOMETRES
0   10 MILES

The Lake George Area of Operations 1755-1759

Robert Rogers   Section 2–4

Lord Loudoun planned a major expedition against the fortress of Louisbourg for the summer of 1757, involving most of the army. Newly promoted Major General Daniel Webb, commander of Fort Edward, was left behind with instructions to guard the frontier. After his recovery, Robert was ordered to New York with three companies to form part of the expedition, leaving Richard and his company at Fort William Henry. In New York they were joined by the recently created fifth company under the command of Captain John Shephard. The 6000-man invasion force embarked for Halifax, where they arrived on 1 July 1757. With the addition of 5000 men from Halifax, Lord Loudoun prepared for the assault on Louisbourg. Scouts reported the presence of some twenty-two French warships in the bay, however, and in the expectation of a strengthened garrison Loudun aborted the operation.

Meanwhile, the French, under the command of the Marquis de Montcalm,* took advantage of the reduced British troop concentrations in the interior and quickly moved against those forts protecting the strategic portage between the Hudson River and Lake George: Forts William Henry and Edward. Montcalm attacked the former with a force of approximately 8000 men on 2 August, and the 2400 British defenders could not hold without reinforcement.† The post commander, Lieutenant Colonel George Monro, sent several urgent dispatches to General Webb for support but to no avail. Webb had 3400 men ready to march the fifteen miles to Fort William Henry, if required, but he feared that they would be overwhelmed. He requested additional militia from Albany and refused to move until they arrived. Monro capitulated after seven days of a valiant defence.

After the surrender many of the garrison, although accorded honours of war and guaranteed safe passage to Fort Edward, were massacred by the Indians. Of 2100 troops surrendered, over 300 lost their lives in the slaughter together with an unknown number of women and children. Montcalm lost control of the situation, and even the bodies of those who had recently died of smallpox were dug up and scalped. Among the latter was Robert's brother Richard, who had died on 22 June. After this incident, Montcalm reprimanded the Indians and they departed. Low on supplies and abandoned by his allies, he was forced to reconsidered any movement south and he withdrew his forces to Fort Carillon. Before leaving, he

---

* See Historical Figures, Annex C.

† The French force was made up of the following according to various sources: 2570 *troupes de terre* (land troops or army), 520 *troupes de la marine* (sea troops or marines, although not in the modern sense) and 190 gunners, 2950 Canadian militia and volunteers and more than 1800 Indians. The British force comprised 850 British Regulars, 100 Royal Artillery, 1400 American militia and 100 Rangers. There was also a large number of women and children at the fort.

ordered his troops to destroy the fort and dispose of the bodies of the dead.*

After returning from Nova Scotia, the Commander-in-Chief ordered Robert to train fifty-six of his most junior officers as rangers under the guise of wishing to expand their level of experience. The real purpose was probably that these young men when trained could lead their own companies and thereby reduce British dependence on "untrained and undisciplined Provincials." Robert gladly undertook this assignment and its challenges along with his regular scouting duties during the fall of 1757. One significant consequence of this endeavour was *The Methods & Practices of the Rangers,* perhaps the first written manual of commando warfare and tactics. (A copy may be found in Appendix II to this section.) The Cadet Company came into existence on 14 September, but it was disbanded by 8 November on the realization that it took more than a short training course to produce an effective ranger. Brigadier General Lord George Howe,† a grandson of King George I, accompanied Robert on a patrol and returned full of praise for the abilities and methods of the ranger corps. Howe was an interested and adept student, going out at least a dozen times. He later insisted that some of the ranger tactics be incorporated during long overdue reforms to the British Army.

It appeared that the British were finally beginning to understand North American warfare. Lieutenant Colonel Thomas Gage,‡ who had been with Braddock at Monongahela, had seen firsthand how irregular troops could be used to great advantage. Like most British officers, however, he was contemptuous of provincial units in general and of Robert and his rangers in particular. He asked Lord Loudoun if he could raise a regiment to emulate the rangers' ability but with the discipline of a regular unit, thus allowing the rangers to be reduced. He even offered to pay all expenses. Loudoun agreed to the proposal but himself found the £2600 necessary for the creation. Named the 80th Regiment of Light Infantry, this unit was the first instance of the concept of light infantry in the British Army. The regiment was severely mauled in its first encounter, however, and Gage became embittered. Senior British officers came to realize grudgingly that the rangers were indispensable; and instead of being reduced Robert's corps was later increased to more than double the size of the 80th, much to the chagrin of Gage.

---

* The story of the surrender of Fort William Henry and subsequent massacre is well presented in the strikingly beautiful 1992 movie *Last of the Mohicans,* although it contains a number of historical inaccuracies. This is the third movie based on the 1826 novel by James Fenimore Cooper, which also spawned a television series of the same name in the mid-1950's.
† See Historical Figures, Annex C.
‡ See Historical Figures, Annex C.

On 17 December, Robert departed Fort Edward with 150 rangers on a winter patrol. Within a few days his men were reduced to 123 when several were forced to turn back due to illness caused by the cold. They came to within 600 yards of Fort Carillon on Christmas Eve, seized some outlying sentries and waited in ambush. There was little activity, and the rangers even fired their weapons to generate some reaction from the defenders. There was no response, and they slaughtered about seventeen head of cattle close to the gates of the fort before returning with their prisoners to Fort Edward. Robert composed a note that was tied to the horns of one of the cows.

> *I am obliged to you, Sir, for the repose you have allowed me to take. I thank you for the fresh meat you have sent me. I shall take care of my prisoners. I request that you present my compliments to the Marquis de Montcalm.*
>
> *Rogers*

During this period Robert was experiencing increasing difficulty with a number of senior officers. The commandant of Fort Edward and commander of the 27th Regiment, Colonel William Haviland,* was another who had little time or patience for the rangers, considering them hardly more than an unruly and insubordinate rabble. He quarrelled publicly with Robert on several occasions over the lack of discipline in the rangers, who were camped just beyond his reach and control on Rogers' Island. In one incident, he had a number of rangers arrested; others came to the jail to forcibly release them. He had a whipping post erected on the island which was cut down by the rangers. These incidents caused clashes between the two commanders that later developed into an intense and deep-seated hatred that almost destroyed the corps.

On 1 January 1758, Robert met with General Abercromby in Albany and threatened to resign if he was not allowed to discipline his men as he saw fit. If not accommodated, he warned that he would accept a position that had recently been offered him as colonel of a provincial regiment. This was a risky step, but he got away with it because he and his men had become invaluable.

On 9 January he met with Lord Loudoun, and the corps was subsequently increased by four additional companies for a total of eight,† with

---

* See Historical Figures, Annex C.
† One company had been disbanded under the terms of the surrender of Fort William Henry.

five additional companies planned. The rangers were to be issued uniforms: short green regimental coats specially ordered by Robert, with woollen or leather Indian-style leggings over their breeches and moccasins. The tam-o'-shanter or bonnet of the Scottish Highlanders was to be the headgear for the men, while the officers were to wear tricornered hats cut down to a jockey-style cap that was far less troublesome in the brush. The cost of the uniform would be recovered from each man's pay, and rangers were to be disciplined only by their own officers. Robert was also permitted to name almost all the officers for the new companies. These were major victories for Robert, but they increased the hostility of regular officers toward the corps.

In early February, Robert developed an imaginative plan to capture Fort Saint-Frédéric. Knowing that the manpower strength at the fort would be reduced for the winter, he proposed to take a force of 400 rangers and wait in ambush for the regular supply convoy. The sleighs would be captured intact and the driver replaced by his men, many of whom spoke fluent French. When the gates of the fort were opened the rangers would overpower the sentries and seize the fort with a minimum of bloodshed. The plan was masterful yet simple, and the rangers would almost certainly have executed it to perfection. The high command was planning for a winter assault on Fort Carillon at the time, however, and his plan was rejected. Although the intended assault was later cancelled, Robert's plan for Fort Saint-Frédéric was not reconsidered. Such an operation might well have altered the strategic balance in the interior and shortened the war, but the opportunity was missed.

By early March it had become common knowledge around Fort Edward that the rangers would soon be engaged in a major patrol, information leaked perhaps intentionally by Haviland. Robert, anxious about the apparent lack of security, expressed concern that the French might know of the planned scout. He believed he might be heading into a trap. In his journals he wrote that Haviland must have his own reasons to order the scout to continue in spite of his concerns.

On 10 March he departed Fort Edward with 183 men and officers, the most experienced of his rangers, on a mission toward the north end of Lake George. Marching by night through deep snow under freezing conditions, hiding by day without fires, apprehensive that the French knew of his coming, he and his men took extra precautions on this mission and went through considerable hardship to avoid detection. About mid-afternoon on 13 March, five miles west of Fort Carillon they ambushed what they believed to be a small war party of 96 Indians travelling along the frozen stream known as Trout Brook. As they followed up the initial attack, however, they quickly determined that this was but the advance party of a considerably larger force consisting of more than 350 French regulars, coureurs-de-bois and more Indians, a force possibly as large as 700 according to some sources. The ensuing engagement became known as the Battle of Rogers' Rock or the Battle on Snowshoes. It lasted for more than three hours with heavy losses on both sides, and more than once the rangers were nearly overwhelmed and destroyed. Heavily outnumbered by a vastly superior force, fighting at close quarters intermingled with a determined enemy, the rangers fell back under great pressure. They retreated toward Bald Mountain in good order to maintain the high ground. Exhausted and surrounded, some of the rangers surrendered. They had been promised protection but were afterwards massacred by the Indians, an enemy who customarily refused to honour the white man's "foolish and sentimental rules of warfare."

As dusk fell, Robert gave the order to disperse and meet at an arranged rendezvous. According to a number of sources, he is said to have led a number of savages away from his wounded men. Pursued toward the top of the mountain, he reached the summit and advanced to the verge of the precipice on the east side 550 feet above the lake. After throwing his knapsack over the cliff, he loosened the thongs on his snowshoes and, reversing his direction, tied them on backwards. He then retraced his steps

Rogers' Rock

(Lake George,
New York)

and escaped down another path to the lake. The Indians following his tracks thought he had jumped. Observing him in the moonlight on the ice below, they believed him to be under the protection of the Great Spirit and gave up the chase. This unusual incident became widely known as "Rogers' Slide" or "Rogers' Leap," and the location has been known as Rogers' Rock from that time to the present.

Robert rejoined the remnants of his patrol, now in the wilderness with little clothing and no supplies. During the battle, many, including Robert, had discarded their outer coats to move more freely. His orders were in his coat pocket, and when the French found them, they assumed that the infamous leader of the rangers was among the dead. The belief was very nearly true. Suffering terribly from hunger and cold, the remnant of the patrol finally reached Fort Edward on 15 March.

This engagement is well documented in primary sources, although the numbers of killed and wounded tend to differ considerably. The reason that Robert and his men were not annihilated was probably a combination of considerable skill and fantastic luck. One of the more accurate sources* suggests that the rangers lost 132 killed and missing with only 51 of the original force of 183 surviving. This source also states French losses were around 180, while another indicates that they were less than 50. Robert credited his unit with more than 150 of the enemy killed and as many wounded. This was the most disastrous engagement of the rangers, not only in lives but in experience, as he lost the cream of his corps.

On 6 April 1758, for his intrepidity at the Battle on Snowshoes and other operations, Robert received from the new Commander-in-Chief, General James Abercromby, a commission as major, and command of all the rangers raised in America.†

Robert continued to patrol, recruit new men and carry out his new and increased administrative duties. In May he dispatched four companies under the command of Captains Stark, Brewer, Hazen and his brother James, a total of 476 men, to Nova Scotia for another expedition against Louisbourg. These companies became part of the 13,000-man army of General Jeffrey Amherst‡ and his second-in-command Brigadier James Wolfe.§ The rangers, along with Fraser's Highlanders, played a significant role during the assault landing at Freshwater Cove, one that perhaps led to the surrender of the stronghold on 26 July.**

---

* *Robert Rogers of the Rangers* by John Cuneo.
† Lord Loudoun was recalled in March 1758 and succeeded by Abercromby.
‡ See Historical Figures, Annex C.
§ See Historical Figures, Annex C.
** For details of this operation see James Rogers, Section 2–3.

By his Excellency James Abercromby, Esq., Colonel of His Majesty's 44th Regiment of Foot, Colonel-in-Chief of the 60th or Royal American Regiment, Major General and Commander-in-Chief of all His Majesty's Forces raised or to be raised in North America, &c. &c. &c.

Whereas it may be of great use to His Majesty's service in operations now carrying on for recouvering His rights in America, to have a number of men employed obtaining intelligence of the strength, situation & motions of the enemy as well as other services for which Rangers, or men acquainted with the woods only are fit: Having the greatest confidence in your loyalty, courage, and skill in this kind of service, I do, by virtue of the power and authority to me given by His Majesty, hereby constitute and appoint you to be Major of the Rangers in His Majesty's service, and likewise Captain of a Company of said Rangers. You are therefore to take said Rangers as Major, and the said Company as Captain, into your care and charge, and duly exercise and instruct as well the Officers and the soldiers, thereof, in arms, and to use your best endeavours to keep them in good order and discipline; and I do hereby command them to obey you as their Major and Captain respectively, and you are to follow and observe such orders and directions from time to time as you shall receive from His Majesty, myself, or any other superior Officer, according to the Rules and Discipline of War.

Given at New York, this 6th Day of April 1758, in the Thirty-first Year of the reign of our Sovereign Lord, George the Second, by the Grace of God, King of Great Britain, France and Ireland, Defender of the Faith, &c. &c. &c.

James Abercromby

Meanwhile, Robert retained seven companies in the interior, four colonist and three Indian,* sending out recruiting parties to replenish the ranks after the significant losses the corps suffered at the Battle of Rogers' Rock. On 8 June Lord Howe arrived at Fort Edward with about half the army. He immediately ordered Robert to scout and make detailed maps of the area surrounding Fort Carillon. On 12 June, Robert left Fort Edward

---

* For the Indian companies of rangers, see Appendix 2 of this section.

with fifty rangers, embarking in whaleboats brought up by wagons to the remains of Fort William Henry. The patrol landed near Coutre-coeur and moved forward to reconnoitre but was ambushed by a French patrol sent out to scout the British positions, which were quickly surrounded. Robert rallied his rangers and retreated in good order to the boats. While covering the embarkation of his men, Robert received a flesh wound in the leg. The wound was not serious, and with the remainder of his rangers he afterwards took part in the disastrous attempt to capture Fort Carillon. The rangers formed the vanguard of the 15,500-man army* that sailed up Lake George on 5 July under command of General Abercromby and Lord George Howe. While moving into position for the assault, the advance party was attacked by a force of some 200 French scouts.

A French advance party reporting on the movements of the British had been slow in retreating, and found itself cut off by Robert's advance party and under attack by Howe's brigade, which was moving up to meet Robert's force. Unfortunately, Howe was killed in the action, and Abercromby lost a valued leader and counsellor. Although they were routed, the French had done considerable damage. The untimely death of Howe, a popular and effective leader, had an immediate and demoralizing effect on the entire army.

On 8 July the British launched a standard frontal assault on a defended position with predictable results. The French successfully threw back wave after wave of attacking troops, inflicting severe losses on the British. Abercromby finally disengaged after sustaining casualties of more than 550 dead and 1300 wounded, with little visible effect on the fortification or the enemy. The army withdrew to Fort Edward with the rangers covering the retreat. This was one of the most devastating defeats for the British army in America.

The rangers continued to patrol and collect intelligence in support of military operations throughout the second half of 1758. In August, Robert and some of his rangers, with about 530 regulars and provincials, were ambushed in the vicinity of Old Fort Anne, near the southern end of Lake Champlain. The attacking party numbered about 450 coureurs-de-bois and Indians under the command of the noted partisan leader Jacques Marin. This was a large war party, and the consequences could have been very serious but for the quick action of Robert and his rangers. After sustaining losses of about 100, the French melted into the forest and

---

* The composition of the British force was 5000 Regulars, 9200 provincials, 800 rangers and 500 Indians. The French garrison at Carillon consisted of about 3100 *troupes de terre,* 150 *troupes de la marine,* 250 Canadian militia and a small number of Indians, according to various sources.

withdrew to Fort Carillon. Although fifty of the British had been killed, Robert was commended for the decisive action that had prevented a total disaster.

Later that year Abercromby was recalled and General Jeffrey Amherst appointed Commander-in-Chief of British forces in America. This was largely because of his exceptional success at Louisbourg and was probably the most significant decision of the War Cabinet. In Amherst, Robert found one of his greatest long-time supporters, and it was useful to have the ear of the commander-in-chief. General Wolfe was also impressed with Robert and his rangers and had the utmost confidence in their abilities. In spite of this, however, Robert had made some very powerful enemies including Sir William Johnson, Colonel William Haviland, Colonel Thomas Gage and Colonel Frederick Haldimand.* These men were ambitious and had come to dislike Robert intensely for a variety of reasons, perhaps including jealousy of his success and favour with the commander-in-chief.

In 1759, the British commenced a three-pronged operation against New France. The Government had finally decided to pour sufficient men and resources into the conflict to end the war. General John Prideaux was ordered to lead one army up the Mohawk River and attack Fort Niagara, while Wolfe advanced up the Saint Lawrence with the fleet and another army to lay siege to Québec. General Amherst would lead a third army up Lake George to assault Forts Carillon and Saint-Frédéric.

The rangers were active in all three aspects of this operation as scouts and in the spearhead of the attacks. Robert and nine companies (six colonials and three Indian) were with Amherst. His brother James and five companies were with Wolfe, and one company was assigned to Prideaux on the Mohawk.† Fort Niagara capitulated on 24 July, Fort Carillon was abandoned on 26 July, and Fort Saint-Frédéric was burned by the French on 4 August, as they retreated in the face of superior forces. At the Battle of the Plains of Abraham, General Wolfe and the Marquis de Montcalm received mortal wounds, but Québec surrendered on 18 September.‡ With Fort Niagara and Québec under occupation, the British consolidated their gains by building a massive fort named Crown Point near the ruins of Fort Saint-Frédéric. Fort Carillon was restored and renamed Ticonderoga, and a new fort named Fort George was started on the former site of Fort William Henry.§ The army then went into winter quarters to prepare for the final assault on Canada the following year.

---

* See Historical Figures, Annex C.

† After General Prideaux set up the siege of Fort Niagara, he was accidentally killed by one of his own cannon. His second in command had been killed earlier, and Sir William Johnson assumed command of the operation.

‡ See James Rogers, Section 2-3, page 38.

§ Although started at this time, this new construction was never finished.

Although operations had ceased on Lake Champlain, there was still one task for Robert and his rangers to perform. The Abenaki Indians lived in an area on the Saint François River about three miles south of the Saint Lawrence, near the present-day village of Odenak. For nearly a century, along with the Pennacook and Caughnawaga tribes, they had brought terror and destruction to the New England frontier. They had looted and burned in savage raids, indiscriminately killing men, women and children, and had carried many captives north to torture or slavery. During this war the tribe had violated flags of truce on several occasions, including the massacre at Fort William Henry. Recently they had attacked an expedition with peace proposals under a flag of truce, and an example was considered necessary. On 13 September, General Amherst ordered Robert to destroy their village. His orders read as follows:

> *You are this night to set out with the detachment, as ordered yesterday, viz. Of 200 men, which you will take under your command, and proceed to Misisquey Bay, from whence you will march, and attack the enemy's settlements on the south side of the river Saint Lawrence, in such a manner as you shall judge most effectual to disgrace the enemy, and for the honour of His Majesty's arms.*
>
> *Remember the barbarities that have been committed by the enemy's Indian scoundrels on every occasion, where they had an opportunity of shewing their infamous cruelties on the King's subjects, which they have done without mercy. Take your revenge, but do not forget that tho' those villains have dastardly and promiscuously murdered the women and children of all ages, it is my order that no women or children are killed or hurt.*
>
> *When you have executed your intended service, you will return with your detachment to camp, or join me wherever the Army may be.*
>
> *Your's &c.*
> *Jeff. Amherst*
>
> *Camp at Crown Point,*
> *Sept. 13, 1759*
>
> *To Major Rogers*

Robert and his rangers then made one of the most remarkable marches through enemy territory in the annals of North American military history. Robert left Crown Point that evening with 190 men in whaleboats and worked silently up the lake past enemy patrols. At the

The Saint-François River Crossing

mouth of the Otter River forty men were sent back with powder burns as a result of an accident. Although he had lost 20% of his command he continued toward the objective, travelling at night on the lake and resting by day. They reached Missisquoi Bay at the north end of Lake Champlain without incident on 23 September, and here they left their boats with supplies for the return journey. Robert then led his men more than 100 miles overland through spruce swamps and dense forest, a vast blank area on contemporary British maps. Two days later the sentries who had been left to watch the boats ran into camp to report that they had been detected.

The rangers were now pursued by a large party of French and Indians. The path of their retreat had been cut off, but Robert was determined to outmarch the enemy, carry out his mission, and return by a different route. He sent word to Amherst requesting supplies be sent to the confluence of the Wells and Connecticut Rivers, a point about sixty miles north of Fort Number Four. If they were to survive these supplies would be vital.

During the night of 2–3 October, the rangers reached the Saint-François and crossed the swollen river by forming a human chain. The sketch above depicts this significant feat. They arrived undetected above the village on the evening of 4 October and prepared for the assault. With 142 rangers, Robert

attacked at dawn the following morning. The surprised village was obliter-
ated in a lightning strike. Over 200 Indian warriors perished and five English
captives were rescued, all at the cost of one man killed and six wounded.* The
Indian women and children were driven into the forest and the village was
burned to the ground. More than 600 English scalps had been found in the
village, and this discovery, added to the infamous actions of this tribe during
the war, more than justified the assault in the eyes of the British.

The raid was a success, but the operation was not yet completed;
Robert still had to get his men home. They learned from the captives that
a large party of the enemy was lying in wait nearby, knowing of a ranger
patrol but uncertain of its whereabouts, movements or intentions. The
French were now alerted to his presence, and Robert would have to move
quickly if he was to save his men. With more than 300 vengeful Indians to
the north and west of his position, a considerable force to the east and
approximately 200 in the rear following the trail from Lake Champlain,
Robert set off to the southeast, toward Lake Memphremagog.

After eight days they arrived at the lake, having long since exhausted
the corn and other provisions captured from Saint-François. The weather had
turned cold with torrential, often freezing, rainstorms, and game in the forest
was scarce, having been decimated by an immense forest fire a few years
previously. Robert divided his command into smaller parties of about
twenty. He thus enabled them to hunt more effectively for food and reduced
the risk that the entire detachment would be discovered and destroyed.
One of these groups was attacked by the pursuing enemy and wiped out;
another was reduced to cannibalism. It was a grueling march through
trackless, unforgiving country, choked with mountains and swamps: a race
to keep ahead of a determined enemy in hot vengeful pursuit through
colder weather threatening early snow. It was a fight against exhaustion,
lameness, sickness and the deterioration of mind and spirit, against
rapidly encroaching hunger and the possibility of starvation.

After eighteen days the remnants of his exhausted force reached the
comparative safety of the Wells River. At the rendezvous they found a fire
still smoldering but no food. Lieutenant Samuel Stevens, the officer sent
by Amherst with the supplies, testified at his subsequent court-martial had
camped several miles south of the location and waited four days. (Robert
suggested that he had probably heard the rangers coming and, fearing they
were a party of French, had retreated with the supplies leaving Robert's
men to die.) It was clear that most of his men could go no farther, and after
five days Robert and three others departed to get food, promising to return

---

* The number of Indians killed during this raid has been a highly disputed issue
among historians for years. The primary objective of the mission was psychological,
however, and it was strikingly successful.

---

in ten days. His party, weak and close to death, manoeuvred down the river on a raft. It was lost over one of the falls; they built another by burning down trees, none having strength to wield an axe.

The group finally reached Fort Number Four on the Connecticut River on 31 October. Within an hour of his arrival Robert dispatched a rescue party north to his men. He followed on 2 November to ensure delivery of the supplies and to begin searching for those of his men still missing. The supplies arrived on 4 November, exactly ten days after he left his men as he had promised.*

On the return trip, Robert lost three officers and forty-six men: thirty-two to starvation and exposure, seventeen to enemy action. The mission, however, was a complete success. They had travelled over 350 miles through hostile enemy territory, mostly on foot, through extremely difficult country, harassed by an aggressive enemy and fighting a running gun battle. In the end they had been reduced to boiling and eating their leather hats and moccasins and in some cases their dead in order to survive. News of the raid spread as if by wildfire throughout the colonies and made headlines in all the newspapers of the day. On 1 December, General Amherst reviewed the rangers at Crown Point to congratulate them on the mission.

Four companies remained on active service during the winter of 1759–60: two at Crown Point, one at Québec and another at Fort Brewerton. The remaining units were temporarily disbanded. In March, Robert was ordered to bring his rangers up to full strength and to divide them among the three armies converging on Montréal.   Six companies were to be assigned to General Haviland on Lake Champlain, two to General Amherst on the Mohawk and one to General Murray on the Saint Lawrence.

On 27 May, Robert was ordered to "harass and distress the retreating French, governing himself as required by the movements of the French army." On 6 June with 200 rangers he engaged a force of about 350 five miles south of Fort de l'Île-aux-Noix. The enemy broke and ran after losong forty men (against sixteen casualties among the rangers). This engagement, known as the Battle of Pointe-au-Fer, was the last large-scale bush encounter and perhaps the most brilliant and successful action by the rangers during the war. After a brief scout of Fort Saint-Jean, the rangers continued to Fort Saint-Thérèse. This fort fell on 16 June without loss of

* The tale of the Saint-François raid, a magnificent exploit of courage and daring, can be found in *Northwest Passage* by Kenneth Roberts and *Robert Rogers of the Rangers* by John R. Cuneo and in other books.   In 1940, MGM produced a film entitled *Northwest Passage,* starring Spencer Tracy, Robert Young and Walter Brennan, based on the book. Although the movie, like the novel, tends to distort the historical data, it graphically depicts the hardships of the expedition and the tremendous courage of the rangers.

The Saint-François Expedition
Copy of the map submitted by Robert which was attached to his report

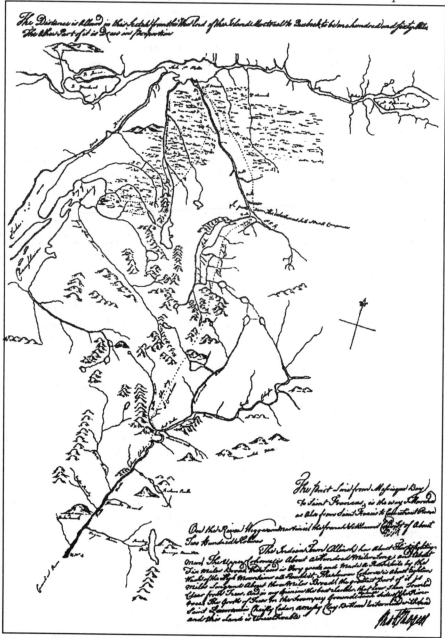

The non-cartographical elements on this copy have been moved to avoid reducing its size of the map.

life, owing to the rangers' quick action in executing a plan similar to that proposed by Robert for Fort Saint-Frédéric in 1758.* The rangers destroyed the fort and village, and rejoined the army at Crown Point on 20 June.

On 11 August 1760, Robert, with 600 rangers and 70 Indians, embarked at Crown Point, the vanguard of Haviland's 3500-man army on Lake Champlain. They joined the armies of Amherst and Murray before Montréal, and New France capitulated without further bloodshed. The surrendered forces were denied the honours of war, however, because of Montcalm's violation of the terms of surrender after the fall of Fort William Henry in 1757. The French regiments retired to Île-Sainte-Hélène and burned their colours rather than hand them over under these terms. British troops entered the city in the evening of 8 September.

Though Governor-General Pierre de Rigaud de Vaudreuil de Cavagnial surrendered all French possessions in Canada with the fall of Montréal, this action did not end the conflict between Britain and France. War continued in Europe until the conclusion of the Seven Years' War in 1763. Hostilities in the French and Indian War in America, however, had ended, although inland forts and posts were slow to hear the news.

On 12 September Amherst did Robert the honour of designating him as the officer to accept the surrender of all the French posts along the Great Lakes. He was to proceed westward with two companies of rangers and take possession of the forts at Détroit, at the Straits of Mackinac and on Lake Michigan.† The forts were located hundreds of miles inland in areas where few Englishmen had penetrated. This was a dangerous and delicate assignment. They had no way to assess the belligerence of the French fort commanders or the strength of the resistance they might present.

Robert left on 13 September with198 men in fifteen whaleboats and along the route made camps near the ruins of Fort Frontenac,‡ Fort Rouillé,§ and Fort Niagara.** (Plaques have been erected at all three locations by local historical societies in commemoration of the expedition.)

---

* For details see page 130.

† The French established a mission called Sainte-Marie-du-Sault, north of the Straits of Mackinac in 1668. In 1683, a fort called Fort de Buade was built near the same location and named after the Governor of New France, Louis de Buade Comte de Frontenac. Both were abandoned in 1701 in favour of a location further south along the river, strait or "détroit", which separated Lakes Huron and Erie. Named Fort Pontchartrain after the Colonial Minister, it soon became known simply as Fort Détroit. In 1702, Fort Saint-Joseph was built at the south end of Lake Michigan. In 1715, Fort Michilimackinac was established on the south side of the Strait of Mackinac. The final fort of any consequence in the area was Fort de la Baie-des-Puants at Green Bay. See map on page 144.

‡ § **: Notes on next page.

On 7 November the rangers made camp at the mouth of the Cuyahoga River, near the present site of Cleveland, Ohio, and Robert became the first British officer to advance so far west.

Pontiac,†† War Chief of the Ottawas, exercised considerable influence and control over the allied tribes of the Great Lakes region. He came into the British camp and demanded to know why British forces were trespassing on Ottawa land. Informed of the French surrender and the nature of the mission in a meeting with Robert, he granted permission for the expedition to traverse his territory and provided an escort of 100 braves.

The rangers broke camp on 12 November and, after some discussion, Détroit surrendered to Robert on 29 November. He dispatched an officer and twenty men to assume custody of posts southwest of Détroit, and on 10 December he started north for Fort Michilimackinac. The season was too far advanced, however, and heavy ice and snow forced him to turn back.

At Detroit Robert met Jean Baptiste Cadotte, a French fur trader who lived at Sault-Sainte-Marie and wielded considerable influence over the tribes. Robert also became acquainted with Alexander Henry, whose later explorations of the interior of America inspired readers, travellers and settlers for generations. With the assistance of these men, Robert negotiated two significant land deals with the Chipewyan Indian Nation, deeds for which were signed by their four senior chiefs at Detroit on 23 December 1760.‡‡ In the first transaction, Robert, Cadotte and Henry acquired a large tract of land amounting to almost 20,000 acres on Saint Mary's River, near the great international locks of today. A map was attached to the document showing the area granted and including such places as Sugar

---

‡ In 1673 the French entered the area and built Fort Cataraqui on the site. This trading post later developed into the elaborate Fort Frontenac that was destroyed by the British in 1758. The area was named Kingston at the time of the Loyalist migration to Upper Canada in 1784. Fort Henry was constructed during the War of 1812 to defend Canada from the Americans. The plaque for Robert's expedition is located on the walls of Fort Henry.

§ Located at what is now Toronto, Ontario, Fort Rouillé was abandoned by the French in July 1759. Fort York was later built on the site in 1793 by Lieutenant Governor John Graves Simcoe and the Queen's Rangers. The plaque is located on the walls of this later fort, which was restored in 1934.

** Built by the French in 1678 and improved over the years, Fort Niagara was surrendered to the British in 1759 following a prolonged siege. The location served as an important post during the succeeding years and as a focal point during the War of 1812. The fort was restored in 1927.

†† The Great War Chief of the Ottawas. See Historical Figures, Annex C.

‡‡ It has been reported that the original documents were restored and placed in the Burton Historical Collection of the Detroit Public Library. Although legible, they are in poor condition. On further investigation, however, only one of the documents could be located. The deed to Robert is located at the Detroit Historical Society.

Island. Each chief signed by making a totem mark behind his name. This deed reads in part as shown below.

In a related deal Robert acquired almost 30,000 acres along the southern shore of Lake Superior for a similar quantity of merchandise. A belt of black wampum was affixed across the bottom of this deed with strips of white beads representing the rivers at either end and in the middle of the belt. A note was appended below the signatures of the chiefs explaining that the belt was presented by the "Head Warriors & Young Chiefs with all their Village," and that they would ever acknowledge the authority represented by the wampum. The document was witnessed by Alexander Henry.

Whereas we the Chiefs of the Chippewas assembled together with our head warriors in Detroit do in the presence of God and with regard to all his angles —————————— to define that all may know —————————— to grant, sell to Major Robert Rogers, John Baptise and Alexander Henry for fifty blankets, Twenty pairs of legions, Twenty pounds of vermillion, Ten barrels of rum, Ten thousand wampum, four barrels of powder and three hundred pounds of shot————— in the Presence of God and with Regard to his Angels ————— it is our Free will and Pleasure ————— to grant and sell to Major Robert Rogers, in Consideration of the Love and Good Will we have to him, as also a Desire we have To Convince the World, that we will Grant him our Bounty for Being the First English Officer that Ever Came into our Country with Troops ————— for One hundred White Blankets, Fifty Stroud Blankets, Twenty Barrels of Rum, forty Pounds Vermillion, Twenty thousand Wampum, and three hundred Pounds of Gunpowder, Two hundred weights of Shott & Ball ————— in the Bounds that God has Given us to Inherit and that Which we have Posses'd under God for Many Generations Back, Long Before any White People Came Amongst us and we look to the Starrs when We Attempt to Count the Years wee have own'd it ————— bounded on the north by Lake Superior; on the east by the Ontonawyon River; on the west by the Copper River and on the south by a Streight Line from the head of one River to the head of the other River ————— Hunting and fishing on said Lands to ourselves when we Please —————

Legions: leggings.
Stroud blankets: blankets made for trade with the Indians.
(Illegible portions are indicated by long dashes.)

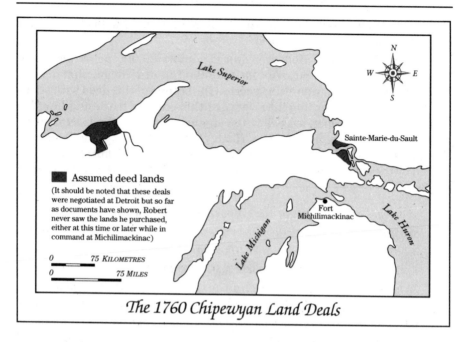

Assumed deed lands

(It should be noted that these deals were negotiated at Detroit but so far as documents have shown, Robert never saw the lands he purchased, either at this time or later while in command at Michilimackinac)

0   75 KILOMETRES
0   75 MILES

The 1760 Chipewyan Land Deals

The region contains perhaps the richest deposits of copper in the America. A portion of the land was sold to Charles Townshend in 1765. In 1835 an attorney came to America from England with copies of the Indian deeds seeking Robert's legal heirs. Apparently no one could establish a satisfactory claim, and the remaining land reverted to its former owners. It is possible that Robert had sold the land and the new owner had failed to register his title. This land is not mentioned as part of Robert's holdings in any references after 1765. These deals were negotiated at Detroit, and it is believed that he never saw the lands he acquired, either in 1760 or later when he was Governor of Michilimackinac. The map above depicts the roughly estimated location of the lands purchased.

Leaving a garrison at Detroit, Robert departed for New York on 23 December. This was "a quick march overland" according to his reports, but it was undertaken in midwinter through what must still have been enemy territory. News travelled slowly in the backwoods and shots were often fired before questions were asked. After brief stops at Fort Pitt and Philadelphia, he arrived safely at New York on 14 February 1761. From newspaper accounts he was clearly the man of the hour. At the age of 29, he had become America's most famous and popular colonial frontiersman. As a final reward for his service, Robert received a commission as "Captain in His Majesty's Regular Forces" with "Command of an Independent Company in South Carolina" from General Amherst. These were predated

25 October 1760 and ensured that he would eventually retire from the army on half pay of five shillings per day. Most of his ranger companies were disbanded at the end of the war, although two participated in the conquest of the West Indies (May 1761–June 1762) but not under his direct command.*

About this time Robert was confronted with a problem that continued to plague him for the rest of his life: exorbitant personal debt. As mentioned above, it was an accepted practice for commanders of provincial regiments and other units to pay and outfit their men from personal funds and afterwards seek compensation. Although Robert was a brilliant commander in the field, he frequently disregarded the necessary paperwork of military command. On reviewing his incomplete and confused records, the Crown now refused to honour many of the debts he had accumulated during the war. To meet his obligations, some going as far back as 1755, he became involved in numerous schemes to raise money. During his brief visit to Niagara en route to Detroit, he formed a trading partnership called "Rogers & Company" with Nicholas Stevens, Edward Cole, John Askins and Lieutenant Caesar McCormick to extract some profit from the expedition. This action was not illegal, or even dishonest by the standards of the day, but it left him open to criticism and perhaps blemished his reputation.†

Along with the Chipewyan land transactions, Robert petitioned the New York Assembly for a land grant based on his military service. The land he wanted was approximately 25,000 acres on Lake George near Fort George, the site of old Fort William Henry. He formed a land company called "Major Rogers & Associates" with his brother James and others to exploit and settle the area. Although the Assembly initially approved it, his right to the land was challenged by the Mohawks, who claimed the entire area. The Superintendent of Indian Affairs, Sir William Johnson, supported their claim and petitioned the Assembly on their behalf. He saw Robert as no more than an opportunist, demonstrating a striking change in attitude from the glowing reports he had made only a few years earlier. It is possible that Johnson and Robert had disagreed over methods of dealing with the Indians and that Johnson saw him as a threat. While James did receive a separate grant of some 3,000 acres further north, Robert's grant was withdrawn by the Crown.

On 30 June 1761, Robert married Elizabeth (30 Jun 1741–11 Dec 1813), the youngest and perhaps the most beautiful of the daughters of the Reverend

---

* See Appendix I to this section and Historical Items, Annex A.

† An example of another trade agreement with McCormick, where Robert invested borrowed money heavily to reap significant potential profit, can be found in Appendix III.

Arthur Browne and Mary Cox.* The Reverend Mr. Browne was an Episcopalian minister and Rector of Queen's Chapel in Portsmouth. The wedding took place in the chapel, celebrated by Elizabeth's father. The newspaper accounts present it as the social event of the year. Throughout their lives Robert called his wife Betsy.

The honeymoon was brief, as Robert was recalled to duty on 23 July and ordered to assume his command in South Carolina and to assist Colonel James Grant, who was dealing with the Cherokee uprising. The Cherokees were the largest and most powerful of the tribes in the Southeast. They were allied to the British during the French and Indian War and occupied territory between the opposing sides. After the war they became dissatisfied with the way they were being treated by their former allies and increasingly upset at being constantly cheated by English traders. These issues led to an incident in February 1760, and the resulting casualties led to hostilities and the uprising a few months later. Robert arrived too late to see any action or make a useful contribution. Grant had defeated the Cherokees by early August in a whirlwind campaign that destroyed most of their villages and food supply.

On 20 August Robert assumed command of his company, attached to Fort Prince George in the western part of the state. For the next fifteen months he conducted scouting operations of the surrounding country from the post; but with the threat of war eliminated, lack of action must have bored him. He was in Charleston in April 1762 for the commissioning of the privateer *Major Rogers,* built and commanded by his brother James,† but little else is positively known of this interval in his life. During his service in the South, he did meet and favourably impress Arthur Dobbs, Governor of North Carolina from 1754 until his death in 1765. When the Commissioner of Indian Affairs for the Southern Department died suddenly, Dobbs petitioned the Crown to have Robert appointed to the position. Although the appointment went to another, meetings with the Governor had a profound influence on Robert's life as shown by ensuing events.

Dobbs had been obsessed with finding the Northwest Passage to the Pacific and by this time had already financed two major expeditions to Hudson Bay in 1741 and 1746. He had also published a number of books and pamphlets on the subject. In Robert he found a willing and interested listener and this was probably the basis of their friendship.

---

* Arthur Browne had four sons and five daughters as follows: Thomas (who died young), the Reverend Marmaduke, Arthur (later Governor of Kinsale), Peter (a major in the army), Lucy (married Colonel Smith), Jane (married Samuel Livermore, a lawyer who later became Chief Justice of the US Supreme Court and represented New Hampshire in Congress and the Senate), Mary (married the Reverend Winwood Serjeant, no relation to the husband of Robert's sister), Anne (married Captain George St. Loe, RN), and Elizabeth, who married Robert Rogers.
† See James Rogers, Section 2–3, page 40.

Elizabeth Browne Rogers
Portrait by Joseph Blackburn
1761

Robert was unable to solve his debt problems in the South and the extended separation from his wife, coupled with boredom from inaction, must have been wearing. A letter to his wife from Edenton, North Carolina, dated 4 May 1762, is revealing.

My dear Betsy

Your letter dated Sixt of February I Received yesterday by Clesh my Servant and obeserve the contents tho I am at a loss at present what to say to you in Regard to my selling my commission and bying another at New York, as I have some time ago wrote to General Amherst desiring leave to Chang but have not as yet had aney answer from him — yet Betsy nothing would give me more pleasure than to be settled in the manor that would be most agreable to Mrs. Rogers.

If I cannot chang my company I shall send for you by some gentleman that I can depend on and you shall have my promis to Return after spending next winter with me at Carolina — I am suar that you will like Carolina much better than you expect as there is a very good set of people there and besides my dear I have a fine house there and a very pretty orang garden in which I should be very glad to have some agreable walks with Betsy, my Dearest Betsy, will you come to me as soon as the scorching heat of Summor is over. I hope to get leave to go to New England if I do go on the Expedition as it will sail from New York if I am ordered by General Amherst to Repair to New York I shall land at Boston and take you with me to New York till the Expedition sails — but it Doth not signify to talk about that matter as I must have General Amherst letters before I can know whether I am to chang my company or go on Service, therefore I will not Say aney more about the matter at present, only I must tell you that I long to see you greately, you are every moment in my mind, I am often with you in Emagenations, I pray God to Grant me the hapiness of Living with my wife and may that Devine Being grant you his Blessing and direct all your way and that you may be Alway free from care and trouble is the prayer of my Dear Betsy.

Your Loving

affeconot Husband

You must Excouse this letter it is wrote in the greatest hury Emagenable

Robt Rogers

The nature of the expedition mentioned in the letter above is not known, but it could have been a reference to operations in the West Indies. It was too early for an expedition to quell unrest in the Great Lakes area, but Amherst may have expected trouble from that quarter. In any event Robert was granted permission to sell his commission, and he subsequently purchased a captaincy in the New York Independents.

On arriving in the North, however, he was besieged by creditors. Concerned for the welfare of his wife, on 20 December 1762 he sold 500 acres of land in Rumford to his father-in-law for the sum of £1000. Much of the money was transferred to Elizabeth in trust. Included in this transaction were a Negro man named Castro Dickerson (age 28), a Negro woman named Sylvia, a Negro boy named Pomp (age 12) and an Indian boy named Billy (age 13).* There can be little doubt these individuals were slaves, although the term was seldom heard in 18th-century usage in the North. (Further evidence that Robert was a slave-owner can be found in Appendix IV.)

In the spring of 1763, the New Hampshire Assembly allowed Robert a portion of his claim for war expenses. With the proceeds of his partnership with Edward Cole and John Askins, things were beginning to look somewhat brighter. Just at this time, however, Arthur Browne sued his son-in-law for over £2600 for lodging and support of his daughter and Robert's servants while he was in the South. Not satisfied with the results of this legal action, Browne attached a lien against all Robert's property. Robert then requested permission to go to England and seek redress for his accounts from the Crown. He was refused by General Amherst, as his services were still needed in America.

Encouraged by the French in Louisiana to believe that they would return, Pontiac organised and united the tribes of the Great Lakes and Ohio River Valley. While hostilities in the French and Indian War had ended with the fall of New France in 1760, the Seven Years' War in Europe was not concluded until 10 February 1763 and the signing of the Treaty of Paris. Hostile British and French forces were still technically at war because of slow communications. Broken promises and the threat of encroaching settlement impelled the Indians to take action. Commencing in April 1763 they attacked in fierce, well co-ordinated raids. Small settlements and western posts, including Fort Michilimackinac, fell quickly to surprise onslaughts, with great loss of life. By late May an Indian army of 2000 braves was laying siege to Fort Detroit.

---

* Several sources mention an Indian boy named Billy. These may refer to the captive Robert brought back from the Saint-François expedition mentioned in the book *Northwest Passage*.

Robert was quickly dispatched to Fort Niagara with forty rangers hastily recruited by his brother James. On 10 July, as part of a 250-man relief force under the command of Captain James Dalyell,* they departed Niagara to reinforce the besieged fort. The expedition arrived on 29 July, and Dalyell insisted that "a major force be sent immediately against these savages, who will melt before superior British firepower." Against the strong recommendations of Robert and several others, the post commander, Major Henry Gladwin, reluctantly consented to the action.

Just before dawn on 31 July, the patrol left the fort. It was ambushed at Parent's Creek, about two miles out. The Indians had been advised of the plan by French settlers living in and around the post and were ready. The skirmish became known as the Battle of Bloody Run, after the creek which is said to have run crimson for hours from the blood of the fallen. According to a number of reports, the conspicuous gallantry of Robert and his rangers greatly reduced the impact of yet another disastrous retreat following an ill conceived attack against overwhelming odds. By seizing a large, solidly built farmhouse close to the river, the rangers were able to cover the disorganised retirement of the regulars, who were being slaughtered by constant withering fire. These rangers were now isolated but were eventually rescued by two bateaux from Detroit. Armed with swivel guns, these boats temporarily drove off the Indians. This enabled the rangers to escape, and they reached Fort Detroit without further casualties. The sketch opposite depicts this battle.†

This was the last recorded action of Rogers' Rangers. For eight years they had served in the war with courage and spirit, earning a reputation that made them the terror of the enemy and the toast of their countrymen. They left an indelible mark on the pages of history as the hardiest and most successful of guerrilla fighters—the Commandos of the Seven Years' War.

Of an original force of 280, sixty-one men had been killed or wounded, including Captain Dalyell, and as many more were listed as missing, prisoners of the Indians, who had suffered few losses. The conflict degenerated into a blockade, a mode of warfare disadvantageous to Indians, who needed to hunt to obtain supplies for their families for the winter. As the siege dragged on many of the tribes became disaffected, and on 31 October, Pontiac called a truce until spring.‡ With the immediate danger to Detroit at an end,

---

* Captain Dalyell, aide-de--camp to General Amherst, was a long-time acquaintance of Robert.

† In 1846 the farm through which the creek ran became Elmwood Cemetery. It was later a Michigan Historic Site with an appropriate marker recording the battle. The marker still exists, but it is not well known and is located in one of the depressed sections of the city.

‡ At that time a treaty was negotiated, and the uprising came to an end.

The Battle of Bloody Run

Major Gladwin reduced his garrison for the winter, and after a brief period at Niagara, Robert returned to New Hampshire. The hostilities had been disastrous for the fur trade, and Robert's interests were no exception. His creditors again pressing for payment, he again applied to various provincial assemblies for consideration of his war accounts, but without success. Furthermore, General Amherst had been relieved by General Gage as Commander-in-Chief. Gage had not forgotten previous disagreements and wartime rivalries, and now even the expenses for Robert's Detroit expedition were being refused by the Crown.

Offered little encouragement of further military service in America, Robert made an unsuccessful stab at civilian life. As a reduced officer he was entitled to land as a reward for his service. On 4 July 1764, he received a grant of 3000 acres at Readsboro, in the New Hampshire Grants. He quickly mortgaged the property for £5600 to pay some of his creditors. However, the royal proclamation settling the long-standing dispute over this area between New York and New Hampshire established the boundary between these colonies as the west bank of the Connecticut River on 20 July. All grants made by New Hampshire in the area known as the New

Hampshire Grants were therefore worthless, as the territory belonged to New York. Robert was worse off than before, with a spiraling debt load and lawsuit after lawsuit facing him.

Convinced that the solutions to his difficulties lay in England, Robert sailed unaccompanied in March 1765 to claim redress for his accounts. He landed in Dublin and travelled on to London, where he that discovered his fame had preceded him and he was the toast of the town. He engaged a secretary named Nathaniel Potter, according to some sources a well educated and clever but thoroughly disreputable individual.* However, he probably was of considerable assistance to Robert in the preparation of his literary works. While in England Robert wrote two books and possibly a play, largely at his own expense. The first editions appeared in 1765–66, and others soon followed.†

The Journals of Major Robert Rogers : London, Oct.1765
A Concise Account of North America : London, Oct. 1765
Ponteach, or the Savages of America : London, Feb. 1766

The first two were considered reasonable works by contemporary scholars and were well received. They contained a wealth of information on North America that was then unknown to the general public. The play, on the other hand, was considered to be of little artistic merit, and few copies have been preserved to the present day. It was, however, only the second drama penned by an American-born playwright to be published in England (the first was by Thomas Godfrey only a few months before). Some would argue that Robert did not write the play; yet its historical accuracy and the parallels to his *Concise Account* leave little doubt that he had a hand in its composition.

On 12 August, Robert presented a memorial to the King's Council urging a search for the Northwest Passage by land. Considering that rangers would undoubtedly be the best suited for such an undertaking, he proposed to send some 228 officers and men in a three-year expedition at an estimated cost of £32,182 sterling. The scheme was to reach the Pacific by proceeding from the headwaters of the Mississippi to the "Great River Ourigan."‡ Very little of the interior or the Pacific coast had been explored

---

* Potter was a native of Elizabeth, New Jersey, and had obtained a degree from Princeton. He was first a schoolteacher at Watertown, Massachusetts, and later a minister in Brookline, Massachusetts. He was dismissed from the latter position in 1759, and the course of his life from that time until he met Robert in London in 1765 is not known.

† These are the accepted short titles of the works. For full titles, see Bibliography.

‡ This was an early Indian name for the Columbia River. Robert's use of this word in 1765 and the word "Oreigan" in his other references may have been the first introduction of these terms into English documents.

North America after the French and Indian War

at this time, twenty-five years after the La Vérendrye expedition and thirteen years before Captain Cook visited the coast in 1778. The proposal was seen as a needless luxury after the expenses incurred during the long war with France and was turned down by the Councillors. Had the plan received official sanction, the name of Robert Rogers could have stood in Canadian and American history books beside the stories of the great explorations of Lewis and Clark (1803–06), Simon Fraser (1807–08) and David Thompson (1808–11). These men explored areas near those outlined in Robert's memorial during the years shown, as detailed on the map opposite some thirty to fifty years later.

Robert also submitted a claim for war expenses that had been refused by various colonial assemblies. While he failed to get the compensation he sought, on 12 October he was informed that he was to be appointed Governor of Fort Michilimackinac, perhaps the most important western British garrison in North America. He was also to receive a commission in the 60th or Royal American Regiment. These two appointments were probably a result of the considerable influence of his backers and major supporters, General Amherst and Sir Charles Townshend, Chancellor of the Exchequer. Michilimackinac was the jumping off point for exploration of the interior, a fact not lost on Robert or his supporters. On 17 October, Robert was presented at Court and is said by Cuneo to have been permitted to kiss the hand of King George III. On 18 December 1765, Robert sailed for North America on the frigate *Resolute,* arriving at New York on 9 January.

General Gage and Sir William Johnson, both of whom bore deep animosity toward him, were incensed at the appointment. As his superiors, neither considered him remotely fitted for this position of executive trust, and they believed him to be dangerous to themselves and to their interpretations of the interests of the Crown. They therefore conspired to put such controls upon him as to make him largely ineffective. From a number of documents it appears that Gage and Johnson may have had their own plans for the interior, and Robert's appointment had created a problem. On 10 January, Gage reluctantly gave Robert his instructions, but severely restricted his authority by making him subordinate to Johnson in all matters relating to the Indians and to the commander at Detroit in all other respects, thus making the execution of the appointment as difficult as possible. While the appointment was couched in military terms to restrict his powers, Robert was not actually in the army, as Gage failed to follow his orders and issue Robert a commission. He later claimed that the appointment was a civil one and used this claim as an excuse for refusing Robert the pay to which he was entitled. Robert appears to have been confused by the hostility shown him.

With his wife Elizabeth and secretary Nathaniel Potter, Robert departed for Michilimackinac by way of Johnson Hall in the Mohawk

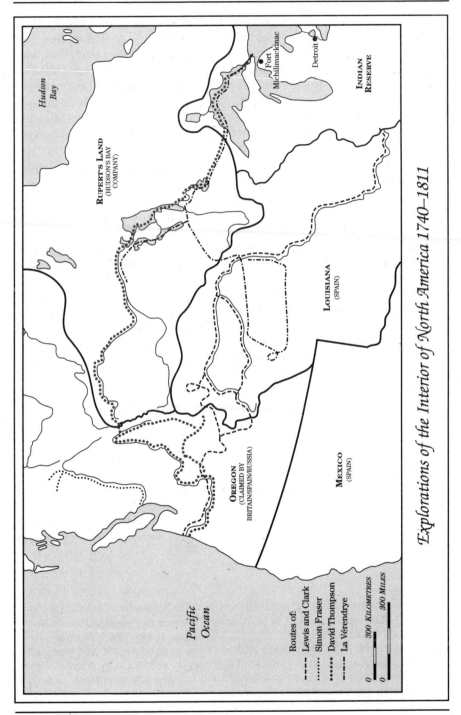

Hudson Bay

RUPERT'S LAND
(HUDSON'S BAY
COMPANY)

Fort
Michilimackinac

Detroit

INDIAN
RESERVE

LOUISIANA
(SPAIN)

OREGON
(CLAIMED BY
BRITAIN/SPAIN/RUSSIA)

MEXICO
(SPAIN)

Pacific
Ocean

Routes of:

Lewis and Clark
Simon Fraser
David Thompson
La Vérendrye

300 KILOMETRES

300 MILES

0

0

Explorations of the Interior of North America 1740–1811

Valley. There, on 3 June, he received his instructions from Sir William Johnson, a copy of which may be found in Appendix VI to this section. He later met with Pontiac and representatives of the northwestern tribes, who were on their way to the major Indian conference at Fort Oswego called by Johnson for 23 July. Robert and his party arrived at his new post onboard the schooner *Gladwin* on 10 August. Although his orders and instructions were very restrictive, Robert considered that he could still accomplish his goals, using profits obtained from the fur trade to finance preliminary explorations.

On 12 September he commissioned Captain James Tute, Jonathan Carver and James Stanley Goddard to map the country south and west of the lakes in preparation for an expedition in search of the Northwest Passage.* The men were also instructed to invite the tribes to a Great Conference at Fort Michilimackinac in July of the following year. While the mission may have been contrary to the intent of his instructions, clearly he considered this a matter of interpretation. All three men had served with him during the French and Indian War, were respected traders in the North-West and later became famous for their explorations.† Unfortunately they did not follow these instructions closely, and they failed to accomplish the mission. This failure resulted in significant difficulties for Robert, as he was counting on their results and on profits from expected new trade alliances to justify the expedition and finance future activity. The men returned from the West in mid-1768, by which time Robert was in serious trouble.

In October 1766, Robert called a large Indian Conference with the Ottawa, Cree and Chipewyan nations. Through this meeting he helped resolve an ancient dispute between these tribes, which also involved the Dakota or Sioux Nation to the west. This was an attempt to improve and consolidate relations between the Indian nations and the Crown. At the conference Robert gained considerable prestige and esteem among both local traders and the Indians of the Great Lakes Region. During the winter he laid plans for the Grand Conference to be held the following summer, to build on what had been accomplished, and to develop a concept being formulated on the future of the West.

---

* Copies of the instructions given them are found in Appendix VII to this section.
† Carver published an account of his *Travels Through the Interior Part of North America in the Years 1766, 1767 and 1768* (London, 1778). The book met astonishing popularity; more than thirty editions were printed, and it was translated into several languages. Large portions of it, however, were actually lifted verbatim from Robert's *Concise Account* published in 1765, and Robert's name is almost excluded from any connection to the project.

Instructions to Major Robert Rogers — Commandant of the Post of Michilimakinac
By His Excellency the Honourable Thomas Gage, Major General and Commander-in-Chief of All His Majesty's Forces in North America, &c., &c., &c.

His Majesty's Pleasure having been signified to me that you should be appointed to Command of Michilimackinac, or some other Post in the upper Country; I do by these Presents appoint you to be Captain Commandant of the Garrison of Michilimakinac, and you are hereby Authorized to take the Command of the said Garrison, and the Officers and Soldiers that compose the same are required to obey you as their Commanding Officer; You are therefore to take the said Charge upon you, and carefully and Diligently to discharge the Duty thereof, by doing and performing all and all manner of things thereunto belonging; And you are to observe and follow such Orders and Directions as you shall from time to time receive from His Majesty, myself, or any other your Superior Officer, according to the Rules and Discipline of War; And for your better guidance and Direction in the great Trust repose in you, you are herewith furnished with such Orders as have been given out during my Command to the Officers Commanding Posts, to which you will pay due attention and Obedience.* I cannot recomment too strongly to you the strictest Oeconomy in the small Expences that may unavoidably be incurred at this Post, now put under your Command, but nothing New or Changeable must upon any Account be undertaken by you of your own head.

As in the course of your Command you must Necessarily have some Intercourse with the Savages, I have thought proper, in this Particular to put you under the direction of Sir William Johnson, Bart., His Majesty's Sole Agent and Superintendent of the Northern Indians, and he will furnish you with proper Instructions for your guidance in your Transactions with the Indians who reside near, and may visit the said Post of Michilimakinac, to which, and all such future Orders as he may Judge necessary to sent you upon this Subject, you are to pay the Strictest Attention and Obedience.

* A copy of the extracts of orders furnished to Robert is in Appendix V of this section.

You will as frequently as possible Report to the Officer Commanding at Detroit, under whose immediate Command you are, the State of the Troops under your Command; sending him the proper Returns, and acquainting him of every Occurrence relative to the better Conducting His Majesty's Affairs in that Country, that you shall think it necessary he should be informed of. You will likewise Correspond with Sir William Johnson, giving him notice of every thing you shall think worthy his knowledge, relative to the Conduct and Temper of the Savages.

Given at Head Quarters in New York this 10th day of January 1766.

Thos. Gage

On 27 May 1767, he sent a lengthy memorandum to the Board of Trade in England recommending the creation of a new colony in the North-West encompassing the Lakes Region and the extensive but as yet unexplored territory to westward. The colony was to have a military/civilian administration, with himself as Governor, responsible only and directly to the King and his Ministers in Council, to be given complete authority over Indian affairs in the colony and to the West. To preserve peace and order, he suggested that a few companies of rangers be placed on permanent establishment. Robert pointed out that the fur trade was beneficial to all sectors of the British economy through the supply of trade goods, and that expanded trade would further enhance improving relations with the Indians. This, he reasoned, could lead to explorations and discoveries of great importance to the Crown. The traders of the region fully supported the proposal, as they saw the advantages of this system of government in the local area and were opposed to dealing with officials far to the East who were unfamiliar with their problems.

Overall, these recommendations were not unreasonable for the time, and if they had been acted upon could well have altered later political divisions in the interior of the continent, including the future border between Canada and the United States. They could also have been instrumental to discoveries in the West years before the Lewis and Clark Expedition of 1803. Robert was in considerable difficulty with his superiors long before the Board of Trade could take any action on his proposal. The Board were probably aware of the arrest and court martial when Robert's proposal came to their attention, and as a result it was not taken seriously. General Gage and Sir William Johnson would have been furious had they known of this document, but there is no evidence that they were ever aware of its existence. Their actions were based upon other issues largely of their own creation.

On 23 June 1767, Lieutenant Benjamin Roberts, one of Sir William Johnson's most trusted aides, arrived at Fort Michilimackinac as Commissary of Indian Affairs. In reality he was sent as a spy for Johnson to ensure that Robert obeyed his instructions, and from other documents it is apparent that Gage was aware of this fact. Lieutenant Roberts had a very poor reputation and had clashed with the commanders of several posts during his service with the Indian Affairs Department. One account of his character suggests that he was thoroughly unprincipled, and that he would stop at nothing to accomplish his ends.* "He was petulant, hot-headed, unreliable, a sycophant, devoid of good judgement and a liar, in addition to having other grave faults" according to one source. The lieutenant arrived at the fort during the scheduled Grand Conference and could do little but watch and report to Johnson.

The conference was attended by over a thousand Indians representing the Chipewyan, Mississauga, Cree, Fox, Huron, Ottawa, Potawatomi, Winnebago and Dakota or Sioux nations. A number of smaller meetings took place during the latter part of June, but on 3 July the tribes gathered in a great formal convention. This was reported to be an extremely successful event, with a great deal accomplished and gifts valued at more than £5000 sterling given to the Indians. It was the value of the gifts and the lack of authorization for the conference that landed Robert in trouble, in spite of his good intentions.

It was not very long before the Governor and the new Commissary clashed over the division of responsibility and authority concerning Indian affairs and trade. After a disagreement, Lieutenant Roberts wrote a very detailed report to Johnson which resulted in another loud confrontation. Robert finally ordered his arrest and sent him to Gage in irons on charges of insubordination. Arriving at New York, Lieutenant Roberts probably informed Gage that the Governor had considerably exceeded his authority and grossly mismanaged government funds; he may have even suggested that he was involved in treasonous activities. Presumably it was only the disreputable character of Benjamin Roberts that restrained Gage from taking action immediately to get rid of Robert.

About that time Gage received a sworn affidavit from Nathaniel Potter, Robert's secretary, whom Robert had recently discharged. He had departed for England on 29 August and died at sea. This document, sworn at Montreal by an angered and embittered man probably seeking revenge,

---

* See *Northwest Passage*, Appendix Edition, court-martial appendix, page 76.

was also of questionable validity. It did support accusations made by Roberts, however, and taken together these documents gave Gage the excuse he needed. On 19 October he issued an order for Robert's arrest on the charge of treason. A copy of the order for arrest is on the next page.

The arrest warrant was received at Fort Michilimackinac on 6 December, and Robert was immediately confined to a cell in the stockade, "a small fireless room open to the full inclemency of that freezing weather." There he remained throughout the winter, transport south to Detroit and on to Montreal being impossible at that time of year. The traders and Indians were in arms over the arrest, and many in the garrison were also sympathetic. Because of the nature of the charges and concern that he might attempt to escape, he was securely bound with seven-pound leg irons, and his sentries were doubled to ensure his continued confinement. Robert and his wife were frequently threatened and often deprived of food and basic necessities of life, according to his statements afterwards.

Finally on 21 May he was placed in the hold of the schooner *Gladwin*, still confined in leg irons, and thus transported first to Detroit then to Niagara and Montreal. He arrived at Montreal on 17 July 1768. At his trial he made the following statement.

I was thrown into the hold of the vessel, upon the ballast stones, still in irons; and in this manner transported the whole distance. When they were taken off, the weight of them was so considerable, and they were fastened so tightly, that my legs were bent. From the pain I suffered, together with the cold, the bone in my right leg was split, and marrow forced its way out through the skin.

The leg irons were removed by the post commander at Niagara, who stated that he was shocked at the condition of the prisoner and expressed surprise that he had lived through the ordeal. From this time, Robert walked with a limp.

From the treatment Robert received, it seems probable that his accusers had little intention of going through with the formality of a trial. Death in custody would have removed the requirement, and any suggestion of harsh treatment would soon be forgotten; an attempted escape, though to relieve his torment, would have firmly established his guilt. A lesser man might have tried to escape and died in the attempt. Robert was a strong individual, however, and had the respect and support of a large number of officers and friends. After Fort Niagara it was difficult, if not impossible, for his enemies to make any further moves to harm him physically.

By His Excellency the Hon'ble Thomas Gage, General and Commander-in-Chief of all His Majesty's Forces in North America &c., &c., &c.

To Captain Lieutenant Spiesmaker, or Officer Commanding two Companies of His Majesty's 2nd Battalion of the 60th or Royal American Regiment doing Duty at Michilimackinac.

Whereas it has appeared from divers Informations, that Major Robert Rogers, Commandant of Michilimackinac, hath contrary to the Trust reposed in him, and his Sworn Allegiance to His Sovereign Majesty George the Third, been holding Dangerous and Traitorous Conferences with His Majesty's Enemies, and forming designs of a most dangerous nature, with intent to raise Commotions and Disturbances in the upper Countries, and to kindle a War betwixt the Savages and His Majesty's Subjects.

I do therefore by these Presents instantly divest the said Robert Rogers of all Command whatever of His Majesty's Fort and Garrison of Michilimackinac, and order that the Command thereof shall devolve to you the Senior Officer of the Companies of the Royal American Regiment doing Duty there; of which all Officers, Non-Commissioned Officers, Private Soldiers and others His Majesty's Subjects at Michimackinac have notice hereby, and are to obey you accordingly, as His Majesty's Chief Commander of the Fort and Garrison of Michilimackinac. And I do hereby order and require you, and you are hereby Ordered, Authorized and required immediately upon the receipt of this to Seize the Person of the said Robert Rogers as a Traitor to his King and Country, and hold him in sure and safe custody, till a proper opportunity offers of conveying him with sufficient Escort either to Montreal or Detroit; And this you are to perform at all events and even to make use of Force, if Absolutely necessary thereto. And for the doing of this, and every part thereof, this shall be to you and all Persons concerned a sufficient Warrant and Authority; And all, and every part of the Garrison under your Command, and all others His Majesty's good Subjects are hereby required to be Aiding and Assisting to you in the execution of this Matter, as they shall answer the same at their Peril.

Given under my hand & Seal at Head Quarters in the City of New York this 19th day of October 1767

Thos. Gage

Robert in Chains

On his arrival at Montreal, he was kept in close custody awaiting his trial while the prosecution prepared their case and gathered evidence against him. A letter to his wife, dated 25 August 1768, has survived and is printed on Pages 164–5. It appears that they were together until Niagara, after which Robert sent her home to her parents because she was carrying their unborn child.

On 20 October 1768, some three months after he arrived in the city, a general court martial was convened at Montreal, and Robert was formally charged according to the Articles of Accusation on the opposite page. The charge of treason suggested in the arrest warrant was changed to mutiny, probably to avoid a public trial. It is likely that there was insufficient evidence to support the original charge.

During the trial Robert acted on his own behalf as in this period for the charges laid, the accused was allowed legal counsel in preparing his case but not during the trial itself. At the outset Robert stated that he had been denied his personal papers and certain principal witnesses necessary to his defence, despite assurances from General Gage that he would be allowed every

The General Court Martial of Major Robert Rogers
Articles of Accusation

1st Article

For having contrary to his Duty and Allegiance to his King and Country, formed Designs of a Traiterous and Dangerous nature of Deserting to the French, after plundering the Traders and others of His Majesty's Subjects, and Stirring up the Indians against His Majesty and His Government.

2nd Article

For holding a Correspondence with His Majesty's Enemies.

3rd Article

For Disobedience of his Orders and Instructions during his Command at Michilimackinac in having undertaken expensive Schemes and projects, and lavished away money amongst the Savages, contrary to his Instructions, but Conformable to the Council given in a Letter to him by an Officer in the French Service and formerly a Captain in His Majesty's Army.

consideration. In fact, many of his papers had been delivered to Gage before the trial and were in all probability deliberately withheld. Robert stated that he wished to continue with the trial, however, because of the length of his confinement and desire to clear his name. After hearing the witnesses and evidence for the prosecution, he defended himself by denying all charges and justifying every action made to look sinister by the evidence. He supplied an exact accounting of all the expenses incurred during his tour of duty as Governor and presented witnesses to his character and conduct. The trial concluded on 31 October. The findings were as follows:

The Court, having taken into consideration the Articles of Accusation preferred against Major Robert Rogers, together with the Evidence in Support of the Charge, as well as what the Prisoner had to offer in his defence, Is of the Opinion, that Major Robert Rogers is not Guilty of any one of the Articles laid to His Charge: and therefore doth acquit him of the same.

Val. Jones
Lieut. Colonel to the 52nd Regiment
President

H. T. Cramahe, Depy J. Ade.

My dearest —

I Received your letter deated at Albany the Second of this Instant — and am happy to find that you were in a Fair way to git home to your Agreable Family at portsmouth.

I also Received the letter you mention To a have wrote me from Oswago — and am much obliged to Captain Worthan for his polite treatment to you while you was at that garison.

In regard to the place of my confinment it is made as agreable for me as possiblie it could by Colo. Jones the commanding officer at this place — I am lodged in that house that was the Marquis devodreels — and have good appartments consined me — but I am still kept under Strict guard.

I dont yet know what time my Tryal will come on. I am informed that Spies make esuly and Roberts Set out from Michelemakenao the 3rd Instant by way of Detroit. I Suppose they will be hear Some time in September — they are trying to do everything that is in their power to hurt me, as is also two great men in New York provance.

I was under the needsessity of Sending a Man to New England not many days Since for theme cartificates that I have already wrote to you about As they must be had — I also wrote to Mr. Livermore desiring his assistance and hope he will come For Should I be cleard I have the fariest actions against My accusers.

I could most heartily wish it was in my powar to be with you to attend you in your presant condision, but my Dearest that cannot be at Least for Some months — but I don doubt you will have a good time, and I hop a Son — that he may Inherit your Fortun — and be a comfert to you in after times.

I do intend going to England as soon as I am cleard but shall first go to portsmouth and that is great post [part] of my desire in having Mr. Livermore to assist me, as I cannot, will attend the actions, and no doubt all the witnesses will be hear at my tryal and he could carry them on as well for me as if I was present.

devodreels: de Vaudreuil's

Robert Rogers

I have wrote to Quebec for a loyer he is last night come to town. I shall stop hear and not close my letter till I see him, and shall let you have in the other part of it what ever occcures that may be worth communicating.

Mr. Williams the loyar I have just Seen. He is clever and I am much Incouraged by him. I dont doubt but I shall be Honourably Accquited and then I Shall have the Happiness of Seeing you this winter. I hop Mr. Livermore will come if he can be hear by the first of october it will be time Enough.

My Duty to your Father & Mother. My Best wishes to Jeanny & Polly — and all Friends I desire to be remmembered to and believe me to be with Esteam my Dearest Dear your Ever

Affeconat Loving Husbant

Robt Rogers

Two copies exist of the official transcript of the proceedings. One is located in the Canadian National Archives at Ottawa; the other is in the Public Records Office in London, England. Complete copies may also be found in the books *Treason? At Michilimackinac* by David Armour, and the special appendix edition of *Northwest Passage* by Kenneth Roberts.

General Gage was clearly disappointed, perhaps enraged by the findings of the Court. Although Robert was acquitted of the charges, Gage did not authorize his release from close custody until February 1769, some fourteen months after his arrest. He was then permitted the freedom of the city though still held under open arrest and forbidden to travel. He was not granted a final discharge until 3 June, and only after the letter on the next page had been received from England, compelling Gage to discharge him seventeen months after his arrest and eight months following his acquittal. This was a poor reward for one who had faithfully served his country.

The portion of the letter that implies some reason to suspect him may have been inserted to protect Gage and the Crown from legal action. Considering the evidence there was no reason for such a statement, unless Gage had embellished the situation in his reports. It seems surprising that it would take a full three months for a letter to come from England and another to be sent to Quebec to order his release. Gage had lost this battle and he was not pleased.

The most damaging evidence against Robert had been a letter allegedly written by Captain Hopkins, a former ranger who went into the French service at the end of the French and Indian War. The letter was dated 9 April

1766, some months before Robert took up his appointment as governor. From documents dated 13 May, it is clear that Gage knew of the letter, perhaps even before Robert, and such knowledge, so soon after the letter was supposedly written suggests cnspiracy. The letter was signed "Maryland". Robert never refused knowledge of the letter or its contents. It simply suggests that if Robert were to consider changing his allegiance on account of poor treatment or injustice at the hands of his superiors, he would probably be well received.

An interesting point concerning the charge of inciting the Indians is that there was little reason for the French to want trouble in the Northwest. They had ceded all Louisiana to Spain at the end of the French and Indian War, and there was never any suggestion that Robert might wish or intend to desert to Spain. If the French had truly wanted the suggested unrest, they would have more actively supported the uprising of Pontiac.

Concerning other aspects of the charges, Robert may have been technically wrong, but the evidence was clearly exaggerated by Gage and Johnson with the express purpose of getting rid of him. In this they were at least in part successful, as the stigma of the charges remained with him the rest of his life despite the findings of the court. The book *Robert Rogers of the Rangers* by John Cuneo convincingly suggests that Gage had an aversion to Robert that was deep, personal, unfair and unrelenting.

The records indicate that Robert always acted in the best interests of the Crown and was truly endeavoring to open up the West. He presented gifts to the Indians only when necessary according to custom and in quantities considerably less than the French had given. He had consistently worked for peace among the tribes and had gained the respect of the Indians and traders of the area.

Elizabeth clearly missed Robert during his long confinement and wanted to be near him. The letter below, dated 24 December 1768, gives a clear indication of how he felt. Their son, named Arthur after his maternal grandfather, was born in Concord and baptized by his grandfather on 12 February 1769.

After his release in June, Robert briefly visited his family in New Hampshire before sailing for England on 18 July. He arrived in London in September and shortly thereafter petitioned the Crown for a Baronetcy and a pension as a "just and reasonable reward for services." Although he was presented at Court and granted an audience, his petition failed to receive favourable consideration. In the succeeding months he submitted a series of petitions for back pay and compensation for expenses for the Indian Conferences and expeditions. The petition for back pay was granted in January 1770 and he received his salary as the Commandant of Fort Michilimackinac for the entire four year period (18 December 1765 to 21 December 1769), a total of £3000. This enabled him to hold his creditors

My Dear Betsy,

I Received your letter of 25th Oct[r]. By the last post, and it Realey gives pleasure to know you are in perfect helth, and it wase obliging in you to write me so paticular — I am sorry you give your Selfe the least uneasyness about your not comming with me to this place and I am convinced that you have done everything for me and much more than you could had you have come to this place.

I have no News as yet from General Gage. Colonol Jones tould me this day that he expected the York post next week, and if his Excellency is pleased to Release me out of confinment, I shall Emediently Set out for portsmouth, and you cannot emagin what pleasure it would give me to be with you at this time when my presence might be of some comfort to you.

My dearest Betsy keep up your spirits for be ashured that my fondness for canot be altered Either by time or accident and nothing that in my powar lays Shall be wanting to contribute to your Ease of mind and hapiness, Remember what I tould you at Neagra when we parted — be asured I will abide by it — pray don't Vex your Self about me, for my Enemys have done me a pease of Service by confining — there is not an officer in this place but what are my friends and I hop to soon have it in my powar to Revenge on my Enemys.

I have wrote by this post to all my friends in England, and dont in the least doubt but I shall son have a better government than Michelemakenae, but as I hope Soon to see you shall leave the particular Eseptations that I have till I can tell you by word and I am, my Dearest Dear your

Affactonat Husband

Robert Rogers

Mrs. Rogers.

at bay, but all attempts to obtain additional compensation from the Crown were blocked at every turn by Gage and his friends. The treasury refused to pay further expenses until Gage certified that they were justified, and this he steadfastly refused to do.

Holding liabilities exceeding £13,000, his creditors soon lost patience, and on 2 June 1770 Robert was committed to the Fleet Prison in London for debt. On 29 September he petitioned for a commission in the British East India Company, but the petition was denied as the Crown had decided that

Horse Guards, 1st March 1769

Sir,

The Proceedings of General Court Martial held in the City of Montreal, in the Province of Quebec, on Thursday the 20th, and continued by several Adjournments to Monday the 31st of October last, having been laid before the King, by which Court Martial Major Robert Rogers was tried upon three several Articles of Charge, to wit,

1st   "For having contrary to his Duty and Allegiance to his King and Country, formed Designs of a Traiterous and Dangerous nature of deserting to the French, after plundering the Traders and others of His Majesty's Subjects, and Stirring up the Indians against His Majesty and His Government."

2n   "For holding a Correspondence with His Majesty's Enemies."

3rd   "For Disobedience of his Orders and Instructions during his Command at Michilimackinac in having undertaken expensive Schemes and projects, and lavished away money amongst the Savages, contrary to his Instructions, but Conformable to the Council given in a Letter to him by an Officer in the French Service and formerly a Captain in His Majesty's Army."

I have the honour to acquaint you that His Majesty is pleased to approve the opinion of the Court in acquitting the said Major Robert Rogers of each of the said Articles of Charge and to Order that he be released from his confinement; At the same time it appears to His Majesty, that there was great reason to suspect the said Major Robert Rogers Entertaining an improper and dangerous Correspondence, which Suspicion the account afterwards given of his meditating an Escape tended to confirm.

I am with respect

Sir,

Your most humble Servant,

Charles Gould

His Excellency;
Major General Gage, Commanding in Chief
His Majesty's Forces in North America

no additional officers would be sent.* He was granted some compensation, a portion of his accounts for the Carver Expedition and his half pay as a retired Captain. This enabled him to pay some debts and obtain his release from prison.†

Very little is known of Robert's activities during the following sixteen months but it is likely that he was attempting to avoid his creditors while trying to gain some influence at Court. The only related item found from this period is an article in the *London Evening Post* dated 1 October 1771, reporting an encounter with a wanted highwayman. The thief was reaching into the coach for a wallet when Robert grabbed him, hauled him through the window and ordered the driver to go on. He collected a reward of £50 when the man was turned over to the authorities.

On 11 February 1772 Robert submitted a revised petition for a major expedition to search for the Northwest Passage. He trimmed his original (1765) projected requirements of 228 officers and men to 58 and the budget of £32,000 to £23,000. While the proposal received some encouragement from several men of influence, Robert could not get the necessary backing, and the petition failed. The route detailed in this petition was virtually the same as that followed by Lewis and Clark in 1803, about thirty years later. These explorers demonstrated that Robert's proposals were entirely reasonable as to route, time, supplies and to a large extent men and funding for such an expedition.

On 16 October Robert was again committed to the Fleet Prison for debt, and it was reported that he was in despair and drinking heavily. On 14 June he submitted a petition for a grant in North America of about sixty square miles in an attempt to free himself from his desperate plight. It also failed. (The document has been attached as Appendix VIII for its historical significance and for its endorsements.) Although family sources suggest that his brother James (2–3) gave a bond for his debts and he was released later that month, this cannot be confirmed from other sources, and he may

---

* English and French Traders arrived in India about 1600 and took sides in the local wars in exchange for trade concessions and territory. The country was in political chaos with assorted rajahs and nabobs fighting each other. By the 1740's the French *Compagnie des Indes Orientales* and the British East India Company each ruled several towns and had armies made up of European officers and native soldiers (sepoys). In war both countries sent regular units to bolster company forces in India.

† A person who could not pay his debts was harshly treated under the legal system of the day. Insolvent debtors were confined in the Fleet Prison until their debts were paid, an ironic situation as they could not work while so incarcerated. Frequently their families accompanied them, and it must have been an interesting place indeed.

have remained in prison until mid-1774. Robert later claimed that between July 1773 and March 1774 he was in the service of the Dey of Algiers as a mercenary and fought in two pitched battles. No evidence has ever been found to support this claim, and it may have been a fabrication to conceal the embarrassing length of his incarceration in the Fleet Prison. Although the letter below mentions the possibility of his arrest, he may still have been in prison when he wrote to his wife on 7 April 1774:

My dear Betsy

In my last letter to Mr. Livermore I sent him a particular Detail of my proceedings from the time I came to England up till last Summor, which no doubt he made you acquainted wth.

And as I have a good oppertunity to convay this Letter Safely to you without any Expence / by the Revnd Mr. Parker / who sailes for Boston the 9th Instant, I shall let you know my progress Sinc General Gages arival in London —

I was advised by my councal to let him alone till the Act of Insolvency took place which is Expected to be in May next and thereby clear my Selfe from the Incolance of creditors that might be indust by General Gages friends to arest me

but on General Gages being apointed Governor of Boston, my council advised me to first send him a memoral, which I did and the coppy of my moral as also General Gages letter in answer are anext to this letter, as also a coppy of my memoral to thier Lordships of his Majestys treasurey, wrote them in consequance of General Gages letter, I have no answer to the last memoral as yet but shall have one tomorow — if it should not be favourable General Gage will be arested on Saturday next for damages, etc.

I shall write you again tomorrow as I expect that I shall Easely have an answer from Lord North which you shall have Vesbatom in my letter tomorrow.

My love to Ally — Mr Mrs Livermore Mrs Mr Sargent, And believe me to be your Most Affacionat friend and

faithfull Husband

Robert Rogers

Vesbatom: verbatim (?)

In the letter to Gage, Robert humbly asked that he approve the accounts already submitted to the Crown. Gage was temporarily in England on leave and General Haldimand was acting in his place as commander-in-chief of British forces in America.* Gage denied his request. On 8 April, as Gage was preparing to return to America, the sheriff served him with a writ demanding £20,000, a suit by Robert that delayed his departure. This civil action alleged trespass, assault, false imprisonment and unlawful conversion of goods from 1767 to 1769. The amount of the suit was based on the ill treatment he had suffered at the hands of Gage's agents and the loss of his goods. Robert later claimed that he had brought the suit at the insistence of his creditors, but he may have intended to compel the Crown to give attention to his petitions in order to spare Gage the indignity of a civil trial. The suit was unsuccessful, however, as the Court found that Gage had acted properly based on the evidence available to him at the time.

Shortly thereafter the Bankruptcy Act was passed, and upon application Robert finally gained freedom from his creditors. He was released from the Fleet Prison on 4 August 1774, after almost twenty-two months according to some accounts. In the following months Robert continued to press for what he saw as just compensation for his services, but all his petitions failed. In April 1775 he again petitioned for an appointment in the British East India Company but was rejected as before.

About this time Parliament voted an award of £30,000 to the explorer who would discover a northern passage through North America, and the dream of the Northwest Passage was reborn. Robert found a new friend and patron in Richard Whitworth, the member of Parliament for Stafford Borough, to whom he appealed for support for a renewed project. Whitworth, unfortunately, was not a patron of political prominence in the House of Commons, but he was enthusiastic for the proposal. One of Robert's petitions to Lord Dartmouth succeeded about this time, and he was granted the retirement pay of a major. Now having sufficient funds to return to America, Robert left the funding for the expedition in his new patron's hands and prepared to travel home full of expectations of success. Before leaving England, however, he was advised by his political friends that he would do well to attempt to repair the breach with Gage if he wished to accomplish anything in America.

Robert sailed from Gravesend on the brigantine *Baltimore* on 4 June 1775 and landed at Baltimore, Maryland, in early August. Fighting had broken out in the Revolutionary War, and his return was viewed with suspicion by both sides. Many thought him a military adventurer eager to sell his services to the highest bidder; a few believed him to be a British spy,

---

* See notes on General Gage and General Haldimand in Historical Figures, Annex c.

as he was drawing the half pay of a retired officer; others considered him a traitor who had escaped justice at his court martial. These suspicions arose from the grudging respect for his abilities held by both sides.

Some historians suggest that he was already a broken man, drinking heavily and probably oblivious to events taking place around him. The evidence suggests otherwise. He was heedless of events because he was utterly obsessed by his dream. In spite of suspicions and speculations he was probably completely absorbed in his project and engaged in seeking volunteers and support for his proposed expedition, an endeavour he could not discuss.

On arrival Robert went to the Congress at Philadelphia to seek permission to travel in the Colonies and settle his affairs. He had not seen his wife and son, then living at Portsmouth, for more than six years. Permission was granted, but on 22 September the Pennsylvania Committee of Safety arrested him. He was paroled on his solemn declaration "not to bear arms against these United Colonies." He was also offered and urged to accept a commission in the Continental Army with the rank of brigadier general. He refused, stating that he was only seeking land upon which to settle and establish a quiet life. His political views at this time are not known; he was probably sympathetic to the American cause, constrained by his sworn allegiance to the King and motivated by his dreams of an expedition that could only be funded by the Crown.

On 5 October, Robert wrote to General Gage and Sir William Howe* to tender his non-military services to the Crown. From the correspondence, it seems he was to be encouraged, but no immediate action was taken on his offer. On 13 November, he called on Doctor Eleazar Wheelock, president of Dartmouth College, to offer his services in seeking land for the College in exchange for a place to settle. (It was in this interview that he claimed to have been in the service of the Dey of Algiers.) Wheelock distrusted him and reported the entire incident to General Washington.† Robert wrote to Washington on 12 December requesting an interview but was refused. Washington ordered that he be closely watched; it seems, that he also distrusted Robert. The letter to Elizabeth below was sent from Medford and dated 17 December 1775.

In two letters to Whitworth during this period, Robert expressed considerable apprehension that any expedition was impossible "without a reconciliation between Great Britain & hur Colonies." He asked for support in obtaining a position in the British East India Company, a pension, or some employment to enable him to support himself and his family, at least until matters were resolved in America. On 4 February

* See Historical Figures, Annex C.
† See Historical Figures, Annex C.

My dearest Betsy,

In my last I tould you that I was going to lay my pass before General Washington which I did the 12th at this place by a letter. Inclosed the copy and the different minuts made theron by the Provincial Congress at New York and New Hampshire and this morning had the satisfaction to have my permit approved of. The answer came by General Sullivan who sent for me to dine with him at winter hill and immediately I left the camp. I am now on my way to Albany and shall make all the expedition that I can but must call at Londonderry for some old deeds that wer forgot there as I came down. From thence through Peterboro. I could not get anythings for Ally, neither did I see Blodget at all and it was necessary for me to come from Medford the moment my business was done and of course don't send you any money. You must do as well as you can till I return which will be as soon as possible, for I will make the greatest haste in my power to get my cash and return with it. It was lucky that I went to Medford and from there wrote to General Washington as many persons had given a very unfavorable representation concerning my coming to America. Some had wrote that I had been to Canada and it was certain that I was second in command to General Carleton but when General Sullivan was sent to Examin into the matter I cleared up every point so that I shall have no further trouble. Stay in America as long as I will.

Please to make my compliments to Mr. Peperill and his lady. My love to Ally and accept of the most sincerest regards from Your ever affectionat and faithful husband

Robt Rogers

1776, Sir Henry Clinton* interviewed Robert and offered him a commission in the British service. He was forced to refuse because of the parole he had given to Congress, and he departed to continue his travels through the northern colonies.

On 25 June, Robert was arrested in South Amboy. Some historians have suggested that Robert expressed a desire to tender his services to Congress at this time but was told that the offer was no longer valid. The truth of this suggestion is not known, but it seems unlikely. There is no

* See Historical Figures, Annex C.

evidence that he ever considered shifting loyalties, in spite of the treatment he had received. Colonial authorities, however, were suspicious and believed he was probably spying for the British, although concrete evidence was never produced. He could not divulge his plans for a Northwest Passage expedition to the Revolutionary Committees, and given their sensitivity to British intentions, it is hardly surprising if they saw treason in all his actions. He was taken under guard to Philadelphia and confined near Independence Hall at the time the Declaration of Independence was being signed. On 5 July, Congress ordered that he be sent to the New Hampshire Assembly for final disposition. Robert considered that these events had freed him of his parole and was consequently able to accept the British offer. On 8 July he escaped from custody as they were preparing to move him. He fled to New York and joined the British colours.

On 6 August 1776 Sir William Howe presented Robert with a commission in the rank of lieutenant colonel and a warrant empowering him to raise a regiment of rangers for the British Army from loyalist refugees to be known as the Queen's American Rangers. By late summer he had recruited close to six companies and had located his headquarters on Long Island, New York. These rangers were not of same the caliber as those of the previous war. Many were farmers and townspeople who scarcely knew one end of a gun from the other, and few had any military experience. Many of those he would have recruited, men of his former ranger companies, were already on the opposing side. A number of his former captains, including John Stark and Moses Hazen, were now senior officers in the Continental Army.* In spite of his men's lack of experience, he undertook to prepare his unit for action.

When General Howe marched on General Washington that fall, the rangers were present. On 21 October the regiment, about 300 strong, was detached to occupy Mamaroneck, New York, on the right flank of the proposed route of the main body. That evening they were attacked by a force of 750 Americans. Although there was considerable confusion on both sides, the rangers stood their ground, and the enemy was forced to withdraw. The rangers were reinforced the next day, and the following week Washington suffered a major defeat at the Battle of White Plains. From this point the Americans adopted the hit-and-run tactics that had already proved to be effective against European methods of warfare. Robert's rangers were employed as infantry, and Robert became disenchanted with the role assigned to his regiment. The Americans were employing tactics he would have used, and Howe refused to listen to his recommendations. This seems strange considering Howe's experience

---

* See Appendix I and Historical Figures, Annex C, for details.

during the previous war, but the British seemed to be unable to learn from "provincials". Early in 1777, Robert either was removed from or willingly relinquished his command.

Robert was first succeeded in command of the Queen's Rangers by Lieutenant Colonel Christopher French and later by Major James Wemyass. By August 1777 the regiment was up to full strength, and on 11 September they played a significant role in the Battle of Brandywine, an action fought just before the British capture of Philadelphia. In that engagement the rangers singlehandedly defeated two American brigades, suffering almost a fifth of the total British casualties, including fourteen of twenty-one officers. For their actions the Queen's Rangers received the following Letter of Distinguished Conduct.

> *The Commander-in-Chief desires to convey to the Officers and men of the Queen's Rangers his approbation and acknowledgement of their spirited and gallant behaviour in the engagement of the eleventh instant and to assure them how well he is satisfied with their conduct on that day. His Excellency only regrets their having suffered so very much in the gallant execution of their duty.*

Wemyass was wounded on 4 October 1777 at the Battle of Germantown, an action in which the rangers again played a distinguished role. He was succeeded by Major John Graves Simcoe, who commanded the regiment for the remainder of the war.* At about this time regimental strength was increased to twelve companies, one of which was cavalry, and they continued to distinguish themselves in several engagements during the war. The unit received regimental colours and was permitted to have the title "First American Regiment" attached to their name through general orders published 2 May 1779, "To reward their faithful services and spirited conduct on several occasions." This was an unusual distinction for a colonial regiment. On 25 December 1782 "The Queen's Rangers, 1st American Regiment, Cavalry and Infantry, with the Gracious approval of His Majesty, were honourably enrolled in the British Army,"† another unusual occurrence.

The corps was reduced in October 1783 at the conclusion of the war but reestablished on 20 December 1791 by Simcoe. They built Fort York

---

* After the Constitutional Act of 1791, John Graves Simcoe was appointed the first Lieutenant Governor of Upper Canada. See Historical Figures, Annex C.

† Quoted in *Rogers' Rangers* by H. M. Jackson, and in *The Queen's York Rangers* by S. H. Bull.

at the present site of Toronto and carried out other duties in the defence and development of Upper Canada. Several units through the years have carried the corps name, the current one being the Queen's York Rangers (First American Regiment). The original colours were purchased from the Simcoe estate in 1923, and they hung in the Metropolitan Toronto Library for more than fifty years. They were later repaired and presented to the current regiment on 18 April 1975.

Elizabeth Rogers petitioned the Assembly of New Hampshire to grant her a divorce on the grounds of desertion and infidelity (as shown in her petition on the following page). An act granting the divorce was passed by the Assembly on 4 March. On 19 November 1778 the Assembly passed an act naming a number of persons, including Robert, who were forbidden to return to its soil. Any who did so were to be seized and escorted to British territory. A second return would result in death.

Elizabeth's petition may not have been heartfelt in spite of her statement, as she did save most of the letters Robert wrote to her from as early as 1761. Many of these have been an invaluable source of information about this period and about Robert's life. Over time many were sold at auctions to private collectors, and a few have been quoted in this work. Had she really felt as wronged as she stated, she would surely have destroyed these documents along with anything else of her life with Robert.

A short time after the divorce Elizabeth married Captain John Roach, a native of Cork, Ireland. He had been master of an English vessel engaged in the fur trade but had sometime before abandoned life at sea. The timing of this marriage suggests that John was perhaps the real reason for the divorce petition, but there is no evidence to confirm this supposition. The couple lived on the Rogers' estate in Concord that had been transferred to Elizabeth's father Arthur Browne in 1761 and then to Elizabeth on his death in 1773. According to several sources, John was famous for his "unholy expletives and excessive potations" (swearing and heavy drinking). Although they were married over thirty years, some documents suggest that this marriage was not a happy one. John died at Concord in May 1811, followed two years later by Elizabeth in 1813 at the age of 72 years. The estate then passed to Robert's only son and remained in the family until purchased by Governor Hill of New Hampshire in 1833.

Few details of Robert's activities from the time he relinquished command of the Queen's Rangers in 1777 until the year 1779 are known. From the papers of General Frederick Haldimand,* Governor of Quebec and Commander of the Northern Department, it has been established that he was in Quebec during October 1778, seeking authority to raise a new regiment

* See Historical Figures, Annex C.

State of New   *To the Honble The Council and*
Hampshire   *House of Representatives in General*
                                    Assembly convened Feb^{ry} ye 11th 1778.

The Petition of Elizabeth Rogers of Portsmouth in said State
Humbly sheweth:

That your Petitioner some time in June A.D. 1761 entered into
Marriage with Col^l Robert Rogers a person at that time of some Character
and distinction (tho' your petitioner married him solely in Obedience to the
will of her parents, friends etc.). That after tarrying with her six days —
he left her, went off to South-Carolina, and there remained seventeen
months, without making any provision for a house or housekeeping — He
then returned tarried four or five months — & went to De-troit where
he remained about a twelve-month leaving her unprovided (save by her
father) as before — He came back — staid a few days — and then went
to England, tarried eighteen months, (she unprovided still) and once more
returned. Notwithstanding all which — your Petitioner desirous of
doing her duty, and in hopes of winning him by gentleness and condescen-
sion, against the remonstrances of many of her dearest connections &
went with him to Mishelmakinow an indian settlement near Lake-
superior — To paint, in their true colours, the sufferings of your
Petitioner during her stay (which was near two years) in that remote and
lonely region, would be a task beyond her ability — 'Tis enough to say that
she underwent every hardship, and endured every species of ill-treatment
which infidelity, uncleaness & drunken barbarity could inflict from one,
bound by the tenderest & most sacred ties to succour, protect and comfort
her. To mention all the particulars would neither consist with the modesty
of the sex, or the respect due your Honours — And to recount all the
tedious steps of this detested pilgrimage would be trespassing on your
Honor's patience Heaven, at last enabled ye Pet^r to return to her friends
after an absence of almost two years.

In the mean time he was taken up and confined of being guilty of High-
Treason but on being sent to Montreal & tried was acquitted and once
more came back to Portsmouth He tarried only a few days — and sailed
for England where he continued for seven years —Your Pet^r remained all

that time at her Father's by whom She was supported 'till his death — Since which she has been obliged to support herself & son not only without the least assistance from His unnatural parent, but under all the disadvantages that arise from this ungrateful Connection.

The last time your Petitioner saw him, which was about two years since, he was in a situation which, as her peace and safety forced her then to shun & fly from him so Decency now forbids her to say more upon so indelicate a subject. — He has since joined the Ministerial Army — and so put it out of his power — even should he incline, ever to return to this Town or to her again.

To sum up all, your petitioner has been during this unhappy seventeen years as miserable as is possible in such connection not only destitute of all the comforts and advantages peculiar to such a state — but undergoing the sorest and heaviest evils.

And is now rendered unable to change her situation or transact any business of importance — For all which reasons and many others which might be mentioned some of which your Honor's own minds will readily suggest — Your Petitioner humbly intreats she may be forever separated — (in this life) from Col' Robert Rogers — and that your Honors would order an act of divorce to issue between them, a vinculo-matrimonii — and your Petitioner, as in duty bound, will ever pray —

Dated Portsmouth January 26th 1778 —

Elizabeth Rogers

(Feb. 12. 1778, hearing ordered for Feb. 17.)
(Feb. 26, 1778, petition granted.)

from the loyalist refugees (as seen from the letter below). Haldimand was already having problems with existing regiments and, seeing no need for another of dubious reliability, denied the petition. His attitude toward Robert was perhaps coloured by his having been a subordinate of General Gage for several years.

Family correspondence suggests that Robert spent some time in England in early 1779. By April he was back in New York with instructions that he was again to be employed. On 1 May Sir Henry Clinton issued a warrant to him to raise a new regiment to be known as the King's Rangers.

To his Excellency Frederick Haldimand, Captain General & Governor in Chief in, and over the Province of Quebec, and the territories depending thereon in America, Vice Admiral of the same, and Lieutenant General of his Majesty's Forces commanding the northern District &c, &c, &c.

The Memorial and Petition of Robert Rogers Leut. Cold Commandant of the Queen's American Rangers humbly sheweth

That there are on the frontiers of new England & New York many loyal & faithful Subjects of his Majesty who are desirous of assisting him in the present war against the Rebels, but are so narrowly watched and garded by Committees and partys of the Rebel Army that they cannot get into New York, but can make their way into this Province; This being represented to his Excellency General Clinton he advised to apply to your Excellency for authority to raise them by way of this Province, and knowing likewise that your memorialist was well acquainted with the frontiers aforesaid, has permitted him to come into Quebec to lay the same before your Excellency.

Your Memorialist therefore, anxious of rendering further services to his King & desirous of distinguishing himself under the Command of so able and experienced an officer as your Excellency, humbly prays your Excellency to take the above into consideration, and be pleased to grant to your Memorialist a Warrant to raise two or more Battallions from the frontiers of the Colonies aforesaid, upon the same footing the Queen's American Rangers were raised at New York, and to serve under the Command of your Excellency —

And your memorialist as bound shall ever pray

Robert Rogers

Quebec Octo' 24th 1778

State of New Hampshire
An Act to dissolve the marriage between
Robert Rogers & Elizabeth, his wife.

Whereas Elizabeth Rogers of Portsmouth, in the County of Rockingham, and State aforesaid, hath petitioned the General Assembly for the said State, setting forth that she was married to the said Robert Rogers about seventeen years ago; for the greater part of this time he had absented himself from and totally neglected to support and maintain her and had, in the most flagrant manner, in a variety of ways, violated the marriage contract but especially by infidelity to her bed; For which reasons praying that a divorce from the said Rogers, a vinculo-matrimonii, might be granted. The principal facts contained in said petition being made to appear, upon a full hearing thereof.

Therefore, be it enacted by the Council and House of Representatives for the State in General Assembly convened, That the Bonds of Matrimony between the said Robert and Elizabeth be and are hereby dissolved.

(Passed by Assembly 28th February, and the Council 4th March.)

This regiment was to be employed in harassing the enemy, an objective Robert knew well. The initial plant in his mind was for the First Battalion to be stationed at Halifax while the second was at Quebec. Unfortunately no one told the local area commanders, and they became understandably upset.

To raise a new regiment of 1300 all ranks at this point in the war would have been a considerable feat even for Robert. That he was entrusted with such a task offers proof that at this time he was not the weak, unreliable individual presented by some historians. The British were at times incompetent, but they were never fools, throwing away on wild schemes money needed elsewhere. It is also very unlikely that they would fund such an endeavour just to be rid of him.

All the loyalist regiments were well below establishment, and there was fierce competition for the small number of available recruits. Although the regiment was part of the Central Department and under the personal patronage of Clinton, Robert sent his brother James (who had been commissioned to command the Second Battalion) into Quebec to recruit

Lieutenant Colonel Robert Rogers

Sir

You are hereby authorized and empowered to raise for His Majesty's Service Two Battalions of able bodied Rangers, each Battalion to be composed of one Major, nine Captains, one Captain Lieutenant, Nine Lieutenants, Ten Ensigns, one Adjutant, one Quarter Master, One Surgeon, Thirty Serjeants, Thirty Corporals, ten Drummers and Five Hundred and thirty Privates, to be divided into Ten Companies, each to consist of one Captain, one Lieutenant, one Ensign, Three Serjeants, Three Corporals, one Drummer, and fifty three Privates, who will be engaged to carry arms under my Orders, or the Orders of the Commander-in-Chief of His Majesty's Forces for the time being, for Two years, or if required, during the continuance of the present Rebellion in North America, to receive the same Pay, and be under the same Discipline as His Majesty's Regular Troops.

The Officers to be approved of by me, and as their Appointments by Commission will depend upon their Success in Recruiting, They are to be instructed to raise the following Numbers to entitle them hereto — vis. A Captain Thirty-two Men, a Lieutenant Sixteen Men, and an Ensign Twelve Men, and is to be made known to them that their Pay will not commence untill half the above number raised and approved.

In like manner when Men raised in either Battalion sufficient to compleat four Companies, a Major will be commissioned to such Battalion, and a Commission as Lieutenant Colonel Commandant of both Battalions will be given you Six Hundred Men being raised.

The same Bounty will be allowed to each Man Inlisted and approved as is given to the Provincial Corps.

All Officers Civil and Military and others His Majesty's liege Subjects, are hereby required to be aiding and assisting you and all Concerned in the Execution of the above Service, for which this shall be to you and them a sufficient warrant and Authority.

Signed at Head Quarters, New York, May 1ˢᵗ 1779.

Henry Clinton

---

from the loyalist refugees. James arrived at Montreal in July on the brigantine *Hawke* and soon ran afoul of the Governor. Haldimand still saw no need for another regiment and denied James permission to recruit in his area of responsibility for a corps over which he would have little or no control. That James arrived with a warrant when Robert had been denied permission for the same thing only a year earlier must have infuriated the Governor. He made it clear the King's Rangers were unwelcome guests and strongly suggested that Robert recall his officers. He would temporarily permit them to receive recruits sent from the lower colonies, but the unit was not to be raised in Quebec. He also stated that he had no authority or funds to provide support. By early September, the rangers were stationed at Fort Saint Johns on the Richelieu River (now Saint Jean, Quebec).

Robert was aboard the frigate HMS *Bloud* on his way to Halifax when a naval engagement at Penobscot took place on 13 August 1779. This British victory forced the Americans to abandon their efforts to capture Fort George. It is probably the last action in the war in which Robert participated.

During the winter he arrived in Quebec, claiming to have raised 700 rangers in Nova Scotia. It turned out that the number was less than fifty, and in the process he had incurred an enormous debt. He wrote several letters to Haldimand over the course of the winter, one of which has been attached as Appendix V to section 2–3. In this memorial, he recommended that James be promoted to the command of another corps under the Governor's patronage, and requested that all recruits for the rangers be so assigned and not held for other units. In response Haldimand suggested that Robert collect his officers and rejoin his regiment in Nova Scotia or New York. James and certain of the other officers would be permitted to remain in Quebec to receive recruits. Robert made himself even more disliked over the winter months, but finally left for Halifax in March 1780.

James continued trying to raise men and sought authority to send parties to the colonies to recruit and gather intelligence. Permission was granted, but rivalry with other corps was intense. James, seeking to distance himself from the actions of his brother, requested permission to resign from the King's Rangers and join some other regiment wholly under the command of the General. The request was denied because his appointment had been made by Clinton, and Haldimand had no authority to grant such a request. In the letter, however, James was extended encouragement, his generally good character was mentioned, and he was promised that the "extraordinary behaviour" of his brother would not be held against him. In reply, James wrote, "the Conduct of my Brother of late has almost unmann'd me," and expressed his sincere gratitude to the Governor.

By early September Haldimand ceased demanding that the rangers return to the Central Department and extended their recruiting privileges to include loyalists in the province who had not joined other corps. He had come to the conclusion that the Second Battalion King's Rangers were there to stay, and if he was going to have them he would find them useful employment.*

The history of the First Battalion King's Rangers is shrouded in confusion and mystery. From the records we have only fragments of the story, and Robert's connection seems tenuous. After leaving Montreal in March 1780, Robert went to Halifax. In June the Commanding Officer at Halifax wrote to General Clinton:

> *LtCol Robert Rogers was confined for the sum of Five to 600£ due to his own mismanagement and it is feared he will not complete his Corps not having enlisted more than 80-90 men.*

The rangers remained a small unit according to all the returns. One of their principal obligations was to perform guard duty on the prison ships in Halifax harbour. Some concerns were raised about their recruiting among the prisoners, but not many men were obtained in this manner. In fact, more were lost through sickness and disease than were gained through all recruiting, keeping the unit around the 100 mark. The rangers were relieved of their guard duty on 24 January 1781.

Robert apparently travelled widely in the Maritimes and to New York, amassing considerable debt in his unsuccessful attempts to gain recruits. In May he was back in the Halifax prison for debt and was released only after his obligations were assumed by his brother James. Robert then made his way to Penobscot, where he boarded a schooner bound for New York. On 10 June this vessel was attacked and captured by the Continental brigantine *Patty,* commanded by Captain Read. Robert was seized, taken to Boston and imprisoned for the remainder of the war.

Hostilities essentially ended a few months later when Lord Cornwallis surrendered his forces after the Battle of Yorktown, though a formal state of war continued to exist for two years. A draft treaty was negotiated in November 1782 and ratified by Congress the following April. On 3 September 1783 the war ended with the signing of the Treaty of Paris. Robert remained in prison until May 1783, when he was exchanged and returned to England with the Royal Fusiliers in HMS *Audacious.*

---

* From this point Robert had little to do with the Second Battalion. The section on James Rogers (2–3) may be consulted for additional information on the activities of this unit.

The King's Rangers

A company of the recreated regiment during a re-enactment at Quebec in August 1994

The remaining story of the First Battalion revolves around Captain Samuel Hayden. Hayden was born in 1752. He initially served in the New Jersey Volunteers and saw action at the Battles of Long Island and White Plains. On 2 May 1779 he received a warrant to raise a company for the King's Rangers, and by summer he had three officers, two sergeants, a corporal and twenty-eight privates. This unit conducted scouting operations in New York and New Jersey until it was sent to join the rest of the battalion in October 1781. By that time Robert was already in American hands, and Hayden, as the senior captain, became the commanding officer of the first battalion. A return in December indicated a strength of 142 all ranks comprising the following:

3 Captains	2 Lieutenants	2 Ensigns
1 Adjutant	1 Surgeon	
9 Sergeants	3 drummers	and 120 Rank & File

In the spring of 1782 the First Battalion was sent to garrison the

Island of Saint John* and performed that duty for the rest of the war. Returns from October 1782 indicate 83 effectives; others in January 1783 list 6 officers and 93 men. The end of hostilities brought a reduction in all Provincial forces, and most of the rangers afterwards settled on the island.

Robert apparently spent the last twelve years of his life living impoverished and improvidently in London on the half pay of a retired major. He was committed to the Fleet Prison on numerous occasions, and records show assignments of his pay to creditors in the years 1784, 1788, 1793 and 1794. A military career of unusual vision and contribution was drawing to an end in misery, partially brought on by excessive use of alcohol as a means of escape.

In midsummer of 1787 Robert had a final altercation with Benjamin Roberts on a London street. Following a heated and somewhat animated discussion, he picked Roberts up, carried him hysterically kicking and screaming across the street to a churchyard, unceremoniously threw him into a freshly dug grave and then kicked dirt in on top of him.

Robert passed his final days in a poor lodging in Southwark, where continuous drinking finally brought an end to his life on 18 May 1795, at the age of 63 years. One newspaper report of his death reads as follows:

> Lieutenant Col. Rogers, who died on Thursday last in the Borough, served in America during the late war, in which he performed prodigious feats of valour. He was a man of uncommon strength, but long confinement in the Rules of the King's Bench, had reduced him to the most miserable state of wretchedness.
>
> The Morning Press
> 22 May 1795

On 20 May 1795 Robert was laid to rest in Saint Mary's Churchyard next to the Elephant & Castle inn, at Newington in the southern part of London. By report, the funeral service was hastily read in the rain, attended by two unidentified mourners who hurried off at the end of the committal service. It appears that some years later the churchyard was paved over for a street; hence no marker exists to mark his final resting place. This area of London was heavily bombed during World War II, and it is unlikely that the exact location of his grave will ever be discovered.

---

* Later to become Prince Edward Island.

Although his last years were certainly the lowest point of his life, Robert Rogers was nonetheless an extraordinary individual, perhaps the most exceptional to emerge from the American colonial period. Robert was a man of considerable energy who inspired intense loyalty but who has not been given his rightful place in the annals of American military history next to heroes such as Daniel Boone or Davy Crockett. Although a backwoodsman of modest origins, he rose to international prominence through exceptional ability, military intuition and courage. He did not create the notion of highly mobile companes operating widely separated from conventional units, but he perfected the concept and the techniques of hit-and-run tactics that would be employed by commando and guerrilla units for more than two hundred years.

He would probably have reached greater heights had not the hardships of debt, alcohol and the jealousy of lesser men beset him. General Thomas Gage and Sir William Johnson succeeded in their character assassination of him by so blackening his reputation that others considered him untrustworthy and by encumbering him with such an enormous debt as to destroy his career and inevitably his life. He displayed exceptional ambition and broad vision, surpassing the smaller minds of men like Gage and Johnson, as well as those of a generation of politicians who failed to grasp the importance of and subsequently act upon his Northwest Passage proposals. His literary works, while not exceptional for their time, were worthy efforts that captured the imagination of the people and are still respected.

Robert was not a saint, but there is no evidence that he was an extraordinary sinner. The charges of counterfeiting early in his career can be chalked up to the naïveté of youth, as there was no recurrence of such activity. Alcohol in large quantities was part of the normal diet of the time, and there is no documentation of unusual abuse until very late in life. Suggestions of infidelity have been made, but other than a single phrase in his wife's 1778 divorce petition, no hint of sexual scandal is attached to his name in any contemporary documents.

As for his land schemes, these were not exceptional for the day. Sir William Johnson and many others acquired vast land holdings in what might be considered questionable circumstances by today's standards. All his schemes were an attempt to ease his enormous debt load, most of which was accumulated in the service of his country. There is no record of his having cheated anyone in any of his trading ventures or land dealings. He was a warrior and a military genius: a man destined to do well in periods of conflict but to suffer from inactivity and other constricting aspects of peace. Robert died forgotten by the country he served, but his fame later grew and endured through the many books and articles written on his life.

Robert Rogers and his Family

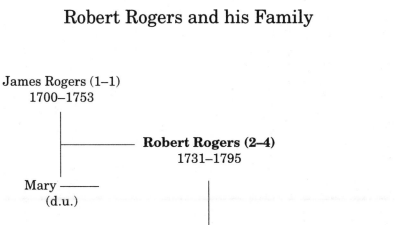

James Rogers (1–1)
1700–1753

———————— **Robert Rogers (2–4)**
1731–1795

Mary ———
(d.u.)

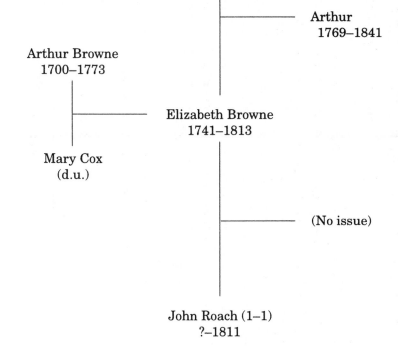

Arthur
1769–1841

Arthur Browne
1700–1773

Elizabeth Browne
1741–1813

Mary Cox
(d.u.)

(No issue)

John Roach (1–1)
?–1811

d.u.—date(s) unknown

Appendix I: Ranger Companies Established During the French & Indian War

The following chart lists the companies in Rogers' Rangers established at various times during the French & Indian War. Each Captain who commanded the company is indicated along with his eventual disposition. The disbandment of each company is indicated by the death or discharge of the last captain to command. Most of the ranger companies were disbanded when no longer required between 1759 and 1761. At the end of the war, however, two companies went on to serve in the West Indies. In addition the list indicates those officers who served in the American Revolutionary War and on which side they served.

◆ indicates an officer who served on the British side during the Revolutionary War.
❖ indicates an officer who served on the American side during the Revolutionary War.

Company	Date Organized	Officers	Remarks
1st "Rogers' Own"	March 1756	◆ Major Robert Rogers	• Transferred to the regular army February 1761.
		Captain James Tute	• Commanded June–November 1760, discharged November 1760.
2nd	July 1756	Captain Richard Rogers	• Died of smallpox 1757. The company was disbanded under the terms of surrender of Fort William Henry.

Company	Date Organized	Officers	Remarks
3rd	November 1756	Captain Humphery Hobbs	• Died of smallpox February 1757.
		Captain Charles Bulkeley	• Killed in Battle of Rogers' Rock March 1758.
		Captain Jonathan Burbank	• Killed in action on a scout May 1759.
4th	November 1756	Captain Thomas Speakman	• Killed at Battle of La Barbue Creek January 1757.
		❖ Captain John Stark	• Retired November 1759.
5th	February 1757	◆ Captain John Shepard	• Resigned because of ill health July 1759.
		Captain James Tute	• Captured September and exchanged November 1759; afterwards commanded the 1st company.
"Cadet"	September 1757	No captain; operated under Robert's personal command	• Disbanded 8 November 1757.
6th	January 1758	◆ Captain James Rogers	• Discharged November 1760.

Company	Date Organized	Officers	Remarks
7th	January 1758	Captain John McCurdy	• Killed in accident January 1759.
		❖ Captain Moses Hazen	• Discharged February 1761.
8th	January 1758	❖ Captain William Stark	• Discharged November 1759.
9th	January 1758	❖ Captain Jonathan Brewer	• Discharged November 1760.
10th	March 1758	Captain Henry Wendell	• Resigned May 1759.
		Captain Joseph Waite	• Discharged June 1762. This unit later served in the West Indies.
11th	April 1758	Captain James Neile	• Resigned January 1759.
		Captain Noah Johnson	• Killed at Battle of Pointe-au-Fer June 1760.
		Captain Simon Stevens	• Discharged February 1761.
12th	March 1760	❖ Captain David Brewer	• Discharged February 1761.
13th	March 1760	Captain Amos Ogden	• Discharged June 1762. This unit later served in the West Indies.

Indian companies

Company	Date Organized	Officers	Remarks
Stockbridge Indian	July 1756	Captain Jacob Cheeksaunkun	• Service: May–November 1756, January–September 1758 and March 1759–October 1760. He was captured in July and held until October 1760.
Stockbridge Indian	January 1758	Captain Jacob Naunauphtaunk	• Service: January–November 1758, March–August 1759. Captured in August 1760 and held until August 1760.
Mohegan Indian	January 1758	Captain Moses Brewer ❖ Captain Solomon Uhauamvaumut	• Resigned November 1759. • Service: May–November 1760.
Mohawk Indian	February 1759	Captain Lotridge	• Service: February–September 1759.

The Indian Companies were on a less regular establishment, and the periods shown indicate dates actually in service. The Indians were seen as unreliable and undisciplined but necessary to the army and to the fulfillment of British intentions. The solution was to attach them to the Rangers in companies of 30 to 50 warriors under an Indian captain. The first two companies were Christianised Indians from Stockbridge, Massachusetts, under the command of their war chief, Captain Jacob Cheeksaunkun, who was simply known as Captain Jacobs. Captain Jacob Naunauphtaunk (son of Captain Jacobs) commanded the second company. The third company consisted of Christianised Mohegan Indians from Connecticut under the command of Captain Moses Brewer. Captain Solomon Uhauamvaumut was the principal chief of the tribe during the Revolution and declared his allegiance and that of his tribe to the American cause. The fourth company consisted of some 50 Mohawk Indians provided to Robert by Sir William Johnson, for which Robert had little use.

Appendix II: The Methods & Practices of the Rangers

The following military treatise on the art of forest warfare and discipline employed by the rangers is a unique and valuable work of Robert Rogers. All the rules had been tried and tested by himself, and many were the direct result of lessons learned from encounters with the enemy. They were written down after Lord Loudoun ordered the formation of the Cadet Company, and as a document became the only manual on effective tactics for the forest warfare conducted in America. It is considered that the British refusal to apply these rules universally to operations prolonged the conflict and postponed the victory that their superior numbers and adequate supply lines should have guaranteed much earlier. These rules have been printed in a number of sources. While all are essentially the same, each contains small variations of text. The following is an exact copy of the letter to Lord Loudoun dated 25 October 1757. For readability some punctuation and paragraphing have been added to this rendition.

The Methods used by Captain Robert Rogers in disciplining the Rangers of his Command in Camp, with their manner of and practices in Scouting & Fighting in the woods; Which is humbly submitted to His Excellency the Earl of Loudoun, that their Errors may be avoided for want of greater Regulardy of found necessary pointed out to them for their Observation and Improvement.

They are subject to the Rules & Articles of War and are ordered to observe all general orders in Camp and to appear at Rollcall every Evening on their own Parade, each of them equipt with a Firelock, sixty rounds of Powder & Ball and a Hatchet; At which time an Officer inspects into the same to see they are duly provided and their Arms in order, so as to be ready to march at a minute's warning; And before they are dismissed from Parade the necessary guards are draughted, and Scouts for the next day appointed.

The manner of marching whenever we go out to the Enemies Forts or Frontiers for discovery is to take a party of about eight or ten and walk in a single file, keeping such a distance from each other as to prevent an Enemy's destroying two of us at one Shot, always taking care to send one man ahead & another on each side of the party, each of them at the distance of about twenty yards from it, with a private Signal to notify the Officer of the approach of an Enemy and of their numbers. Upon seeing an Enemy I could encounter, I would endeavour for the best ground & Shelter from Trees, and make the most of it. If I have the first fire, it's more than probable we gain our point; For immediately after it, we shall rush the Enemy and in their surprise no doubt make Prisoners by disconserting of them; But if the Enemy were superior, I would retreat so as to maintain the rising ground or advantageous post till their was a moral certainty of securing another and gaining a third, fourth, &c, which is a pretty sure method of harassing them & making our Escape; However lest their numbers should make it practicable to surround us, we then should scatter, every one taking his own Road and making to the Rendervous appointed for that Evening; Which is every Morning altered and fixed for the ensuing night in order to get the party together after separation by day.

On going over mossy or soft ground, we change our position & march abreast of each other to prevent an Enemy from tracking us, as they could do if we kept in a Single File, till we get over it and then resume our former order of travel till it's quite dark before we encamp; Which we generally do if possible on a piece of ground that will afford our Sentries the advantage of discovering or hearing an Enemy at a considerable distance, keeping half such a party the whole night awake. In this manner we proceed and continue on to the place we are to reconnoitre, and just before we come to it send a man or two to look out the best ground for making observations and after Effecting our design therein, we endeavour to take what prisoners we can, and after Captivating of 'em we keep them separate till their examined, and then return home in a different Road from the one we came in, taking particular care to halt only on rising ground that we may have a prospect of discovering a party in our Rear and be enabled to alter our Course or Scatter as the exigences of the circumstances may require.

When we set out with a party of three hundred to Scout, and distress the Enemy, and get into the woods; I divide them into the following order: Leading with one third in the Center, the next Senior Officer with one hundred on my Right at twenty yards distance, and the other hundred at the same distance on my left is led by the Third Commanding Officer of the party; Which Divisions are marched in the Indian or single File, as are the Guards taken out of the whole, which are ten or twelve men in front of each Division at about thirty yards distance, and two men thirty yards before each of them, besides two Flankers on each side of twenty five men each, at about forty yards distance from the Main Body, and two or three without at the same distance from them to prevent their being ambuscaded, also a Rear Guard consisting of a Sergeant and eight, with orders to halt on all Eminencies, where any party following us might be seen, until the whole were well forward. These Guards have Orders upon discovering an Enemy to send and acquaint the Commanding Officer of it that he may make the proper Dispositions for Attacking or defending.

Robert Rogers   Appendix II to Section 2-4

In case of an Enemy's approaching in front on level ground, I would give orders that the three Divisions or Main Body make a front with the Advance Guard and as an Officer will be appointed to command of each Flank Guard, they are at the time of putting ourselves in a Line Abreast, to keep the same distance from us as in marching to prevent the Savages from pressing too Hard upon either of our wings or surrounding us; Which is their usual method if their numbers will admit of it; And to support & strengthen our Rear Guard.

If I am obliged to receive the Enemy's Fire, it is our Custom to fall or squat down that their Balls may go over us before we discharge at them, and in case their Body is equal to ours, our party extends itself occasionally; But if the Enemy are superior to our numbers we always take care to strengthen our Flanking parties to make them equal with theirs, and if possible to beat them back to their Main Body; Which if I luckily do, I order a third of my party on each Flank to push with the greatest Resolution; Heading myself with the Center and advancing in front with the said Division from Tree to Tree for Security to ourselves; With one half of the party before the other & both Divisions in a Line abreast about ten or twelve yards distance from each other. If the Enemy push in upon us the Front Fires whilst the Rear Reserve theirs till the front has discharged and then their Opportunity by advancing and doing the like, by which time the front who fall back in the Rear after their first fire, advance loaded and in readiness to discharge again; In doing which the Rear are preparing also to perform it a second time; Which will keep up a constant fire & prevent the Enemy from coming in upon us, provided this Order is duly complied with, as the French could not possibly forever break us, more especially as our Flanking parties would strictly observe it till Victory was decided either for or against us.

If we have the good fortune to oblige them to retreat, I pursue them in the following order Viz: Keeping out my Flanking parties while I do my utmost in their flight to keep them off the Risings and as much as possible confine them to the Hollows, that we may the better surround them, which if I do they will consequently be obliged to surrender themselves to us; But if I am obliged to retreat from them our front Line of the Center and Flanking parties fire first and retreat about ten or twenty yards behind the second Line and become the Rear of the party; Then the second Line fires and retreats in the same manner, by which time the first Line will be in readings to perform the same thing over again and so in like manner during our retreat we continue covering & securing each other till we have got quite clear of the Enemy.

Robert Rogers   Appendix II to Section 2–4

When the Rear is attacked, the Center and Flankers Face to the Rear about and form themselves to oppose as in the foregoing Method & Order, and the then advance parties become Rear Guards; And when attacked in Flank we alter and face Right or Left as the occurance makes it necessary, which will always make a Rear of one of our Flank Guards; And provided I found we had not strength enough to repulse the Enemy, I would retreat with my Flanking parties out, and whenever the ground gave me the advantage, I would improve it by firing a Volley at them, which ground I should be very carefull to look for in order the better to defend & secure our Retreat; But if they were to surround us, I would form a Square and if possible make a Stand till darkness of night would give us an opportunity of making our Escape compleat.

If I was attacked in broken ground and found I could not make a Stand to advantage I would retreat to a better situation in an irregular scattering manner so as to make the Enemy conceive I was flying and when I had recovered the spot I imagined would answer our purpose, I would then let them approach very close & pour in a Volley upon them & immediately afterward those nearest in front should fall in upon them with their Hatchetts and with the rest if possible surround them in their surprise.

At night when Camping with such a party, I fix my Centries in such a manner that they are not to be relieved till morning, putting six men in the place of one Centry, allowing one of 'em only at a time to keep up an hour, who is to call up another to relieve him & so on till the whole six have stood their Tour of duty; And all of them are to be close to the Centry that they may be ready to relieve without noise; Where are to be as still as possible that he may better hear the approach of an Enemy, and if he discovers any, he is to sent one of the guard to acquaint the Commanding Officer of the party of it, who will put the whole in reading to receive them; And so in the same manner I fix all my occasional Centries. And as soon as light appears, I awake my people, as that is the time that the Savages chooses to fall on their Enemies, and send out small parties to take a Scout round the Camp to look if there are any Tracks of an Enemy that might have been near us in the Course of the night; Which parties come in and join us about Sunrise; And then we march the whole Body in the order before mentioned until occasion of refreshment, which I always do by a Spring or Riverlet & post my people so as to prevent being surprised, and for our greater security send a small Party to lay by the path we came in at some distance behind us to observe if an Enemy is pursuing; Besides placing Centries at all convenient places as occasion and the situation we are in make it requisite; And when the Main Body are refreshed, I relieve the out Centries and party that they may refresh also before I march.

If I have to cross Rivers, I take care not to do it at the usual Ford lest an Enemy might have discovered us, and laid an ambush in those places, therefore avoid them by going over where they cannot suspect us, and endeavour to surprise them by coming on them the other side of the water. If I am to pass by Lakes, I keep at some distance from the edge of the water that the Enemy cannot get us betwixt the woods and the water; As in case of being waylaid there, we should have nothing to Shelter us from their Fire. And if they pursue my Rear, I take a turn round till I come to a good place and waylay my own Tracks and fix my ambush in such a manner as to gain the first Shot at them. In coming near our own Forts when we are returning from a Scout, I shun all Roads or paths contiguous to them, lest the Enemy's parties might get or be ahead of mine, and so go another Road to keep clear of their ambuscades; Which if we fell into, we could not so vigorously resist after the fatigues of our Journey.

Preparing for a Winter Scout

This sketch by Gary Zaboly depicts an inspection by Robert of his Rangers outside Fort William Henry before their march north to the Battle of La Barbue Creek in January 1757.

When I go out in pursuit of any party that has done mischief near our Forts or Incampments, I would not follow them directly on their own Tracks, lest the Enemy might discover us by their Rear Guard, which they would be naturally induced to keep to prevent a Surprise; For in case of their being followed & saw their Adversaries close after them, they would waylay in their own Tracks and have a chance for the first fire and a very good prospect of beating their pursuers; But in order to frustrate their hopes of gaining such an advantage, I would take a different Route by going round & getting ahead of them to some narrow passes I conceived they would go through, where I would lay an ambuscade which of course must give us the fire, and as it would be entirely unexpected to meet any party ahead of them in their return home, I doubt not this method better answering our purpose than coming on them in their own Tracks, and that there would be almost a certainty of destroying and overcoming the most of their party.

If I am to go on Canoes or any other Boats by water, it's my practice not to sett off before night that we may the better pass undiscovered by parties on Hills or other places commanding a prospect of the Lakes or Rivers we are in; And in padling or rowing, order that the Boat next the stern most waits for her & the third for that, the fourth for the third and so on to the Boat leading ahead, that we may keep together to assist each other on any Emergency and prevent Separation. A man is appointed in each Boat to look out for Fires which will discover themselves at a great distance at night, and from the sizes of which we could form a Judgment of the numbers that kindled them, and if I imagined them to be the Enemy's Incampment & thought I was able to cope with & overcome their party, I would in such case, provided the Lake or River was not more than gun Shot across, post a quarter of my party on the opposite side to the Enemy, and with the other Three quarters cross the water at some distance from them, leaving a small guard with the Boats, and with the remainder endeavour to surround them or come on their backs about break of day and surprise them with a Vigorous attack; On which it's probable they'd push for their Boats & make to the other Shore, where my reserved party will be ready to receive & distress them in a very sensible manner, more especially as I should follow them close to the water and harass them at their standing betwixt our two Fires.

But if I could not form a pretty exact Judgment of the Enemy's Force and was dubious whether I was strong enough to attempt them, I would go about a mile's distance and conceal my Boats until the morning, when we might possibly get a Chance of making a true discernment of their number at the time they took Boat & put off; And as I should find the Course they took and be capable of knowing if it was practicable to engage or surprise them, I should with such a prospect follow them in the Evening, and when I came in sight of their Fires order my Boats to be hid on the opposite side to the Enemy and at some distance short of them, then march round ahead of and waylay them along the water where the River is narrow and where I imagined they must come by, extending my people just as far as to command all their Boats at one and the same time; And when the opportunity offered surprise them with a Volley, which Circumstance & Situation would give us the advantage of a second discharge before they could be in reading to fire at us, and give them such a panic that they would be very apt to make the best of their way off, especially as they'd be uncertain of our numbers & could not with any prudence attempt landing under our Fire.

On the other hand if I did not see any Fires, I would go on in the manner first mentioned until day break and then draw up and conceal my Boats and keep my people from making Fires or any noise that might discover them throughout the day. In the Evening I would set off and go in the beforementioned order by water to the place where I intended to begin my march by Land, and after hiding our Boats in a very secure place, take to the Woods and conduct ourselves in the manner set forth in the former part of these Methods and Practices.

There are many other different Methods used which cannot be so intelligibly express in writing as they arise in consequence of occurrences that cannot be foreseen and are only to be judged of and directed on the Spot by the Officer commanding the party, whose presence of mind must be his only guide to prompt him to his Duty by preserving his party or distressing the Enemy as his situation and in the circumstances may make requisite.

We give out our parole and countersign in the Woods in order to know one another in the dark night, likewise appoint a station for every man to repair to incase of being attacked at night, and if the Officer is prudent in doing this, his caution will prevent considerable mischiefs that otherwise ensue from his neglect of it.

Dated at Fort Edward the 25th October 1757 and humbly presented to his Excellency the Right honourable the Earl of Loudoun, Major General and Commander in Chief of His Majesty's Troops in North America, &c, &c, &c.

By:

His Excellency's

Most Obedient and Most
devoted humble Servant

Robt Rogers

Appendix III: The Rogers / McCormick Trading Agreement

Lieutenant Caesar McCormick served in Rogers' Rangers during the French & Indian War and was acting adjutant of the ranger detachment during the expedition to Detroit in 1760. He was one of the four original members of the trading partnership "Rogers & Company" that was formed at Niagara during this period and later became a respected trader in the area. McCormick was at Detroit during the time of the Pontiac Uprising in 1763. He joined Robert and the rangers when they arrived. The agreement below was written in Robert's own hand. The original is located in the Rogers' Papers in the Ontario Archives in Toronto. It is believed that this document was a separate extension of the original agreements among the four men.

Articles of Agreement

made at Albany this Twenty fifth day of March 1761,

between Robert Rogers, Esq., on the one part and Cesar Cormick on the other part, Viz. —

Its agreed between the two parties that they carry on a trade together in Copartnership betwixt this place and Detroit and the neighborhood thereof with the Indians and inhabitants thereabouts; In which copartnership each party is Equally to divide & share both gains or losses during the copartnership. It is agreed that the said Rogers shall furnish the said Cormick Four Battues loaded with goods for said Trade. Cormick to proceed with the goods to Detroit & dispose of the same there & in the neighborhood to the best advantage. It is further agreed that the said Rogers shall cause the said Cormick to be furnished with goods from time to time at Albany, provided the said Cormick applys in writing to Mr John Askins, Merchant, in Albany. It is agreed also that Cormick proceed at once to Detroit with Four Battoes loaded and to keep the said Battoes constantly passing from Chewchady to Detroit carrying up and bringing down Furs, skins, &c., which skins are to be delivet to Mr John Askins at Albany or to his order. The said Cormick agrees to remain at Detroit the Ensuing Winter to sell of Goods and to purchase Furs, Skins, &c. For the benifit of the two parties.

It is agreed the copartnership shall continue Four Years, Cormick to keep proper Books & accounts and to make each year returns of all Furs & Skins bought & sold. The said Rogers to take no further trouble than accur his share of the Profits & share equally all losses.

Finally it is agreed between the said Rogers & Cormick That for the faithful fullfillment of their respective agreement, This Instrument doth firmly bind both the said parties in the sum of Five Thousand Pounds sterling to be recovered from the party That shall fails.

Cesar Cormick

Robᵗ Rogers

Appendix IV: Newspaper Articles on Prince — Servant to Major Rogers

The term "slave" was one seldom seen in 18th century usage in the northern colonies, but slavery was not uncommon in the area. Indentured servants were frequently treated as slaves until their passages had been paid. In this case there can be little doubt that Prince was a slave owned by Robert Rogers and from the dates of the articles it appears that he had been bought some time before Robert's service in the South. What happened to Prince or the other slaves mentioned in the main part of this narrative is not known. These articles were researched by Gary Zaboly and are used with permission.

The Boston Weekly Post-Boy, April 28, 1760:

Ran away from the Widow Rogers of Rumford, in N.H., about a Month ago, a Negro Servant Man, belonging to Major Robert Rogers, named Prince, of middling stature, about 30 years of age, has had the Small-Pox, looks very serious and grave, & pretends to a great deal of Religion. Since his Departure, he has sold the most of his Cloaths, & now is but meanly dressed; he was in the Service the last Year. & has offered to inlist sundry Times, pretending himself to be a Free-man; He was lately taken up, but by his incriminating Discourse made his Escape again.

Whoever will take up & secure said Servant, & convey him to the Widow Rogers at Rumford, or to Capt. James Rogers, or to Col. Doty at the Sign of the Lamb in Boston, shall have FIVE DOLLARS Reward, & all necessary Charges paid.

Bost. Ap. 23, 1760   James Rogers

The Widow Rogers: Robert's mother.

The Boston Weekly Post-Boy, November 22, 1762:

Ran away from me the Subscriber at Londonderry, in the Province of New Hampshire, on the 18th of September, a Negro Man Servant named Prince about 40 Years of Age, about 5 feet 5 inches high, speaks good English, had on when he went away a green Coat, blue plush Breeches, diaper Jacket, several pair of thread Stockings with him; he looks very serious and grave, and pretends to be very religious; He is the property of Major Robert Rogers and has been several Years in the Service to the Westward, and pretends to be free.

Whoever will take up said Slave, and bring him to me, or to Captain Jonathan Brewer at Farmington, shall have FIVE DOLLARS Reward and all necessary Charges paid by me.

James Rogers.   Dated at Londonderry, October 8, 1762.

Appendix V: Extracts of Orders by General Gage

The following is a copy of the document attached to the instructions issued to Major Robert Rogers on his appointment to the command of Fort Michilimackinac. It consists of extracts of orders that had been issued by General Gage to the commanding officers of posts in the interior during the period of his tour as commander-in-chief. This document was presented as evidence at the court martial of Major Rogers and used in an attempt to convict him on the charge of disobedience of orders. These orders give an indication of how the Crown viewed Indian issues during this period and how Gage intentionally placed severe restrictions on the post commanders.

Extracts of Orders given by His Excellency the Honble, Thomas Gage, Major General and Commander-in-Chief of all His Majesty's Forces in North America, to the Officers Commanding Posts, relative to their Treatment of Indians.

New York, 17 January 1765.

As the Indian Traders will be provided with particular Passes by their respective Governors, the Officers Commanding in the several Posts and Forts will endeavor to make them comply with the Conditions upon which their Passes shall be granted. Care to be taken in the opening of the Trade, that Traders are guilty of no Impositions upon the Indians.

When the Traders bring Spirituous Liquors to any of the Forts or Posts where they intend to remain and trade, the said Liquors are to be taken into Store, marked with the Traders names, and receipts given them for the quantity put into Store, and no Spirituous Liquors are to be Sold to the Indians in the Posts or near them; But when Indians shall have finished their Trade and going away, the Traders to have as much of their Spirits out of Store, as they shall have Sold to such Indians, upon their engaging to carry it at least Two Leagues from the Post, and then deliver it to the Indians. And in order to prevent Disputes concerning Liquors put into Store, the Stores are to be fastened with Two Locks, and the key of one kept by the Commissary or Commanding Officer, the other by the Person on whom the Traders shall fix upon for that purpose. The Officers Commanding at the Posts will at all times inform Sir William Johnson of everything which shall come to their knowledge relative to Indian Affairs, which shall be worth his notice.

Presents are not to be made to Indians but on Occasions which shall render such measures unavoidable, and when it so happens, the occasion of the Presents, and the quantity delivered to be Certified by the Commanding Officer, and two other Officers next in Rank to the Commander where so many shall be, likewise by the Commissary if any such Person in the Post; And when there is a necessity to take up Liquors or other Goods from the Traders for those purposes, the Current price of the Goods to be Certified in like manner in the Trader's Bill; These Certificates to be transmitted to the General's Secretary.

When any Deputy of Sir William Johnson's shall be in the Post, he must be employed in delivering the Presents; the Occasion, Quantity, and Price to be Certified as above.

Returns to be sent to Head Quarters of the number of Boats, Waggons, Teams, Horses, or Oxen belonging to the King.

New York, 6th October 1765.

Indians may be fed when Provision is given them by the worst Sort.

Appendix VI: Instructions from Sir William Johnson

The following is a copy of the instructions issued to Major Robert Rogers on his appointment by Sir William Johnson, Superintendent of Indian Affairs, to the command of Fort Michilimackinac. These instructions were presented at his court martial by the authorities in an attempt to condemn him for disobeying orders.

INSTRUCTIONS to Major Robert Rogers, Commandant of Michilimakinac respecting his Conduct towards the Indians.

On your arrival at Michilimackinac you will acquaint the Indians who may resort to that Post, that you are to receive your Orders concerning Indian Affairs from me, that I heartily wish them well, and hope they will continue to behave as Friends, and Men who regard their Engagements, and that so long as they do so, they may be assured of my Friendship and good Offices, and that His Majesty will not permit any of His Subjects to wrong them. To which end you are to report to me all matters relative to them, and I expect they will pay no attention to idle Stories or Reports brought amongst them, as they may be assured, I shall Communicate any thing necessary for their Information.

You are to inform yourself as soon as possible concerning the Leading Men of the several Nations around your Post, and to do your utmost to become acquainted with their Sentiments, and you are carefully to avoid giving any Umbrage to the Indians, and Studiously to prevent any Quarrels from arising between them and the Soldiery or Traders; And you are to hear their Complaints, and to do your utmost to redress them should and Traders use them ill, or over reach them in Dealings, Reporting the Persons guilty to me without favour of affection; And you are in all things to conduct yourself so as to acquire the Confidence and esteem of the Indians, and to discover and Plots concerting by them, or any other Persons, tending to disturb the Public Tranquility.

And lastly, you are to send me exact Copies of your Proceedings with them once in Six Months, as also to give me the speediest notice in your power of any Material Occurences respecting Indian Affairs in that Quarter, and on your Report to me after your Arrival there touching the foregoing Articles, you shall be furnished with such further or other Instructions as the Circumstances of Affairs may require.

Given under my hand at Johnson Hall this 3rd day of June, 1766.

W. Johnson

Appendix VII: Commissions and Instructions on Explorations

In 1766 Robert Rogers, Governor of Fort Michilimackinac, commissioned Captain Jonathan Carver,* James Stanley Goddard and Captain James Tute to explore and map the country west of the Great Lakes, in preparation for an expedition in search of an overland route to the Pacific: a Northwest Passage. The documents below are copies of the instructions issued to these men. Numerous sources make it clear that Robert wanted to lead the expedition himself and may have planned to join them during the second or third year. To accomplish this, however, he was counting on the opening of trade to show the Crown and his sponsors that significant profits could be realised from the opening of the West. The men conducted some exploration but failed to follow their instructions precisely, and as a result the items upon which Robert was counting could not be shown. At his court martial, the prosecution used these documents to show how Robert had exceeded his authority by ordering the explorations and incurring cost to the Crown. Various versions of these instructions can be found in numerous sources, including the Proceedings of the Court Martial. The documents below are taken from what are possibly copies of the originals and are full of misspellings.

By Robert Rogers Esq'r, Agent to the Westeron Indians and Governor Commandant of His Majesty's Garison of Michilimakinac and its Dependances

To Captain Johnothan Carver Esq'r

WHEREAS it will be to the Honour and Dignity of the Nation as well as for the good of His Majestyis Service to have some good Suravees of the Intieriour parts of North America, espiessiely to the West and North West from this Garison,

I do by Virtue of the Authority given me apoint you for that purpose at Eight Shillings starting this day (untill Discharged); And you are heareby directed to set out from this Post Emidiently and proceed along the North Side of Lake Mssigon to the Bay, and from thence to the Falls of St Antinoies on the Missispee, taking an Exact Plans of the Cuntery by the way marking down all Indian Towns with their Numbers as also to take Survaies of the Diffront Posts, Lakes and Rivers as also the Mountains, and at the Falles of Saint Antoines, and about that, as far as you can explore this Winter, and make your Reports to me early in the

---

* Carver later became famous for his part in the expedition. He published an account that was remarkably popular and was translated into several languages.

Spring. Should you Recive orders from me to march further to the Westward with any other Detachment that I may send this fall or Winter, you are to do it, and send back your Journals by Mr. Browe or some other safe hand, — but should you not Recive any you will Return by the Illen Way River and from thence to St Joseph and from thence along the east side of Lake Misegan to this place taking all the way exact Plans of the Cuntry and for so doing this shall be your Sufficient Warrant.

Given under my hand at

Michilimakinac 2/12nd August 1766

Robt Rogers

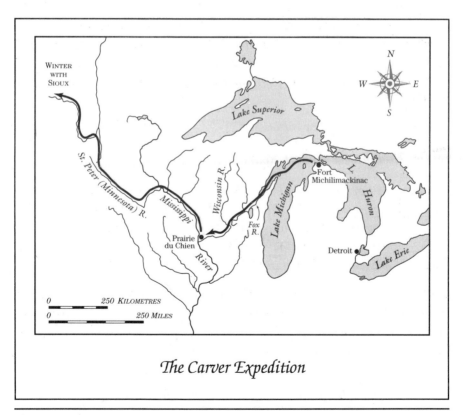

The Carver Expedition

By the Honourable Robert Rogers,

Major and Governor of the Lakes Huron, Missigan, and Superior and the Surrounding Country to the Heads of the several Bays and Rivers that Discharge their Waters into said Lakes, Subordinate Agent and Superintendent to Sir William Johnson for the Western Indians, Captain Commandant of Michilimakinac and its Dependencies &c. &c.

To James Stanley Goddard Esq'r

I do by Virtue of the power and Authority to me given appoint you Secretary to a Detachment under the Command of Captain James Tute (as also one of the Council to the said Detachment) ordered for the discovery of the River Ourigan and the North West Passage at Eight Shillings Sterling per day, & over and above an equal Share of the reward offered by the Government for that Discovery, and you are hereby ordered to Do, Act, and Perform the Office of Secretary for the Detachment to the utmost of your power by keeping exact Journals, and entering every useful remark that you think can attend to future knowledge of the Country, which you pass through, as also to take down the Talks of the Indians, their Numbers, &c. And for so doing this shall be your Sufficient Warrant and Authority to demand your Payment at your Return.

Given under my hand and Seal this Twelfth day of September 1766 at Michilimakinac.

Robt Rogers

By the Honourable Robert Rogers,

Major and Governor of the Lakes Huron, Missigan, and Superior and the Surrounding Country to the Heads of the Several Bays and Rivers that Discharge their Waters into said Lakes, Subordinate Agent and Superintendent to Sir William Johnson for the Western Indians, Captain Commandant of Michilimakinac and its Dependencies &c., &c., &c.

INSTRUCTIONS To Captain James Tute, Esq'r, Commanding a Party for the Discovery of the North West Passage from the Atlantic into the Pacific Ocean if any such Passage there be, or for the Discovery of the Great River Ourigan that falls into the Pacific Ocean about Latitude Fifty.

You are to set out immediately with this Detachment and with them proceed to La Bay from thence to the Falls of St. Antonies and further up the said River to a Convenient place to Winter amongst the Souex, carrying with you the necessary Articles now delivered to your Care for Boons to gain the Friendship of the Indians, and to remain and dismiss from Time to Time as you approach on your Way, and pass the Country they are best acquainted with. You are when you arrive at the Falls of St. Antonies to endeavour to find out where Mr. Bruce Winters, and from him take Captain Jonathan Carver under your Command who is to be Draftsman for the Detachment. He with Mr. James Stanley Goddard and Interpreter is to make up a Council, which you may on every occasion that appears necessary order that they may with you Consult the Expediency of the Voyage by which with these Instructions you are to guard yourselves, Mr. Goddard has an appointment as your Secretary for Indian Affairs, he is to be second in Command, Mr. Carver third, Mr. Reaume has my Appointment for your Interpreter and fourth in Command.

You will from where you winter, early in the Spring endeavour to get some good Guides from the Souex and proceed with your Party to the North West, and make what Discoveries you can during the Summer, and at the close of which you will fall in with your Party to Winter at Fort La Parrie, at which place you shall have sent you a further supply of Goods next fall, that you may take of them what is Necessary to carry on the Expedition, and from Fort La Parrie you will Travel West, bearing to the North West, and do your endeavour to fall in with the great River Ourigan which rises in several different Branches between the Latitudes of Fifty Six and Forty Eight, and runs Westward for near three hundred Leagues, when it is at no great distance from each other joyned by one from the South, and a little up the Stream by one from the North; About these Forks you will find an Inhabited Country, and great Riches, the Gold is up that River that comes in from the North at about three days Journey from their Great Town, near the Mouth of it at the South West side of a Large Mountain, but there is not any Iron Ore that is known to be workt among them. From this Town the Inhabitants carry their Gold near two Thousand Miles to Traffick with the Japancies, and it's said they have some kind of Beasts of Burden.

From where the above River joins this great River Ourigan it becomes much Larger, and about four hundred Leagues as the River runs from this Town above mentioned it discharges itself into an Arm or Bay of the Sea at near the Latitude of Fifty four and bends southerdly and enters into the Pacific Ocean about Forty eight, nine, or Fifty where its narrow, but to the North West where you join this Bay of the Sea at the entrance of the River Ourigan the bay is wide and supposed to have a Communication with the Hudson Bay about the Latitude of Fifty nine near Dobsie's Point. From the above Description you will do your utmost Endeavour to find out and discover the said Country, and take all possible means to obtain a Draft of it, as well as by the way reporting from Time to Time to me all your proceedings at every opportunity sending such Sketches or Plans as your Draftsman has taken, and you are further to make all the Interest you possibly can with the different Nations that others may pass after your Return to open a Trade across the Continent to those People equally advantageous to themselves as to us. On your way should you have occasion you may draw Bills on me at any time for the purchase of Goods and Merchandise of Traders that you may meet, or for the Payment of Indians that you may employ for carrying on the Expedition, should your Goods that you have with you, and those I shall send you next Fall to Fort La Pierre not be Sufficient, and such Drafts at a Small sight shall meet with due Honour.

And when you have any thing to send back, as no doubt the Indians will give you Presents, take care to convey them to me by some careful Person that will honourably deliver them here. And over and above Eight Shillings Sterling per day, you are entitled if you discover a North West Passage from the Atlantic to the Pacific Ocean, Twenty Thousand Pound Sterling to be paid to the Detachment, which is equally to be divided amongst them by the Honourable Lords of His Majesty's Treasury of England, and for the other discovery of the River Ourigan, you will be Considered by the Government, and paid according to the Value of the Discovery that you make to be likewise divided amongst the Detachment.

You must take great Care not to be deceived by the Rivers Missisure, or by the River that falls into Hudson's Bay, or by other Rivers that empty into the Gulph of Californie. As every attempt of this kind is attended with some difficulty, wherever that appears to you call to mind your Courage and Resolution, and not let that fail you in the attempt, Consider the Honour it will be to you and the Detachment with you, besides the great Advantages that must arise to the undertakers of it. Behave in it like a Man that is devoted to his King, and brave out every difficulty, and you may be sure of Success.

You are to take great Care not to leave the least Suspicion among the many different Nations of Indians that your design is any other than to open a Trade with them; Beware of their Women not to take them without Consent of their Chiefs; Pay them punctually for what you have of them which is the sure way to have success. And when you have made all the Discovery you can you must return *to this place in the Way and manner you think most Convenient and easy for yourself and Party, either by Hudson's Bay or back the Way you go out across the Country observing proper Place for Posts, going and coming. But I strongly recommend it to you not to touch at any of our Hudson Bay Posts, as they may detain you and make advantages of your Journey to themselves; But should you find out a North West Passage as I do not doubt but you will, or a short Carrying Place, cross over to Fort La Parrie where you may be assured to meet Relief. I hartily wish you Success and that God may preserve you and the Detachment through this Undertaking, and that you may meet the reward of a deserving Officer at your Return, over and above the money offered for the Discovery, to effect which my good Offices shall not be wanting to every individual. You are strictly Commanded to make your Report to me at your Return, where ever I may be, or in case of my Death to the Honourable Charles Townsend, or in case of both our Deaths, to the Honourable Lords of Trade and Plantations, and for so doing this shall be your Sufficient Warrant and instructions.*

Given under my hand and Seal at Michilimakinac this 12th September 1766.

Robt Rogers

A Group of Rogers' Rangers at Fort Niagara, July 1984

Back row: Captain Tim Todish, Gary Rhowmine, Terry Todish, Dr. Tod Harburn, Major John Jaeger, and Jerry Shoger. Front row: Larry Conkle, Bob Howells

Robert Rogers   Appendix VII to Section 2–4

Appendix VIII: Petition for a Land Grant in North America

Robert Rogers, encumbered with an enormous debt load, was committed to the Fleet Prison on 16 October 1772, where he had been incarcerated numerous times. It was reported that he was in despair and drinking heavily. On 14 June, in what must have been a desperate attempt to free himself from his creditors, he submitted a petition for a land grant in America about sixty miles square. Considering his previous success rate, he must have known this petition was not likely to succeed. The document has been included here for its historical significance and its endorsements.

The Petition of Major Robt Rogers

To

His Majesty In Council

For

A Grant of Lands in North America

To the Kings most Excellent Majesty in Council

The Petition of Major Robert Rogers

Most Humbly Sheweth

That your Petitioner had the Honor to Command Your Majesty's Rangers in America during all the Services of the last War, and for a Considerable Time after was on various Services In the Course whereof he always made it his invariable Rule not to spare his Person or his Purse in fulfilling the Orders of the Generals under whom he Acted.

That your Petitioner in that Station hath incurred Debts on Account on such Services to the amount of Thirteen Thousand pounds and upwards which have not yet been paid or reimbursed to him tho' long sollicited.

That your Petitioner is at this Time Deprived of his Liberty and in Close Confinement in the Fleet prison for the above Debts Contracted Merely and entirely on Account of the Above Service.

That your Petitioner has heretofore been presented with Certificates of his good Behaviour by many Officers of Rank whose names are hereto annexed, which Certificates are ready to produced when required.

That your Petitioner hopes the Circumstances of his Case may induce your Majesty to Grant him a Tract of Lands in North America situated on the Banks of some great and convenient River of Lake in Lieu of his Claims, on obtaining which your Petitioner has great hopes that he may have it in his Power to Compromise with his Principal Creditors so as to obtain his enlargement and make some Provision for his future Support.

That your Petitioner being very desirous to pay or satisfy his said Creditors and being also in the greatest Distress for want of almost every Necessary and far distant from his Family and Friends from whom he might expect Relief, And greatly injured in his Health by his long Confinement and fearing to be daily more so; and having no other Effects or Method to pay his Creditors, therefore most humbly Hopes that in Consideration of the many great and signal Services he has rendered to his King and Country during the late War and since that Time the large Unsatisfied Claims which he has upon Government and his Ardent desire to render Your Majesty and his Country fresh Services from whom he always Endeavoured in the most Loyal Manner to Deserve well he may be indulged with such a Grant upon the Terms hereinafter mentioned only.

Your Petitioner therefore most Humbly prays that Your Majesty will be graciously pleased to Grant him and his Heirs Sixty Miles Square of Your Majesty's Common Lands on the Banks of or near to any of the Great Lakes or Rivers in North America or any other Quantity thereof in Lieu and full Satisfaction of his Claims, Your Petitioner Undertaking and Submitting to such Modes of Cultivation Population or other Terms of Improvements as may be thought necessary, or to make such Order in the premises as to Your Majesty in Your Great Wisdom and Goodness shall seem Meet.

And Your Petitioner as in Duty bound shall ever pray

Robert Rogers

Fleet Prison
Monday, 14th June, 1773

We whose Names are hereunto Subscribed, the Creditors of the Petitioner Robert Rogers, do humbly recommend the Petitioner to his Majesty's Royal Consideration.

> *Wm. Neate*
> *Champion Dickason*
> *Allen MacPar & Co*
> > *for themselves & as Attornies to Grig*
> > *Cunningham & Co of New York*
> *C. Hayley & Hopkins*
> *Henry & Thos Bromfield*
> *Peter Fowler*

The Names of the Generals and other Officers Alluded to in the foregoing Petition who have Certified for Major Rogers:

> *The Right Honble Lord Loudon*
> *The Right Honble Earl of Eglington*
> *General Webb*
> *General Abercrombie*
> *The Right Honble Sir Jeffery Amherst*
> *The Honble General Monckton*
> *Colonel Amherst*
> *The Honble Colonel Harvey*
> *The Honble Colonel West*
> *Colonel Grant*
> *Colonel Abercrombie*
> *Captain D'Arcy, Aide de Camp to General Amherst*

Annexes: Historical Items, Events and Figures

These annexes highlight some of the historical items, events, figures and other significant points mentioned in this work. A detailed knowledge of these points should enhance an understanding of the Rogers family and the historical period. The first section consists of significant or interesting items not generally known or appreciated and placed in this annex solely for enlightenment. The second section comprises short descriptions of historical events that had some impact on the period, arranged in chronological order. The third section holds short biographies of prominent historical figures arranged in alphabetical order for ease of reference.

Annex A: Historical Items & Other Significant Points

Independent Companies: During the Colonial period provincial regiments and other units were frequently raised on an as-required basis and usually broken up or disbanded soon after the threat no longer existed. These units were funded entirely by the provincial assemblies. Royal regiments, on the other hand, were created by the Crown and certain "independent companies" were raised for the defence of a particular province. These companies were intended for garrison duty in a particular area and were not generally trained for tactical operations, although exceptions occurred. These units were part of the royal establishment, formed under a royal warrant. Officers held royal commissions and were senior to provincial officers of the same rank. These units were funded by the Crown although the provincial assemblies were expected to contribute to the war chest. An example of an independent company was Gorham's Rangers, described below.

Rogers' Rangers was a special provincial unit, created for tactical operations, and fell somewhere between the two definitions above. Though the rangers were unique, they were not a royal unit nor raised under a royal warrant. They were funded by the Crown, but their officers did not hold a royal commission. Unlike independent companies, they were intended not for garrison duty but for full tactical operations. The Rangers enjoyed considerably more freedom than regular units, which contributed to their effectiveness, but at the end of hostilities they were subject to being disbanded like other provincial units. After the war, Robert was given a captain's commission in the South Carolina Independent Company which he afterwards sold to purchase a captaincy in the New York Independent Company. He lost this commission later when the unit was disbanded.

Successive French, British and American Military Command in North America

Colonial America

William Shirley	1741–1756
Edward Braddock	1754–1755
John Campbell (Lord Loudoun)	1756–1758
James Abercromby	1758–1759

New France (Canada)

Baron de Dieskau	1755–1756
Marquis de Montcalm	1756–1759

British North America

Sir Jeffrey Amherst	1759–1763
Thomas Gage	1763–1772
Frederick Haldimand (Acting)	1772–1774
Thomas Gage	1774–1775

Successive French, British and American Military Command in North America

The United States	America	Canada
George Washington 1775–1785	Sir William Howe 1775–1778	Sir Guy Carleton 1775–1778
	Sir Henry Clinton 1778–1782	Frederick Haldimand 1778–1784
	Sir Guy Carleton 1782–1783	

The United States	British North America
President George Washington 1789–1797	Lord Dorchester (Sir Guy Carleton) 1785–1795

Gorham's Rangers: Gorham's Rangers were raised on a royal warrant in 1744 by Joseph Gorham of Massachusetts. The original purpose of the unit was the defence of Annapolis Royal (Port Royal) just before the first siege of Louisbourg. One of three companies of Rangers, Gorham's was the only one kept in service after King George's War (1744–1748). It was later titled "His Majesty's First Independent Company of American Rangers." It was not part of the Rogers' Rangers corps but took part in the sieges of Louisbourg (1758) and Quebec (1759). In 1760, Gorham was promoted major of the two companies stationed in Nova Scotia, his own and Benoni Danks' that had also been at Quebec. He was later appointed major of a "Battalion of American Rangers on Regular Establishment," a position Robert never achieved. Three companies were with Lord Rollo on his attack on Cuba in 1762. Successful but diminished by sickness and casualties, the companies were drafted into other regiments left to garrison Havana. Gorham raised another company that formed part of the garrison of Halifax until November 1763. That summer most of his men were drafted into the 17th Regiment. The majority were killed or wounded moving up the river to relieve Detroit during Pontiac's uprising.

Annex B: Historical Events

The English Civil Wars and Commonwealth [1642–1660]: The struggle between King Charles I and Parliament in 1640 over the distribution of powers and religious freedom led to a division of the kingdom into two formidable factions. Civil war broke out in 1642. The English and Scottish Parliaments signed the Solemn League and Covenant in 1643, and the Scots became allies of the parliamentary forces, the so-called "Roundheads." Led by Oliver Cromwell, the army decisively defeated the "Royalists" at the Battle of Naseby in 1645. In 1646 the king surrendered to the Scottish army and the First Civil War ended. A new government was created and England was proclaimed a Commonwealth ruled by Parliament.

In 1648 the Scots signed a secret treaty with Charles and, with Irish support, rose in support of the king, marking the beginning of the Second Civil War.   Cromwell's army crushed the rebellions in Scotland and Ireland; as a result, the army became the supreme power in Great Britain. The king was brought to trial and beheaded in 1649.

A form of military dictatorship was established, and Cromwell became Lord Protector. Those who opposed it or disagreed with its policies were expelled from the House of Commons. The title and offices of the king and the House of Lords were abolished.   Cromwell adopted an aggressive commercial and colonial policy that led to a successful war with the Netherlands (1652–1654), but unpopular domestic policies and under-representation in Parliament led to discontent throughout the country. After Cromwell died in 1658, the power of the army and parliament quickly declined, and the people agitated for the return of the Stuarts. The king's son was crowned Charles II in 1660 at the Restoration.

The War of the Spanish Succession [1702–1713] "Queen Anne's War": When King Charles II of Spain died childless, the grandson of King Louis XIV of France ascended to the Spanish throne as King Philip V. This event greatly antagonised England and Holland, which were in growing competition with France, and Holy Roman Emperor Leopold I, who had claimed the succession on behalf of his son. A European war broke out in 1702 with England and most of northern Europe aligned against France, Spain, Bavaria, Portugal and Savoy. The conflict spilled over into the North American colonies of the major powers, where it was known as Queen Anne's War. French forces destroyed the English settlement at Bonavista, Newfoundland, and captured St. John's early in the war. British forces later gained control of Port-Royal and with it all of Acadia in

Opposite: a recreated unit of King's Rangers following the 1st Foot Guards, near Mount Independence, Vermont, 1994.

1710, but the following year a British fleet was wrecked in an abortive attempt to sail to Quebec. The Treaty of Utrecht in 1713 settled a number of succession disputes and granted England considerable territory. While France retained Île St-Jean (PEI) and Île Royal (Cape Breton), they ceded Acadia to the English and restored to them all of Newfoundland and the Hudson Bay drainage basin. This war marked the end of French colonial expansion in America and the rise of the British Empire, although the French went on fighting to hold what they had acquired.

The War of the Austrian Succession [1739–1748] "King George's War": From 1713 to 1739 French overseas trade increased astronomically, largely because of almost exclusive access to the Spanish Empire. British trade stagnated during the same period, and, to oust France from her vast market, England declared war on Spain (the War of Jenkins' Ear) 19 October 1739. War with France would have quickly followed had it not been for the outbreak of hostilities between the continental powers over the accession of Maria Theresa to the Imperial Habsburg (Austrian) throne. Britain and France were drawn into the conflict on opposing sides . This proved a disaster for both. A British army was driven off the continent after being soundly defeated in Flanders, and French maritime trade was eventually ruined by the Royal Navy. In North America the conflict was known as King George's War, and it raged between the frontier settlements of New England and New France. An Anglo-American force captured Louisbourg but was no more able to conquer Canada than the French and Canadians were able to conquer the English colonies. In 1748 the Treaty of Aix-la-Chapelle ended the war but in reality settled nothing. Britain exchanged Louisbourg for Madras, India; the Netherlands was ceded to Austria; and Silesia went to Prussia as part of the settlements. No powers were satisfied with their respective allies, and changes in alliances were made by the time of the outbreak of the Seven Years' War.

The Seven Years' War [1756–1763] "French and Indian War": The Seven Years' War, the first truly global conflict, started in America in 1754 when a Virginia major of Militia, George Washington, ambushed a small French detachment in the Ohio Valley. Eventually the protagonists were Britain, Prussia and Hanover against France, Austria, Sweden, Saxony, Russia and Spain. Britain's war aims were to destroy the French navy and merchant fleet, seize her possessions and eliminate France as a commercial rival. They therefore declined to commit their main forces on the continent, leaving that part of the war to allies, and concentrated on America. Although fighting had broken out in America, war was not officially declared until May 1756. The first years saw numerous French successes, including the defeat of Braddock (1755), securing of Lake Ontario (1756), destruction of Fort William Henry (1757) and the crushing defeat of the

British army at Ticonderoga (1758). The tide of war began to turn in 1758, however, as the British took Louisbourg. Ticonderoga, Niagara and Quebec fell the following year and in 1760 France lost all of New France to Great Britain with the surrender of Montreal. This essentially ended the war in America, but the conflict continued elsewhere for some time. The Treaty of Paris (1763) redrew the map of the colonial powers around the world. Guadeloupe and St-Pierre and Miquelon were retained by France but Canada and Cape Breton became British territory. To persuade Spain to sign the treaty, France also ceded the vast Louisiana territory to Spain in compensation for the loss of Florida to Britain.

Pontiac's Uprising [1763]: In the spring of 1763 the Indian war chief Pontiac* ignited hostilities against Britain by leading an alliance of Ottawa, Huron, Potawatomi and Ojibwa against Fort Detroit and a number of other forts in the west. This conflict is sometimes known as Pontiac's Conspiracy. The Fort was held under siege and the uprising spread. On 29 July at the Battle of Bloody Run, Pontiac's braves routed a British force of 260, and only the action of Rogers' Rangers prevented complete disaster.† As the siege dragged on, Pontiac's forces began to leave for their families to provide for the coming winter. News of the formal treaty between England and France at the end of the Seven Years' War removed all hope of French assistance in his struggle. A series of treaties was signed in July 1765, with the prestigious Pontiac as a key signatory. He insisted that making peace did not entail the surrender of the Indians' lands.

The American Revolutionary War [1776–1783]: The American War of Independence was the inevitable result of lack of understanding between Great Britain and her colonies, caused by a growing feeling of nationalism in America coupled with resentment of necessary though unpopular fiscal policies of the mother country. The conflict cut across ethnic, religious, class and occupational lines, and at least some members of every group could be found on both sides during the war. Not all of Britain's sixteen colonies in America supported the revolt. Quebec, Nova Scotia and Newfoundland, for a variety of reasons, refused to participate and remained loyal to the Crown.

The basic causes of the revolution started earlier in the century. The conclusion of the French and Indian War ended the threat to the peace and security of the southern colonies. By the mid-1760's they had evolved into self-conscious, self-reliant, self-willed and independent communities, who considered themselves capable of administering their own affairs. America was prosperous and enjoyed an exceptionally high standard of living. The

---

* See Chief Pontiac in Historical Figures below.
† For a description of this battle see Section 2–4, page 150.

colonies, with nearly one fifth of all British subjects, had a low, almost nonexistent rate of taxation, while the people of the mother country were heavily taxed. Financially burdened with a crippling national debt from a war fought largely on behalf of her colonies, Britain enacted measures to tax directly those who benefited from the war. This, however, was viewed by the colonists as "taxation without representation". Officials also levied heavier duties under the provisions of existing Trade and Navigation Acts to which the colonies strenuously objected as being exceedingly harsh. In 1774, Britain passed the Quebec Act that restored French civil law, recognized the Catholic religion and extended the boundaries of the colony to the Ohio River. This was considered an attempt to revive the old French threat, a restriction to the westward expansion of the colonies, and unacceptable interference in their internal affairs. While other sources of conflict were present, those of security, taxation and perceived oppression are considered the major causes of the Revolution.

Americans do not see the war as a fratricidal conflict, but prefer the image of an entire people rising up united against their British oppressors. Such was certainly not the case. Nearly 500,000 colonists, some 20% of the population, remained loyal to the Crown. These people shared the same grievances but objected to mob violence and the extralegal actions taken to achieve the aim. Another large segment of the population preferred to remain neutral and to simply live with the daily struggle for existence. The vast majority had no intention of separation, but the situation deteriorated so rapidly that independence became the only option. The Revolution was in fact a civil war fought within a war for colonial liberation. In the end the British found they could not continue to pour money into a losing cause and withdrew from the southern colonies, recognizing their independence. The three northern colonies accepted thousands of Loyalist refugees, and out of the ashes of the conflict two great nations were born.

Annex C: Historical Figures

Abercromby, James [General]: James Abercromby was born in Scotland in 1706 and like many another Scot made the army his career. He was elected to the British House of Commons in 1734 for the area of Banff. He entered the army as an infantry officer and was a colonel by 1746. He was promoted major general in 1756 and sent to America as second in command to General John Campbell, Earl of Loudoun. In 1758 he was appointed commander-in-chief. That year he led an army of some 15,000 men up Lake Champlain and by early July was laying siege to Fort Carillon (Ticonderoga). After a series of futile assaults and the loss of nearly 2,000 men, he was forced to withdraw. In the eyes of his superiors, he had revealed such incompetence that he was recalled and replaced by Sir Jeffrey Amherst. In spite of this potentially career-destroying setback, he was promoted lieutenant general in 1759 and general in 1772. He was later named King's Painter for Scotland and Deputy Warden of Stirling Castle, both life appointments. He died in Scotland in 1781.

Allen, Ethan: Ethan Allen was born in 1737 in Litchfield, Connecticut. He first worked as a lead miner. He saw service with the British during the French and Indian War, probably in the colonial militia. In 1769 he moved to the New Hampshire Grants and became a prominent figure in the struggle between New York and New Hampshire for control of the region. The area, which eventually became the State of Vermont, had been claimed by both provinces for more than 100 years, and both had issued grants to prospective settlers. In 1764, an Order in Council finally awarded the entire territory to New York. In 1770, Allen organized a band of farmers known as the "Green Mountain Boys," named after the range of mountains near their farms. They were initially formed to resist New York authorities trying to evict residents who had received their land grants from New Hampshire. This group was a notoriously rough bunch, reluctant to take orders from anyone but Allen, who commanded them as their colonel.

On the outbreak of the Revolution in 1775, he offered the services of his unofficial militia against the British. After some discussion as to who was in charge, he accompanied Benedict Arnold on the attack and capture of Fort Ticonderoga on 10 May 1775. Allen later rendered valuable service under General John Philip Schuyler during the expedition into Canada. He was captured near Montreal in September 1775 but was eventually exchanged for Archibald Campbell, Commander of the 2nd Battalion, Fraser's Highlanders, in May 1778. Following his release he returned home and was appointed a Lieutenant colonel in the Continental Army and a major general of militia.

He wrote a number of books and pamphlets, mostly controversial. With his brother and other Vermonters, he devoted much of his time to the territorial dispute, including direct negotiations with the Governor of Canada in 1781. Ostensibly to establish Vermont as a Canadian province, these negotiations were probably designed to force Congress to establish a new state.* For this activity, he was charged with treason but the case was never proved. Having failed to obtain statehood for the area or its annexation to Canada, he quietly settled on his farm at Burlington, where he died in 1789. The region came into existence as the State of Vermont in 1791.

Amherst, Sir Jeffrey [Field Marshal, 1st Baron Amherst]: Jeffrey Amherst was born in Kent in 1717. He entered the army as an ensign in the Coldstream Guards in 1731 and served with distinction during the War of the Austrian Succession (1740–47) as aide-de-camp to General Ligonier and the Duke of Cumberland. He was promoted colonel in 1756, and major general in 1758, and in 1759 he was placed in command of the expedition against Louisbourg. Following the successful conclusion of that operation, he was promoted lieutenant general and appointed to succeed James Abercromby as commander-in-chief of British forces in North America. He commanded the army that advanced up Lake Champlain to take Ticonderoga while General Wolfe attacked Quebec and Sir William Johnson captured Niagara. The following year he directed the three armies converging on Montreal and accepted the formal capitulation of New France. For all these accomplishments he was knighted in 1761 and appointed Governor General of British North America.

In November 1763 he returned to England to answer criticism of his handling of the Pontiac uprising. He was later appointed Governor of Guernsey in 1770. Although he was initially chosen to succeed General Gage as commander-in-chief in America in 1775, he could not bring himself to accept partly because his wife was an American. In 1776 he was ennobled as 1st Baron Amherst and in 1778 promoted to the rank of general. Twice serving as Acting Commander-in-Chief of the British Army (1772–1782 and 1783–1793), he was the Government's principal military adviser during the Revolution. On Lord Howe's request for recall, the Government again turned to Amherst but again he declined, saying that insufficient forces had been assigned to ensure victory. When France entered the war, he recommended that distressing the French should be England's principal objective, with the result of further reducing the forces available for the American theatre. In 1780, he assisted in the suppression of the Gordon riots and was created a Baron of the United Kingdom in 1788. He was confirmed as Commander-in-Chief of the British Army in 1793 and

---

*   For information and further details on the Vermont negotiations, see Section 2–3, page 58.

promoted to field marshal in 1796, the year of his retirement. He died the following year at "Montreal," his estate in Kent.

Arnold, Benedict [Major General]: Benedict Arnold was born in Norwich, Connecticut, in 1741. He ran away from home at the age of 14 and joined a provincial regiment in the French and Indian War. He soon deserted, however, and later became a merchant in New Haven. On the outbreak of the War for Independence he joined the Colonial forces and assisted Ethan Allen in the capture of Fort Ticonderoga. He later took part in the unsuccessful siege of Quebec in 1775, for which he was made a brigadier general. He commanded the American fleet at the Battle of Lake Champlain (1776) which, although defeated, delayed the British advance from Canada. At the Battle of Ridgefield his horse was killed under him; for his gallantry in this engagement he was promoted major general. He fought with distinction at the Battle of Saratoga. Although General Washington greatly admired him, he had influential enemies. He was deeply embittered in 1777 when five of his inferiors in rank were promoted over his head. In 1778 he was placed in command at Philadelphia, and in the same year he was court-martialled for embezzlement, for which he received a reprimand. In 1780, having already gone over to the British, he sought and obtained command of the key fort at West Point. He conspired with Major John André to deliver the fortress but was discovered and escaped through the British lines. He was subsequently given a command in the British Army and led raids in Virginia and Connecticut. After the war he went to England and lived in poverty until his death in 1801.

Braddock, Edward [Major General]: Edward Braddock was born in 1695. He entered the army in his father's regiment, the Coldstream Guards, and rose to command the regiment in 1745 as lieutenant colonel. He saw service in France (1746) and the Netherlands (1746–47). He was promoted major general in 1754 and appointed commander-in-chief of British forces in America. He arrived on 20 February 1755 at the beginning of what became the French and Indian War. With 2500 men, he set off to assault Fort Duquesne (now Pittsburgh), a French fort on the Ohio River. Leaving 1300 men and most of his artillery at a base camp, he advanced with a light column of 1200 men and officers including Lieutenant Colonel Thomas Gage, Daniel Boone, Colonel George Washington and Captain Horatio Gates. Seven miles from their objective the force was ambushed by 900 French regulars and their Indian allies, an engagement became known as the Battle of Monongahela. The result was a resounding British defeat with 914 casualties (65%) to only 28 French killed or wounded. Among the British wounded was Braddock himself, who died a few days later on 13 July at the Great Meadows near Fort Necessity. The survivors were led to safety by Colonel Washington.

Burgoyne, Sir John [General]: John Burgoyne was born in London 1723 and schooled at Westminster. He joined the Horse Guards in 1737 but, after several years without promotion, he resigned in 1741. In 1744 he rejoined the army by purchasing a commission in the 1st Royal Dragoons and served as a coronet during the War of the Austrian Succession (1740–47). Promoted lieutenant in 1745, he purchased a captaincy in the Royals in 1747. In 1751, he eloped with Lady Charlotte Stanley, daughter of the 11th Earl of Derby who disapproved of the match. Burgoyne sold his commission to pay his debts, and the couple moved to France. In 1755 they returned to England with their daughter, born in 1754. In 1756, Burgoyne bought a captain's commission in the 11th Dragoons and took part in the raids on the French coast. For distinguished service, he was transferred to the elite Second or Coldstream Guards in 1758. His subsequent rise in the army was due to a large extent to the influence of his father-in-law. He was promoted lieutenant colonel in 1759 and received permission to raise a cavalry regiment to be known as the 16th Regiment of Light Dragoons. The King and Queen later reviewed his regiment, and it was renamed the Queen's Light Dragoons. In 1761 he was elected to Parliament, first for Midhurst, later Preston, which he represented until the time of his death. As a brigadier general, he rendered further distinguished service along the Spanish–Portuguese frontier.   He returned to England and became a severe critic of British colonial policy in America.

Burgoyne was promoted major general in 1772 and sent to America to serve under General Gage in May 1775. He was in command of a battery at the Battle of Bunker Hill. On 5 December 1775, he returned to England to attend his wife who was gravely ill (possibly asthma). In April 1776 he returned to America as second in command to General Sir Guy Carleton, Governor of Quebec. After helping to repel the American assault on Canada, he clashed with Carleton over the prosecution of the war and returned to England, arriving shortly after the death of his wife. Promoted lieutenant general, he returned again to Canada in March 1777 to command the invasion force established to proceed down Lake Champlain and link with General Howe's army at New York. After a series of indecisive battles, he retreated to Saratoga, and running short of supplies, surrendered his army to General Horatio Gates on 17 October.* This was the turning point in the war, for it encouraged France to enter the conflict in support of the Colonies. After his surrender, Congress refused to honour the Convention of Saratoga that would have permitted the defeated troops to return home. The following year Washington granted Burgoyne permission to return to England. There he was subjected to harsh attacks in Parliament and in the press and deprived of his command. He was later

---

* For details of this expedition, see Burgoyne's Campaign in Section 2–3, page 52.

appointed Commander-in-Chief of Ireland in 1782 but held the position for only a brief period. He afterwards devoted himself to his lifelong interest in the theatre and died in 1792.

Campbell, Lord John [Earl of Loudoun]: Lord Loudoun arrived in New York on 23 July 1756 and succeeded Governor William Shirley as commander-in-chief of British forces in America. He planned an attack on Louisbourg for 1757, but while the army was preparing at Halifax, scouts reported a large French fleet in the area, and the attack was aborted. In the meantime, the Marquis de Montcalm attacked and destroyed Fort William Henry at the foot of Lake George. Loudoun was impressed with the Rangers and ordered Robert to train a number of regular officers in ranger tactics. These trainees were chosen by Gage and he was subsequently ordered to create the 80th Regiment to act as Rangers using these officers. The plan was intended to reduce the need for undisciplined provincials, but it failed to achieve the desired results. Loudoun was recalled in March 1758 and succeeded by General Abercromby.

Carleton, Sir Guy [General, 1st Baron Dorchester]: Guy Carleton was born in Ireland in 1724. He entered the army in 1742 and was a colonel when he fought under General Wolfe at Quebec. During this campaign he was badly wounded while commanding the Grenadiers at the Battle of the Plains of Abraham, and he was wounded again in subsequent engagements. He made a name for himself as one of the bravest and most talented officers in the army. In 1766 he was appointed Lieutenant Governor of Quebec, and in 1768 he succeeded James Murray as Governor. More than any other British officer who served in America, he understood the problem of governing a far-flung empire composed of diverse peoples. Local established institutions and traditions had to be preserved and loyalty obtained by persuasion not compulsion. Endorsing and acting on these principles, he was viewed with distrust by the English settlers but much respected by the French. He was one of the architect of the Quebec Act in 1774. Against the advance of General Montgomery in 1775/76 he fought a rear guard action, surrendering the forts along Lake Champlain and the Richelieu River, and eventually withdrawing from Montreal to the fortress at Quebec, narrowly escaping capture. Although they surrounded the city, the Americans had insufficient forces to secure their objective and were forced to withdraw in May when the advance party of Burgoyne's reinforcements arrived from England. Carleton began pursuit as far as Crown Point, driving the Americans out of Quebec. He defeated Arnold in the Battle of Lake Champlain, but by October he decided that it was too late in the season for further action and withdrew to Canada. For his success in defending Quebec he was created a Knight of the Bath. He was nevertheless relieved of military command by Burgoyne for the following year's campaign although he retained his civil authority as Governor. He was enraged at this turn of events and demanded recall. This was refused, but in 1778 he was relieved by General Haldimand as Commander-in-Chief of the Northern Department. He resigned from the governorship as a result of differences with Lord George Germain, Secretary of State for the Colonies. In 1782 he relieved Sir Henry Clinton as commander-in-chief of America near the end of the war, and had charge of the evacuation of New York by British and Loyalist forces and their dependants in November 1783. After spending some time in England, he was created Baron Dorchester and appointed Governor-in-Chief of British North America in 1786. He opposed the division of the Province of Quebec into Upper and Lower Canada, provided for in the Constitutional Act of 1791. He asked to resign and was finally granted permission in 1795. In 1796 he left Canada to retire to private life and died in England in 1808.

Clinton, Sir Henry [General]: Henry Clinton was born in Newfoundland in 1738. He was the grandson of the sixth Earl of Lincoln, cousin of the second Duke of Newcastle, and son of Admiral George Clinton, Governor of Newfoundland (1731–1741) and Governor of New York (1741–1751). He attended school in America and served for a time in the New York Militia. He went to England and in 1751 obtained a commission in the 2nd Foot Guards. In 1756 he was promoted captain and appointed as an aide-de-camp to Sir John Ligonier, commander-in-chief of the British Army. He was promoted lieutenant colonel in 1758 in the 1st Foot Guards. Clinton was wounded in Germany in 1762 while acting as an aide to Prince Ferdinand of Brunswick at the Battle of Johannesburg. He was subsequently promoted colonel and posted as second in command of Gibraltar. He married in 1767 but his wife died in 1772 following the birth of their fourth child in the year he was promoted major general. In 1775 he was sent to America under General Gage and was active at the Battle of Bunker Hill. He was ordered south in command of an expedition into North Carolina, and after receiving additional troops under Lord Cornwallis, he moved into South Carolina. Following his failure to take Charleston, he rejoined Sir William Howe for an attack on New York in August 1776. After the defeat of Washington at the Battle of Long Island, he was knighted and promoted lieutenant general for his part in the engagement. He was subsequently appointed second in command to Lord Howe, and on 4 February 1778, after Burgoyne's humiliating defeat, he was appointed commander-in-chief in America when Howe was recalled. In 1780 he captured Charleston and the entire southern army of the United States. After Lord Cornwallis was forced to surrender his army at Yorktown in 1781, Clinton resigned his command and returned to England. He was relieved by Sir Guy Carleton. Clinton was promoted general in 1793 and Governor of Gibraltar in 1794. He died in office at Gibraltar in 1795.

Cornwallis, Charles [Lieutenant General, 1st Marquis Cornwallis]: Charles Cornwallis, the son of the 1st Earl Cornwallis, was born in London and educated at Eton. He served as an aide-de-camp to the Marquis of Granby during the Seven Years War. Although opposed to the taxation of the American Colonists, he accepted a command in the Revolutionary War. With an inferior force, he defeated General Gates at Camden in 1780 and more than held his own against vastly superior forces at Guilford in 1781. Later that year he was besieged at Yorktown and forced to surrender his army. From 1786 to 1793 he was Governor General of India and commander-in-chief of British forces, distinguishing himself by victories over Tippoo Sahib. As Lord Lieutenant of Ireland (1798–1801), he was responsible for the crushing of the 1798 rebellion. As plenipotentiary to France, he negotiated the Peace of Amiens in 1802. He was reappointed Governor General of India in 1804 and died at Ghazipur the following year.

Dieskau, Jean Hermann [Major General, Baron de Dieskau]: Baron Dieskau was born in Saxony in 1701 and entered the French army young. He became an aide-de-camp to Maurice de Saxe and in 1748 attained the rank of major general in the infantry. In 1755 he was sent to Canada as commander-in-chief of the French forces in America. In September of that year he suffered a humiliating defeat at the hands of the English under Sir William Johnson at the Battle of Lake George. He was wounded during the action and captured, to be held prisoner until 1763 when he was exchanged and returned to France. He was succeeded as commander-in-chief by the Marquis de Montcalm.

Gage, Thomas [General]: Thomas Gage, the second son of Thomas, 1st Viscount Gage, was born in Sussex, England in 1719. He entered the army in 1740. He saw action against the Scots at the Battle of Culloden and became known as a brave but not notably talented officer. As a lieutenant colonel commanding the 44th Regiment, he was in the vanguard of Braddock's force at the Battle of Monongahela in 1755, an engagement in which he was severely wounded. Gage thus saw at first hand how irregular troops could be used to advantage, but like most British officers he was contemptuous of provincial units. In 1757 he asked Lord Loudoun if he could raise a regiment to emulate the ability and talents of Rogers' Rangers but with the discipline of a regular unit. This would reduce the need for undisciplined provincial units such as the rangers. He even offered to pay all expenses himself. Loudoun agreed to the proposal but found the £2600 necessary for creation of the unit, using officers trained in the Ranger Cadet Company.* This unit was named the 80th Regiment of Light Infantry. It marked the beginning of the concept of light infantry in the

---

* For details on this company and the beginning of the animosity Gage bore toward Robert Rogers see Section 2–4, page 128.

British Army. The regiment was severely mauled in its first encounter, however, and Gage became disillusioned. Gage served under Abercromby at Ticonderoga (1758), Johnson at Niagara (1759) and Amherst at Montreal (1760). He was promoted to major general in 1760 and appointed Military Governor of Montreal, subordinate to James Murray at Quebec, and his unyielding character and stern efficiency soon brought him to the attention of colonial authorities. In 1763 he relieved Amherst as commander-in-chief of British forces in America, and in 1770 he was promoted lieutenant general. He was absent on leave in England (1773–74) at the time of the Boston Tea Party, having been temporarily relieved by General Haldimand. On his return in 1774 he was also appointed Governor of Massachusetts. In rigorously enforcing unpopular British measures, he unknowingly aggravated an already tense situation. He became increasingly alarmed at the growing unrest in America and was responsible for ordering British forces to Concord and Lexington to destroy a suspected cache of military supplies. He showed himself to be totally incompetent to deal with the admittedly difficult situation that led to the outbreak of the American Revolution. Lord North and the Cabinet were very critical and felt he should have done more to suppress disturbances in America. He was in command at the Battle of Bunker Hill, but was subsequently relieved 16 September 1775. The military command in America was split between Sir William Howe at Boston and Sir Guy Carleton at Quebec. Gage was promoted general in 1782, but his career was effectively over after his return from America. He died in London in 1787.

Gates, Horatio [Major General]: Horatio Gates was born in Maldon, Essex in 1728. He entered the British army and served in America under Braddock. He escaped with difficulty from the Battle of Monongahela in 1755. On the establishment of peace in 1763, he bought an estate in Virginia. He sided with the Americans during the Revolutionary War and in 1775 was made Adjutant General. In 1776 he assumed command of the army that had retreated from Canada. In August 1777 he took command of the Northern Army and forced the surrender of General Burgoyne at Saratoga. Success gained him a reputation, and he sought to supplant Washington as commander-in-chief. In 1780 he commanded the Army of the South but was routed by Cornwallis near Camden, and Congress relieved him of command. He retired to Virginia till 1790, when he emancipated his slaves and settled in New York.

Haldimand, Sir Frederick [General]: Frederick Haldimand was born in Switzerland in 1718. He served as a Swiss mercenary in the armies of the King of Sardinia and Frederick the Great, and saw action in Prussia and Holland before transferring to the British Army in 1754. He went to America as lieutenant colonel in command of the 60th or Royal American Regiment in 1756. At Ticonderoga (1758) he was wounded while serving under General Abercromby and was promoted colonel. The following year Haldimand served under General Prideaux and Sir William Johnson and was present at the fall of Fort Niagara (1759). He commanded the regiment in the advance on Montreal (1760) under General Amherst. After the surrender of New France he was twice appointed military governor of Trois-Rivières (1762 and 1765) and served as Governor of West Florida (1767–1773). He was promoted major general in 1773 and appointed second in command in America. He relieved General Gage while the later was absent on leave in England. During this period the Boston Tea Party took place. He was recalled to England in 1775 and remained there until his promotion to lieutenant general and appointment as governor in Canada and Commander-in-Chief of the Northern Department in 1777. He succeeded Sir Guy Carleton in 1778 and served in this capacity until 1786, although he left the province in 1784. At the end of the Revolutionary War, he was responsible for the settlement of the Loyalist refugees in what is now Ontario. He was knighted for his services to the Crown in 1785 and died in Switzerland in 1791.

Haviland, William [Brigadier General]: William Haviland was a lieutenant colonel in 1755, commanding the 27th regiment of Foot. As a colonel in 1757, he was the post commander of Fort Edward and clashed with Robert Rogers (2–4) in numerous confrontations over the lack of discipline among the rangers. He developed a deep-seated hatred for Robert and his rangers that almost destroyed the corps, and on at least one occasion the commander-in-chief had to intervene. Haviland was placed in command of Fort Ticonderoga in 1759. In the following year he was promoted brigadier general to lead the forces advancing on Montreal from the Champlain Valley. After the French and Indian War he disappeared into obscurity.

Howe, Lord George [Brigadier General, 3rd Viscount Howe]: Lord George Howe, a grandson of King George I, was a popular and effective leader in America. On several occasions he accompanied Robert Rogers (2–4) on patrols and returned full of praise for the abilities and methods of the ranger corps. He was an adept student and insisted a number of the ranger tactics be incorporated during reforms to the British Army. In 1758 the rangers formed the vanguard of the 15,500 man army that sailed up Lake George on 5 July, under command of General Abercromby and Lord George Howe. While moving into position for an assault on Fort Carillon (Ticonderoga), the advance party was attacked by a force of some 200 French scouts. Although they were routed, the French had done considerable damage: Howe had been killed. His untimely and probably unnecessary death had an immediate demoralizing effect on the entire army.*

---

* For details on this operation see Section 2–4, page 134.

Howe, Sir William [General, 5th Viscount Howe]: Howe was born in London in 1729. He was the younger son of 2nd Viscount Howe, brother of General Lord George Howe (3rd Viscount) and of Admiral Lord Richard Howe (4th Viscount later Earl Howe, First Lord of the Admiralty). On leaving Eton in 1746 he obtained a commission in the Duke of Cumberland's Light Dragoons. He served with distinction and was quickly seen as the most ingenious junior officer in the service. He was known as a strict disciplinarian and a respected tactician, well liked by his officers and men. During the French and Indian War he served under General Wolfe at Louisbourg and Quebec, performing brilliantly in command of an infantry battalion which Wolfe described as "the best trained in America." Returned to England, he became a Whig Member of Parliament for Nottingham (1758–1780) and opposed Government policy in America. He was promoted major general in 1772 and sent to America in the spring of 1775 as second in command to General Gage. He commanded the assault at the Battle of Bunker Hill. That summer he relieved Gage as commander-in-chief in America. Howe was responsible for withdrawing British forces from Boston and relocating their headquarters to Halifax. During the summer and fall of 1776, he successfully attacked New York and reestablished his headquarters in the southern colonies. The next year's plan called for his army to move north and join Burgoyne's force at Albany, thus effectively splitting New England; but having received no instructions from England (as he later maintained), Howe proceeded with his own plan to march south to take the American capital at Philadelphia. On 25 September he entered the city, three weeks before Burgoyne's surrender at Saratoga, but he was in no position to send relief forces because of Washington's efforts to dislodge him. During the following months, he became more and more frustrated with the lack of progress, caused mainly by a shortage of troops, and demanded recall. During this period he was severely criticized for inactivity. On 4 February 1778, two days before the Franco-American Alliance was signed, he was relieved by Sir Henry Clinton. In England, he claimed that he had not received sufficient support from the home government and demanded that a parliamentary committee enquire into his conduct in America to clear him of suspicion and innuendo. The committee's findings, however, were inconclusive. On the outbreak of war with France, he was placed in command of the Northern and later the Eastern Districts of England. He was promoted Lieutenant General of Ordnance in 1782 and general in 1793. He died in 1814 at Plymouth, where he had been Governor for several years.

Johnson, Sir John [Major General, 2nd Baronet]: John Johnson was born 5 November 1742, the eldest son of Sir William Johnson (below) by his first wife, Catherine Weisenberg. He was knighted in 1765 and succeeded to the baronetcy on the death of his father in 1774. He inherited his father's estate in the Mohawk Valley of New York, but owing to his loyalist sympathies, he was forced to flee to Canada in 1776. He organized and commanded the King's Royal Regiment of New York that played an active role in the Revolutionary War. At the end of the war he settled in Canada and succeeded his cousin Guy Johnson as Superintendent of Indian Affairs in British North America. He greatly assisted the settlement of the Loyalists, particularly along the upper St. Lawrence River. Because of his many duties, he was forced to rely on James Rogers (2–3) to oversee the needs of his regiment.* He was appointed to the Legislative Council of Quebec in 1787 and to that of Lower Canada in 1796. During the War of 1812 he commanded the six township battalions of the Quebec militia. He died in 1830 at the age of 88 years, and the title passed to his third son.

Johnson, Sir William [Major General, 1st Baronet]: William Johnson was born in the Manor of Killeen, County Meath, Ireland in 1715. His father, Christopher Johnson, was one of the poor tenant farmers on the estate of the Warren family, but his mother, Anne Warren, was the daughter of the Earl of Fingal. In June 1737, William was offered an opportunity to manage the estate of an uncle, Admiral Peter Warren, consisting of some 14,000 acres in the Mohawk Valley of New York. He arrived in America in 1738 to assume his responsibilities and became very friendly with the Iroquois. In 1739 he was attracted to Catherine Weisenberg who was an indentured servant of a neighbour. He obtained her indenture and she became his housekeeper and mistress from 1739–1745. In 1742, William was adopted by the Iroquois League and given the name "Warraghiyagey" which means "The man who undertakes great things." In 1743, he was appointed "Superintendent of the Affairs of the Six Nations for the Colony of New York" by the Governor of New York, Admiral George Clinton. In 1745, "Catty" was in failing health and William married her on her death bed, thus making their children legitimate. The following year he obtained from the Mohawks for the sum of £14 a fifteen-year-old French Canadian prisoner named Angélique Vitry. She became his mistress and remained so until 1749, when she was returned to Canada to be reunited with her family. There were no children of this union.

In 1750, William was appointed to the Governor's Council, but within a year he had become so disillusioned with the Colonial government's treatment of the Indians that he resigned his positions. In 1752 his uncle Admiral Peter Warren died and left William his estate, which added to his existing holdings, amounted to a considerable property. In 1754, William married Degonwadonti, better known to history as Molly Brant. She was the daughter of Chief Nicholas Brant of the Mohawk tribe and brother of Joseph Brant, war chief of the tribe. On 14 April 1755, at the instance of

---

* For details see Section 2–3, page 72.

the tribes, William was appointed Superintendent of Indian Affairs in the Northern Department by King George II. In this position he was directly responsible to the Crown for the conduct of Indian affairs and not to any of the colonial governments. His area of responsibility included the colonies of Virginia, Maryland, Pennsylvania, New Jersey, New York, Connecticut, Massachusetts, New Hampshire, Nova Scotia and Quebec. In addition, he was promoted to the provincial rank of major general and subsequently accepted the command of the Crown Point campaign. On 31 December, the King personally proclaimed his rank and position to be permanent as "Colonel, Agent and Sole Supervisor of the Six Nations of Indians and all other Nations and all other Tribes" and stated that no person in America had the power to discharge him from this office. In addition, in recognition of his services to the Crown and his victory at the Battle of Lake George, he was awarded £5000, and the King conferred a baronetcy upon him. He died at Johnson Hall, Johnstown, New York, on 11 July 1774, at the age of 59 years. The title fell to his eldest son, Sir John Johnson. The position as Superintendent of Indian Affairs was assumed by his nephew and son-in-law Guy Johnson.

Montcalm de Saint-Véran, Louis-Joseph de [Lieutenant General, Marquis de Montcalm]: Montcalm was born at the Château de Candial in France in 1712. He entered the army at the age of nine and served with distinction during the War of the Austrian Succession (1740–47). He was promoted Maréchal de Camp in 1756, and then relieved Baron de Dieskau as commander-in-chief of French forces in America. In this position, he was subordinate to Governor Vaudreuil, to whom he developed open hostility because of his corrupt administration. He seized Oswego in 1756 and destroyed Fort William Henry in 1757. On the advance of superior forces under General Abercromby in 1758, he slowly withdrew up Lake Champlain, avoiding a major confrontation which he could not win because of shortages of troops and supplies. Though heavily outnumbered, he conducted a successful defence against British attacks on Fort Carillon, in effect a sweeping victory against Abercromby's invading army. That year he was appointed lieutenant general, the second highest rank in the French army. Montcalm was a competent field commander and strategist, but British control of the sea deprived him of essential reinforcements and supplies. On the advance of General Amherst the following year, he withdrew to Quebec but was forced to engage forces under General Wolfe at the Battle of the Plains of Abraham 13 September 1759. During this action he was mortally wounded and died the following day.

Montgomery, Richard [Brigadier General]: Richard Montgomery was born in Dublin, Ireland. He served in the British Army in the French and Indian War and afterwards settled in New York. On the outbreak of the

American Revolution he was appointed brigadier general in the Colonial army. He served under General Philip Schuyler during the expedition to Canada in 1775 and was in command at the capture of Montreal. He was killed leading the assault on Quebec; Benedict Arnold succeeded him.

Pontiac [Chief of the Ottawas]: Pontiac was born about 1720 probably near Detroit. He rose to become Chief of the Ottawas and leader of the confederation of tribes of the Ohio Valley and Lake Region. He distinguished himself in service with the French and may have been present with the French and Indian forces that defeated Braddock near Fort Duquesne at the Battle of Monongahela in 1755. In the spring of 1763, he initiated hostilities by leading an alliance of Ottawa, Huron, Potawatomi and Ojibwa against Fort Detroit. This conflict is sometimes known as Pontiac's Conspiracy. The fort was held under siege as the uprising spread. On 29 July at the Battle of Bloody Run, Pontiac's braves routed a British force of 260, and only the action of Robert Rogers and his Rangers prevented a complete disaster.* As the siege dragged on, his forces began to leave to provide for their families for the coming winter. News of the treaty between England and France at the end of the Seven Years' War removed all hope of French assistance in his struggle. Several treaties of peace were signed in July 1765. The most important signer was Pontiac, who maintained that in making peace the Indians were not surrendering their lands. Those still hostile to the British, however, turned against him and even expelled him from his own village. He led a wandering life until he was murdered in 1769 by a Peoria assassin in Illinois country near the present site of St. Louis.

Shirley, William [Major General]: William Shirley was born in Sussex in 1674. He was educated at Cambridge and became a lawyer. In 1731 he moved to Boston, Massachusetts, where he was seen as an upholder of British Colonial interests in America. In 1741 he was appointed Governor of the Colony, a position in which he ably served until 1756. In that year he was removed from office, largely because he had authorized an unsuccessful assault on Fort Niagara during the French and Indian War. In 1761 he was appointed Governor of the Bahama Islands, a post from which he retired the year before his death in 1771.

Simcoe, John Graves [General]: John Graves Simcoe was born at Cotterstock in England in 1752, the son of Captain John Simcoe of the Royal Navy. His father commanded the ship H.M.S. *Pembroke* and served with distinction under Admiral Saunders during the French and Indian War. His ship was in the fleet which took part in the attack on Quebec in 1759, but Captain Simcoe died of pneumonia during the siege of Quebec. John Graves Simcoe was educated at Eton and Oxford but left university in 1770 before graduation to enlist in the British Army. After serving in

---

* For details on this battle see Section 2–4, page 150.

England and Ireland he sailed for America and was appointed to command the Grenadier Company of the 40th Regiment at Halifax. As a lieutenant colonel in command of an irregular corps, he was severely wounded at the Battle of Brandywine during the expedition to capture Philadelphia. Later, as a captain in the 40th Foot, he offered to raise a corps of black soldiers but was turned down. He was soon promoted major and given command of the Queen's Rangers (1777–1781) a corps raised by Robert Rogers.* In 1781, he was elected to Parliament for Saint Mawes in Cornwall. In 1791, Simcoe was appointed the first Lieutenant Governor of Upper Canada, a new province created by the Constitutional Act out of the former Province of Quebec. He chose Newark (Niagara) as his capital and began a policy of granting land to American settlers, confident that they would become loyal subjects and foster economic growth. In 1794 he founded York (Toronto), intending it to be the capital, and laid the foundation of a road system. He left the province in 1796. He was later appointed Governor and commander-in-chief of the forces at Santo Domingo (Dominican Republic), but ill health obliged him to return to England. He was promoted lieutenant general in 1798 and appointed to command at Plymouth and the Western District to defend against an expected invasion from France. In 1806 he was appointed Commander-in-Chief for India, but he died at Exeter before he could take up the appointment. The colours of the Queen's Rangers were later obtained from his estate and returned to Canada.

Stark, John [Major General]: John Stark was born in Londonderry, New Hampshire, in 1728, He served as a captain in Rogers' Rangers during the French and Indian War and was a close friend of Robert Rogers. In the American Revolutionary War he chose the Continental side. He commanded the New Hampshire Regiment at the Battle of Bunker Hill (1775) and forces at the Battles of Princeton (1776) and Trenton (1777). His greatest victory was the Battle of Bennington (1777), after which he was promoted brigadier general. He was promoted to major general in 1783 and died at Manchester, New Hampshire, in 1822.

Washington, George [General, later President]: Washington's family arrived in America in 1657 after the English Civil War. George was born in Virginia in 1732, He became a surveyor in 1749 and conducted extensive explorations and surveys of Culpeper County . In 1753 he was given the rank of major and appointed adjutant of one of the Military Districts into which Virginia had been divided. He was later selected to deliver an ultimatum to the French who were building forts in the Ohio Valley. In 1754 he was responsible for the ambush of the party of Ensign Coulon de Jumonville de Villiers, who the French claimed was bringing proposals to

---

* For details on this regiment see Section 2–4, page 174.

reduce tensions on the frontier. This action was one of the sparks that ignited the French and Indian War. As a lieutenant colonel, he later led a militia force to build a fort at the forks of the Ohio but found Fort Duquesne already established by the French. His force was defeated at Fort Necessity while awaiting instructions and reinforcements. After this engagement and under criticism by the Governor, he resigned his commission. He was later asked to serve as an aide-de-camp to General Braddock with the rank of colonel. During the campaign and the subsequent Battle of Monongahela, his actions in leading the survivors out of the wilderness probably prevented a total disaster. As a result he was appointed to command the Virginia Regiment with the rank of colonel. After the war he was elected to the House of Burgesses in 1759, and he was one of the representatives from Virginia at the First Continental Congress. He was appointed Commander-in-Chief of the Continental Army in 1775. After the Revolutionary War, Washington became the first President of the United States of America in 1789. He died at his home at Mount Vernon in 1799.

Wolfe, James [Major General]: James Wolfe was born in Kent in 1727, the eldest son of General Edward Wolfe. He joined the army at 14 and was commissioned in his father's regiment of Marines. He later transferred to the 12th Foot Guards and saw action at the Battles of Dettingen (1743) and Culloden (1746). He was wounded at the Battle of Lawfeldt (1747). From 1749 to 1757 he was stationed in Scotland on garrison duty and progressed in rank, being promoted lieutenant colonel of the 20th Regiment in 1750 and colonel in 1756. Having served with distinction during the War of the Austrian Succession (1740–47) he had gained a notable reputation before coming to America in 1758. He was promoted brigadier general and appointed second in command to General Amherst for the Louisbourg campaign. During the assault on Louisbourg, his distinguished and active role led to his promotion to major general and selection as commander of the combined military and naval expedition against Quebec in 1759, at the age of only 31 years. Although he won the battle, he was mortally wounded and died on the field 13 September 1759. Samuel Holland, a close friend who was with him when he died, praised his "consummate judgment and profound wisdom united to bravery, skill and integrity."

Bibliography

A BATTLE FOUGHT ON SNOW SHOES: Mary Cochran Rogers, published by the Author, Derry, New Hampshire, 1917.

A CONCISE ACCOUNT OF NORTH AMERICA: *Containing a description of the several British Colonies on that Continent, including the islands of New Foundland, Cape Breton, &c., as to their Situation, Extent, Climate, Soil, Produce, Rise Government, Religion, Present Boundries and number of Inhabitants supposed to be in each. Also of the Interior and Westerly Parts of the Country, upon the rivers St. Lawrence, the Mississippi, Christino and the Great Lakes. To which is subjoined, an account of the several Nations and Tribes of Indians residing in those Parts, as to their Customs, Manners, Government, Numbers, &c., Containing many useful and Entertaining Facts, never before treated of.,* Major Robert Rogers, Printed for the Author, and sold by J. Millan, bookseller, near Whitehall, London, 1765.

A HISTORY OF CANADA: Carl Wittke, McClelland & Stewart Limited, Toronto, 1935.

AMERICA'S FIRST FIRST WORLD WAR—THE FRENCH & INDIAN WAR — 1754–1763: Timothy J. Todish, Suagothel Productions Ltd., Grand Rapids, 1982.

ANGLICAN REGISTERS OF REV. JOHN LANGHORN, 1787–1814: Loral and Mildred Wanamaker, Ontario Genealogical Society, Kingston Branch, 1980.

AS SHE BEGAN—AN ILLUSTRATED INTRODUCTION TO LOYALIST ONTARIO: Bruce Wilson, Dundurn Press, Toronto, 1981.

ATLAS OF WARFARE: John Pimlott (editor), Bison Books Corp., Greenwich, Ct., 1988.

BATTLES AND LEADERS OF THE AMERICAN REVOLUTION: American History Illustrated, Acorn Press, 1989.

CHAMBERS BIOGRAPHICAL DICTIONARY (5th edition): Magnus Magnusson (General Editor), W & R Chambers Ltd., Edinburgh, 1990 reprinted 1992.

CHRONICLE OF CANADA: Elizabeth Abbott (editor), Chronicle Publications, Montreal, 1990.

DICTIONARY OF CANADIAN BIOGRAPHY (Volume IV) 1771–1800: Francess G. Halpenny (Editor), University of Toronto Press, Toronto, 1979.

DICTIONARY OF CANADIAN HISTORY: David J. Bercuson, Collins Publishers, Don Mills, Ontario, 1988.

EXPLORING ROGERS ISLAND: published by the Rogers Island Historical Association, Fort Edward, New York, 1969.

FORT TICONDEROGA—A SHORT HISTORY: S. H. P. Pell, Fort
Ticonderoga Museum, Fort Ticonderoga, 1978.

FORT WM HENRY—A HISTORY: Stanley M. Gifford, Publisher unknown, Lake George, New York, 1955.

HISTORY OF BROME COUNTY, QUEBEC, Volume I & II: Rev. Ernest
M. Taylor, Montreal, 1908.

HISTORY OF THE TOWN OF DUNBARTON, NEW HAMPSHIRE, 1751–
1860: Caleb Stark, published by G. Parker Lyon, Concord, 1860.

JAMES ROGERS OF LONDONDERRY AND JAMES ROGERS OF
DUNBARTON: Hon. Josiah H. Drummond, S. C. & L. M. Gould
Publishers, Manchester, N. Y., 1897.

JOURNALS OF MAJOR ROBERT ROGERS: *Containing an account of
several excursions he made under Generals who commanded upon the
Continent of North America during the late war, From which may be
collected the material circumstances of every campaign upon that
continent from the commencement to the conclusion of the war,* Major
Robert Rogers, Printed for the Author, and sold by J. Millan, bookseller
near Whitehall, London, 1765.

KING'S MEN—THE SOLDIER FOUNDERS OF ONTARIO: Mary Beacock
Fryer, Dundurn Press, Toronto and Charlottetown, 1980.

LOYALIST REGIMENTS AND THE SETTLEMENT OF PRINCE
EDWARD COUNTY: H. C. Burleigh, Bayside Publishing Company,
Bloomfield, Ontario, 1977.

LOYALISTS OF THE AMERICAN REVOLUTION, Volumes I & II: Lor-
enzo Sabine, Genealogical Publishing Company, Inc., Baltimore, 1979.

MILITARY HISTORY: Published by Empire Press, Leesburg, Virginia.

    A. *Proud Regiments Routed,* by Jon Guttman, October 1992.

    B. *Stinging Defeat Suffered,* by Arthur B. Fox, February 1993.

MUZZLELOADER: Rebel Publishing Company Inc., Texarkana, Texas.

    A. *The Siege of Fort William Henry, Part One,* by Tim J. Todish,
Nov/Dec 92.

    B. *The Siege of Fort William Henry, Conclusion,* by Tim J. Todish,
Jan/Feb 93.

    C. *A Short History of Robert Rogers, Part One,* by Tony Hunter,
Mar/Apr 93.

    D. *A Short History of Robert Rogers, Part Two,* by Tony Hunter,
May/Jun 93.

E. *A Short History of Robert Rogers, Part Three,* by Tony Hunter, Jul/Aug 93.

F. *A Short History of Robert Rogers, Part Four,* by Tony Hunter, Sep/Oct 93.

NORTHWEST PASSAGE (Appendix Edition): Kenneth Roberts, Doubleday, Doran & Company Inc., Garden City, New York, 1937.

NOTICES FROM THE NEW HAMPSHIRE GAZETTE 1765–1800: Otis G. Hammond, Hunterdon House, Lambertville, New Jersey, 1970.

ONTARIAN FAMILIES—*Genealogies of UEL and other Pioneer Families of Upper Canada:* Edward Marion Chadwick, Hunterdon House, Lambertville, New Jersey, 1983.

PIONEER LIFE ON THE BAY OF QUINTE: Author unknown, Rolph and Clark Limited, Toronto, 1904: Facsimile edition by Mika Publishing Company, Belleville, Ontario, 1983.

PONTEACH, OR THE SAVAGES OF AMERICA, A TRAGEDY: Author unknown but believed to be Robert Rogers, Printed for the Author, and sold by J. Millan, opposite the Admiralty, Whitehall, London, 1766. Caxton Club Edition with introduction by Allan Nevins, The Caxton Club, Chicago, 1914.

PRIDE OF PLACE—*A Story of the Settlement of Prince Edward County:* Brenda M. Hudson, Mika Publishing Company, Belleville, Ontario, 1982.

REDCOATS AND REBELS, THE WAR FOR AMERICA, 1770–1781: Christopher Hibbert, Grafton Books, London, 1990.

ROBERT ROGERS OF THE RANGERS: John R. Cuneo, Oxford University Press, New York, 1959.

ROGERS' RANGERS: Lt. Col. H. M. Jackson MBE (editor), Publisher unknown, City unknown, 1953.

ROGERS FAMILY MEMORIES: Robert Zacheus Rogers. An unpublished paper detailing the history of the Rogers family from 1700 to 1895. The original paper was dated February 1875 with revisions in March 1876 and January 1895. Although it contains numerous errors, this was an excellent document for the time, and it sparked research for the present work.

ROGERS: RANGER & LOYALIST: Walter James Rogers, Barrister of the Inner Temple, Londo. A paper on the life of James Rogers read before the United Empire Loyalists' Society at Toronto, 14 December, 1899. Published in the Transactions of the Royal Society of Canada, Second Series 1900–1901, Volume VI Section II, Hope & Sons, Ottawa, 1900.

SETTLEMENT OF UPPER CANADA: William Canniff, originally published by Dudley & Burns, Toronto, 1869: facsimile edition by Mika Publishing Company, Belleville, Ontario, 1971.

THE AMERICAN WAR OF INDEPENDENCE 1775–1783: John Williams, Invasion Publishing, London, 1974.

THE ANCHOR ATLAS OF WORLD HISTORY: Hermann Kinder and Werner Hilgemann, Anchor Books, Garden City, New York, 1978.

THE COLONIAL CLERGY AND THE COLONIAL CHURCHES OF NEW ENGLAND: Frederick Lewis Weis, Lancaster, Massachusetts, 1936.

THE COLOURS OF THE QUEEN'S RANGERS: Prepared by Cedric Jennings Ltd, published by The Queen's York Rangers, Toronto, 1975.

THE CONCISE ILLUSTRATED HISTORY OF THE AMERICAN REVOLUTION: Joseph P. Cullen, Eastern Acorn Press, 1992.

THE CONQUERORS: Allen W. Eckert, Little, Brown & Company (Canada) Ltd., Toronto, 1970.

THE DEFENCE OF CANADA: Gwynne Dyer, McClelland & Stewart Inc., Toronto, 1990.

THE GEALE/ROGERS PAPERS: Trent University Archives, Reference Finding Aid 170 82-022. Deposited by members of the Geale and Rogers families in 1983.

THE GENERALS OF SARATOGA: Max M. Mintz, Yale University, Vail–Ballou Press, Binghamton, N. Y., 1990.

THE HISTORICAL ATLAS OF CANADA, Volume I: R. Cole Harris, University of Toronto Press, Toronto, 1987.

THE HISTORY OF LONDONDERRY, N.H.: Rev. Edward L. Parker, Perkins & Whipple, Boston, 1851.

THE HISTORY OF LONDONDERRY: Addison E. Cudworth, The Vermont Historical Society, Montpelier, Vermont, 1936.

THE HISTORY OF ROGERS RANGERS (Volume I), THE BEGINNINGS *January 1755–April 1758:* Burt Garfield Loescher, privately published, San Francisco, 1946.

THE HISTORY OF ROGERS RANGERS (Volume II), GENESIS ROGERS RANGERS—THE FIRST GREEN BERETS *April 1758–December 1783:* Burt Garfield Loescher, privately published, San Mateo, 1969.

THE HISTORY OF ROGERS RANGERS (Volume III), OFFICERS & NON-COMMISSIONED OFFICERS (2nd edition): Burt Garfield Loescher, privately published, San Francisco, 1985.

THE HISTORY OF STANSTEAD COUNTY, QUEBEC: B. F. Hubbard: Lovell Printing & Publishing Company: Montreal, 1874, Facsimile edition by Heritage Books, Maryland, 1988.

THE HISTORY OF THE TWENTIETH BATTALION (CENTRAL ON-TARIO REGIMENT)—*Canadian Expeditionary Force in the Great War (1914–1918):* Major D. J. Corrigall, Stone & Cox Limited, Toronto, 1935.

THE ILLUSTRATED HISTORY OF CANADA: Robert Craig Brown (editor), Lester & Orpen Dennys Ltd., Toronto, 1987.

THE LOYALISTS IN ONTARIO: William D. Reid, Hunterdon House, Lambertville, New Jersey, 1973.

THE QUEEN'S YORK RANGERS: Stewart H. Bull, The Boston Mills Press, Erin, Ontario, 1984.

THE ROGERS' PAPERS: Ontario Archives, Toronto, Reference MU 2552. Papers of James Rogers and some of his descendants (1765–1902) acquired from Colonel James Zacheus Rogers.

THE ROLLS OF THE PROVINCIAL (LOYALIST) CORPS, CANADIAN COMMAND, AMERICAN REVOLUTIONARY PERIOD: Mary Beacock Fryer & William A. Smy, Dundurn Press Limited, Toronto, 1981.

THE SETTLEMENT OF THE UNITED EMPIRE LOYALISTS ON THE UPPER ST. LAWRENCE AND BAY OF QUINTE IN 1784: E. A. Crickshank, published by the Ontario Historical Society, Toronto, 1934, Reprinted 1966.

THE SNOW FLAKE—*The History of Dunbarton, N. H.:* John B. Mills, published by the Dunbarton Historical Society, Dunbarton, 1980.

THE WILDERNESS WAR: Allen W. Eckert, Little, Brown & Company (Canada) Ltd., Toronto, 1978.

TREASON? AT MICHILIMACKINAC—*The proceedings of a General Court Martial held at Montreal in October 1768 for the Trial of Major Robert Rogers:* David A. Armour, Mackinac Island State Park Commission, 1967.

TRUMBULL'S HISTORY OF THE INDIAN WARS: Henry Trumbull, Phillips & Sampson, Boston, 1846, Facsimile edition by Coles Publishing Company, Toronto, 1972.

UNITED EMPIRE LOYALISTS—PIONEERS OF UPPER CANADA: Nick and Helma Mika, Mika Publishing Company, Belleville, Ontario, 1977.

WHERE THE WINDS BLOW FREE: Alice M. Hadley, published by the Dunbarton Historical Committee, Dunbarton, New Hampshire, 1976.

WILDERNESS EMPIRE: Allen W. Eckert, Little, Brown & Company (Canada) Ltd., Toronto, 1969.

Index

Note: Names in transcribed documents have been indexed only if they appear in the main text.